Horace: The Odes

HORACE

THE ODES

Latin text,
facing verse translation,
and notes

Colin Sydenham

Duckworth

First published in 2005 by
Gerald Duckworth & Co. Ltd.
90-93 Cowcross Street, London EC1M 6BF
Tel: 020 7490 7300
Fax: 020 7490 0080
inquiries@duckworth-publishers.co.uk
www.ducknet.co.uk

ISBN 0 7156 3431 3

Typeset by Ray Davies
Printed and bound in Great Britain by
CPI Bath

Contents

DW, tibi, namque tu solebas …

Foreword

Philip Howard

So, why Horace?

He is an ancient European male who has been dead for 2,000 years. He wrote in a language that is generally (erroneously) described as dead. Even Latin scholars admit that Horace is difficult. He and his work boast of being the pick of the bunch: in other words, elitist. Worse still, he fails our other fashionable modern shibboleth. He is *irrelevant*. Isn't he?

Not so fast, My Masters. Horace still resonates even in our brisk and barbarian times. The quotation dictionaries cite Horace more often than any other classical author. His tags are so familiar that they have become naturalised English: *Carpe diem, Eheu fugaces, Dulce et decorum, Nil desperandum, Nunc est bibendum, Integer vitae* …. Horace has even leapt across the language barrier into English. For he is the reason that we speak of a purple patch, Homer nodding, no smoke without fire, the groves of Academe, the last rose of summer …. He piled Pelion on Ossa. He first smiled at the crusty old codger praising times past. From Horace the mountains are in labour, but a silly little mouse is born. You can drive out Nature (or Horace) with a pitchfork (or ministerial judgments that he is irrelevant). But he keeps on coming back.

For Horace is an honorary Englishman. In his works, the middle-class provincial, son of an Italian freedman (ex-slave), suggests characteristics on which the English (rightly or wrongly) pride themselves: humour, good manners, urbanity, common sense, friendship, loyalty, gentle melancholy at the passing show. For centuries English schools taught Horace as though he were an English scholarship boy who had the misfortune to live beside the Tiber instead of the Thames. Even before Shakespeare, Horace defined what it means to be human. We read Horace not just because twenty centuries have judged him (correctly) to be a classic. But also because he teaches us better than anyone (except Shakespeare) about life and love, tragedy and comedy, politics and celebrity, and this package tour on the Ship of Fools on which we are all willy-nilly passengers. We cannot read an Ode of Horace without recognising something of ourselves and our world. He is more fundamentally relevant to life today than all other modern publications, official, professional or amateur on the internet.

So, why Sydenham?

Horace has been translated more often into more languages than any other author, apart from the problematic but in any case august author(s) of the Bible. Generations of schoolboys as well as poets from Milton to Michie have had a shot at turning Horace into English. *Versifico quia impossibile est.* We keep on trying because it is impossible. Odes 1.5, the Pyrrha Ode, that bitter-sweet poem of lost love that still makes the hair on the nape of the neck bristle, has been translated so often that a brilliant book was 'assembled' of its many versions in multitudinous languages by Ronald Storrs in 1959. In 1931 Professor Conington climbed the Mount Soracte of versification by translating Horace's Satires, Epistles, Art of Poetry and Odes (apart from those that might bring a blush or snigger to a schoolchild's cheek) into rhyming verse. He still reads well.

I met Horace at the same time that I met Sydenham, when the last two of us were King's Scholars at Eton College, beneficiaries of the bounty of *Rex Henricus* ('*Sis amicus, Nobis in angustia ...*'), King Henry VI. Few monarchs have left better legacies to the nation than Eton and King's College, Cambridge. We little Tugs (*Gens Togata,* the tribe that wears gowns and is excused fees) began Horace with the Epistles, then moved on to the Odes for a treat. We had a division (lesson) called Long Horace ('Long Horrors'), in which we read not just Horace, but Homer, Virgil, and the other classics through fast in Greek or Latin, without pause for construe or context. Our beaks (teachers), Richard Martineau, David Simpson, Stephen McWatters, Brian Young, Francis Crusoe, were humane scholars who could have been university dons (some of them later went on to become dons). For our scholarship exams to university, we learnt to turn English verse into Horatian lyrics, in order to distinguish our versification from common-or-garden Ovidian elegiacs. 'The world's a bubble ... *Est bulla mundus ....*'

Colin won his scholarship to King's, where he studied under the great Horatian scholar, L.P. Wilkinson (who in his spare time was the Cambridge recruiter of spooks – more successful than his predecessor). Colin became a Chancery barrister and later a composer of chess problems. But his first love is Horace. He became Secretary of the Horatian Society as long ago as 1980. For a generation he has run that amiable congregation of brothers and sisters who are in thrall to the Poet Horace, with the punctiliousness of a chess problemist and the conviviality of a Roman clubman. He is a pillar of the *Flaccidi(ae),* offshoots of the Horatians who construe an Ode over dinner at the Garrick Club, to the alarm and amusement of the Club servants. And all the while, in his limited spare time, he has been translating the Odes. Into verse that rhymes. Into a different metre to represent each of Horace's various and intricate metres taken from the

Greek. This is a work of meticulous scholarship and versification to bring tears of admiration to the eyes.

I remember, when I was younger and sillier, observing (mischievously?) to Colin that I wondered whether Horace sometimes bunged a word into an Ode just because it scanned, for example as a dactylic colon, dum, diddy, dum diddy, dum, rather than because it carried a relevant meaning. As we did in our schoolboy verses. As even Shakespeare sometimes let metre take priority over sense. Colin looked at me with the pained disapproval of a King's man meeting a coarser sensibility from Oxford.

Colin's translations are exact scholarship. They fill a hack in my inexact inky trade of daily journalism with wistful envy. Here you may find controversial interpretations. How could you not, with a poet as complex as Horace? But you will find none of the solecisms and other casual mistakes which form the element in which I earn my daily bread. But these are more than punctilious versions of the Odes. Colin will deny the following. But these sympathetic, moving and often beautiful translations reveal depths that we traditionally educated Englishmen are trained to conceal beneath our buttoned-up, and often aggressive and dictatorial, carapaces. They convey emotions that convoluted men, such as Horace himself, could convey in no other way. These are the real stuff, as well as scrupulous translations. Alpha plus, Colin. But better even than that. Poetry.

Acknowledgments

I owe more than I can express to David West, who introduced me to the idea of translating and has taught me so much about the Odes; also to that select band, the Flaccidi, with whom I have shared such stimulating evenings; and to all my friends in the Horatian Society, who provided an excuse for maintaining an acquaintance with Horace during a period when I was thinking more of other things. My warm thanks also go to my friends and ex-colleagues at 4 Breams Buildings (as it then was), who, in return for trifling services, presented me with that indispensable standby, the OLD, and especially to Robert Bailey-King for his unstinting encouragement. Finally, I record with gratitude that the beautiful picture of Mons Lucretilis on the cover is the fruit of tireless researches undertaken on my behalf in Rome by Elizabeth Jones.

Translator's Preface

Why?

'But hasn't it been done before?' they ask. To which there is only one answer: Yes, more times than it is possible to know or count. Then comes the supplementary: 'So why are you doing it again?' Here metaphors crowd in: the Odes of Horace are inextricably interwoven into the tapestry of English literary history, and every generation needs to rediscover them afresh; in this new Dark Age of classical learning the new century stands at greater risk than any since the Renaissance of losing touch with them. 'Yes, yes, but there are plenty of modern translations available. What has yours to offer that they have not?' This question deserves an answer.

Novelty

Translators of the Odes tend to fall into two categories, the scholars and the poets, and they have the strengths and weaknesses of those backgrounds. The scholars are expert at every shade of meaning, but in trying to catch everything they may lose spontaneity. The extreme to which they tend is the crib. The poets will be impressed by Horace's Muse, but may be distracted by their own, with results sometimes brilliant, but frequently uneven. The extreme to which they tend is the imitation. I am neither a scholar nor a poet, and my translation lies between these two extremes. I have been content to allow some elements of meaning to escape, and no private Muse has distracted me, since I have none. But is there any positive virtue that I claim? There is one. I have adopted a disciplined and consistent method, which I will summarise here and elaborate in the Introduction.

There are two elements to my method. First, I have written in verse which rhymes and scans. This in itself is unfashionable enough to be rare these days, but I make no apology for it; it is a calculated attempt to present in English dress a discipline of comparable strictness to Horace's metrical practice. Secondly, for each of Horace's metres I have devised my own equivalent English metre, and have used these metres consistently, matching my Alcaic equivalent to his Alcaic, my Sapphic equivalent to his Sapphic, and so forth. This is such an obvious strategy for representing Horace's verse that it seems strange to be claiming it as a novel virtue. But the fact is that in recent times translators, when they have not written in prose or free verse, have tended to subordinate Horace's metrical choices to their personal inspiration, and thus to sacrifice an element in the impact of the whole.

This approach, with its twin disciplines, constitutes my claim to attention.

Introduction

This book provides a verse translation of the Odes of Horace alongside the Latin text, together with explanatory material to help the reader appreciate them within the context of Horace's life and times. It is intended primarily for the inexpert rather than the expert. It is not a literary commentary, and is not concerned with the learned topics appropriate to such a commentary. Accordingly the function of this Introduction is simply to set the scene, to tell the reader what kind of translation to expect and to describe the structure and contents of the book.

1. A Brief Life of Horace

Appreciation of the Odes must start with a working knowledge of the main events in Horace's life. They are well established; he tells us plenty about himself in his own writings, and there is also an early anonymous Life, which is believed to be based on a biography by Suetonius (written *c.* 100 AD). For easy reference a chronological list of the main events relevant to the Odes and Horace's life is set out in Appendix 1.

Quintus Horatius Flaccus was born in 65 BC in Venusia, a town in Apulia in central southern Italy. His father owned a small farm and worked as an auctioneer's agent. Horace makes much of rising from humble beginnings, and of being taunted in his youth for being the son of a freedman (a former slave). But his father could afford to buy him an excellent education, in Rome and then at university in Athens, and modern scholarship suggests that the period of slavery from which his father was freed may have been short-lived and somewhat technical, the result of being on the losing side when Venusia resisted Rome in the Social War in 88 BC. Be that as it may, after the assassination of Julius Caesar in 44 BC Brutus, one of the leading conspirators, withdrew to Athens, where he recruited Horace, among a number of other able young Romans, to the republican (or anti-dictatorship) cause. Thus it came about that Horace fought on the side of Brutus and Cassius when they were defeated by Octavian and Mark Antony at Philippi in 42 BC.

Horace returned to Rome with his wings clipped. Nevertheless he was able to purchase a comfortable post as a treasury official, and he started to write poetry and to meet poets, including Virgil, who in 39 BC published his *Eclogues*. In about 38 BC Virgil introduced him to the circle of the powerful and immensely wealthy Maecenas, a trusted adviser of Octavian, who became his patron and lifelong friend. In 35 BC he published his first book of *Satires*, hexameter poems after the model of Lucilius (180–102 BC) and in about 33 BC he received from Maecenas an estate in Sabine country east of Rome, substantial enough to afford him a measure of financial security. In 31 BC the defeat of Antony and Cleopatra at the naval battle of Actium left Octavian as undisputed master of the Roman world, and he took the name of Augustus in 27 BC. By this time Maecenas had become Augustus' right-hand man, the overseer of Rome when the great man was away, and through Maecenas Horace was brought into contact with the emperor. Augustus recognised his quality and offered him a post as his personal secretary, but Horace declined, giving poor health as an excuse. Augustus took the refusal in good part, and probably enriched Horace, as he certainly did Virgil, since he understood the value of distinguished poetic support for his regime. Horace's *Epodes*, iambic poems inspired by the Greek of Archilochus (seventh century BC) and his second book of *Satires* came in 30 BC, and there followed the first three books of *Odes* in 23 BC. These he considered his great achievement, importing to Roman culture and the Latin language the themes and metres of the great Greek lyric poets such as Alcaeus, Sappho (both writing *c.* 600 BC) and Pindar (*c.* 520–440 BC). But their reception disappointed him, and in a mood of disillusionment he returned to hexameters with his first book of *Epistles* in 19 BC.

Then came the most satisfying moment of Horace's career. In 17 BC Augustus, to mark his own achievements, revived the Secular Festival. A hymn was required for public performance as a central part of three days of solemn ritual, and in the absence of Virgil, who had died in 19 BC, Horace was chosen to write it. His Secular Hymn, written in the Sapphic metre, is not among his greatest works, but the quasi-laureate status which resulted from public recognition restored his self-esteem and appeased his discontent over the Odes. By this time Maecenas, who had been too close to a plot against Augustus, had ceased to be an intimate of the emperor, but Horace no longer needed patronage, being a wealthy man in his own right.

In 13 BC the fourth book of Odes appeared, prompted partly by Augustus' express wish for the military exploits of Drusus (his currently intended heir) and Tiberius (his ultimate successor) to be celebrated. It is different in tone from the first collection in several ways; most notably, Augustus has superseded Maecenas as the chief object of praise. From the same period come the second book of Epistles, and probably the *Art of Poetry* (the Epistle to the Pisos).

Maecenas died in 8 BC, enjoining Augustus in his will to 'remember Horace as you will me'. Within two months Horace too was dead. Both left their property to Augustus. They were buried close to each other on Maecenas' estate on the Esquiline Hill in Rome.

Autobiography?

Because the Odes are mostly written in the first person they are in some sense a self portrait. It is tempting to suppose that their people and events represent genuine people and events in Horace's life. It is wise to remember, however, that this is at best unknowable, and perhaps an illusion. Horace is a master of image manipulation, and what he shows us is what he wants us to see. Where events are real he presents them in literary dress (e.g. his part in the battle of Philippi in 2.7, *O saepe mecum*). Where names are obviously fictional (e.g. Pyrrha, Tyndaris, Lyde etc.), we cannot know if they are pseudonyms for real people in his life, or whether the parts they play are anything other than imaginary. For those who care to seek consistency in the characterisation of such parts there is help in Appendix 5, which lists the fictional characters appearing in each ode. Although there are some superficial correspondences (e.g. the Lyce to whom Horace is cruel in 4.13, *Audivere, Lyce*, could be the Lyce who is cruel to him in 3.10, *Extremum Tanain*), there are also some hopeless inconsistencies (e.g. the beautiful Chloris of 2.5, *Nondum subacta*, can hardly be the aging Chloris admonished in 3.15, *Uxor pauperis Ibyci*) which undermine any theory of a sustained pattern. On the other hand there are aspects of Horace's self portrait which are not mere smoke and mirrors: his sense of humour, his enjoyment of wine and good fellowship, his teasing of his friends, the warmth of his relationship with Maecenas, the seriousness of his poetic ambition, his pride in public recognition. The image is part of his art, but that does not make it wholly invention.

2. The Translation

Duties of the Translator

Three people participate in the process of translation: the author of the original text, the reader of the translated text and the translator. The job of translation can be considered in terms of duties owed by the translator to each of these parties.

Duty to the Author

The duty to the author comes first, since the whole enterprise is inspired by the value of his work. It is a duty of fidelity. This cannot mean complete fidelity, in the sense of reproducing every word, allusion and nuance, not only because complete understanding is not possible, but because, even if it were, it would not be completely reproducible; languages do not correspond with sufficient exactness. Nevertheless there are degrees of fidelity, and the duty is to convey the form and content of the original so far as reasonably possible.

Form was my starting point. It had to be verse, but what sort of verse? A prime characteristic of the Odes is the unwavering discipline of their versification. The number of syllables to the line, and the metrical quantity of each, is absolutely predictable. A translation in free verse fails to convey this fundamental quality to the reader. The duty of fidelity, therefore, has led me to adopt similarly disciplined verse forms, to devise a different metre to correspond to each of Horace's metres, and to ensure that all my versions are of exactly the same length as the originals.

The choice of actual metres, however, has been affected by the other two duties. Duty to Horace alone might logically require the importation to English of the same metres that he imported from Greek to Latin, a mammoth task to which the English language is ill-suited (see further below), and for which I have no appetite. Instead I have taken the more congenial course of designing metres which look the same as Horace's on the page, but are mostly based on the standard English blank verse line. Metres constructed round this basic unit imitate the length of Horace's metres, rather than their movement, but they have the great merit of coming naturally to the language, the reader and the writer.

I have also embraced the other traditional discipline of English verse, rhyme, though only in moderation. Rhyme is an admirable tool for binding verse together and for making a sharp point, but it is also a demanding taskmaster for the translator, who has to find his rhyme within the parent text. The greater the concession to rhyme, the greater the compromise with the sense. My practice, therefore, has been to have only one rhyme to the stanza, and not to attempt the tyrannies of two, except in the single (long-line) metre which I have consciously borrowed. A more detailed analysis of metres will be found in Appendix 2.

Duty to the Reader

In the scale of duties the reader must come next, since the work is undertaken for his benefit, not the translator's. Here it is necessary to distinguish between two broad categories of reader, the expert and the inexpert. This book is principally designed for the inexpert, the reader who has encountered Horace's reputation, and wishes to know what he says in the Odes, but who has no Latin, or not sufficient to tackle them in the original. I hope that these readers will find it an advantage to have the English version set out opposite the Latin, stanza for stanza, and that they may be encouraged to explore the much greater merits of the original. But they must not expect to find the exact correspondence of a crib. Milton wrote a famous version of 1.5 (*Quis multa gracilis*) 'rendred almost word for word … as near as the Language will permit', but the result is a style more likely to alienate than attract (his version will be found in the Note on 1.5). My approach has been, if anything, the opposite. Rather than seek to force uninflected English to emulate the characteristics of inflected Latin, I have tried to express Horace's meaning in the way most natural in English. This can involve a wide departure from the literal, changing constructions, altering the order of phrases, and so forth. My object has always been to produce a version which can be read with pleasure. In rejecting Milton's approach I have given the interests of the reader priority over the strict duty of fidelity.

The same applies in another area. Horace is an endlessly allusive poet. He is constantly referring to contemporary personalities and events, to places and peoples no longer recognisable, to gods and demigods, to figures and stories of myth, legend and history; even winds are usually identified by name rather than direction. To explain such mysteries a body of notes is inevitable, but in order to keep them within bounds, and to spare the reader the constant need to refer to them, I have not hesitated to eliminate non-essential allusions from my text, or to substitute some non-specific equivalent, where decently possible. Attalus, for example, whose historic munificence figures as a byword at 1.1.12 (*Maecenas atavis*), is not named in my version. This is another departure from fidelity in the interests of the reader.

The truly expert, the professional Latinists, do not need this book, and are very likely (as one of them put it to me) 'allergic to translations of the Odes'. They will know much more about them than I do; they will have their own special touchstones here and there, and they will find that I have missed the point, or got it wrong. If they happen to pick up the book, the best I can hope is that they will put it down without disgust. But there is a more numerous sub-class here: the comparatively expert, the dwindling, but still enthusiastic, band of those with a smattering of schoolroom or self-taught Latin, who wish to rediscover Horace, or meet him for the first time. My hope is that they will find the English in some degree worthy of the original.

Duty to the Translator

Last comes the translator's duty to himself. Not everyone would put this duty so low. According to Poole and Maule (*Oxford Book of Classical Verse in Translation*, 1995, p. xiv), 'far too many nineteenth-century translations are written on their knees, as it were', and they contrast 'Pound and the modernists', who 'will not have anything to do with this cripplingly reverential position'. I should be sorry to think that my respect for Horace had crippled my efforts, but there is a boundary between translation and imitation and, tempting as the pastures on the further side may be for some, this book is intended to occupy the territory on the near side.

The translator's duty to himself is never to be content with second best. The text and the chosen disciplines must be respected: metres must be observed and rhymes must be genuine. The language must lie within a consistent register, capable of accommodating Horace's changes of tone, but above all it must feel like English. The duty is owed to Horace too, whose standards are so high.

Apart from sloppiness there are other temptations which need to be resisted. One is to palliate features which offend modern sensibilities. The passage of 2,000 years has created a huge cultural gulf. To Horace political correctness was more than a matter of using acceptable language. To offend a patron could mean the loss of livelihood; to offend the emperor could mean death (witness the fate of Licinius Murena, the addressee of 2.10, *Rectius vives*). There are many subjects on which Horace's attitudes differ from those prevalent in twenty-first-century Britain: examples are gods, emperors, patriotism, empire, patronage, women, boys, slaves, animals. The reader is entitled to survey such differences through clear glass; the occasional temptation is to tint with rose. An obvious example is provided by the handful of odes in which Horace attacks aging women. In the first and bleakest of these (1.25, *Parcius iunctas*) the temptation is to soften the uncompromising language, but there is no excuse for this departure from fidelity; it would deceive the reader. As it happens the reader can be consoled by the later ode (4.13, *Audivere, Lyce*) where a note of tenderness creeps in.

Another temptation is to make small additions with the object of steering the reader more actively in what the translator perceives to be Horace's direction. This is a form of overtranslation, a sin less venial than the omission of non-essentials. There are, however, a few contexts in which I have yielded to the temptation on the ground that Horace's meaning is likely to be missed without the extra nudge. An example will be found in the last stanza of 1.22 (*Integer vitae*), where my excuse is that so few modern readers seem to appreciate the mischievous subversion which is being practised there.

The Languages

There are two more participants in the process of translation: the languages of the author and of the translation.

So far as the Latin is concerned the translator is able to stand on the shoulders of the giants who have gone before. The text has been set in order by the great Bentley and others, and few serious difficulties remain; the meaning has been elucidated by generations of learned commentators. These distinguished scholars, however, have not always been in complete agreement, so that the translator cannot avoid choices, frequently over the meaning, less frequently over the text, between their divergent views. What is perilous, though sometimes tempting, is to reject their guidance and to adopt a text or meaning which cannot be defended by scholarly authority. I have consciously yielded to this temptation only once in relation to the text (see below) and perhaps two or three times in relation to the meaning.

As to the handling of the English language, two of the ways in which it differs from Latin have required policy decisions. First, Latin has a precise system of inflection, which enables thoughts to be expressed in few words, and the order of the words to be varied very widely. English has little inflection and is encumbered by small intractable words (articles, pronouns, auxiliaries etc.) without which it degenerates into pidgin. As a result English tends to require more words, and the range of acceptable variation in word order is very much narrower. Milton's experiment with 1.5 shows how hostile English is to efforts to imitate the order of the Latin words. So, rather than work against the grain of the language, I have not attempted to depart from a natural English word order, except to an extent normal in English verse. Secondly, there is a fundamental difference between the ways the languages handle metre. English metres are stress-based. This is a relatively fluid and flexible system, in which many syllables do not have unchanging values, but can be heavily or lightly accented according to the needs of sense and rhythm, and within limits the internal pattern of the line may vary. Latin metres are quantity-based. This is a more rigid system in which a vowel is long or short according to fixed rules, and in most of Horace's metres the pattern of the line admits of no significant variety at all. When Horace imported Greek metres into Latin he was at least starting from another quantity-based system. It is a much longer leap to the stress basis, and although I acknowledge the logic of attempting to import Horace's metres into English, I consider that the genius of the English language is bound to frustrate the effort. Despite the advocacy of Leishman (1956) and the work of Lee (1998), I have shrunk from the labour of trying to confine the English language to the straitjacket of Horace's practices, and have preferred the native disciplines that I have described.

It was the long-standing usage of English poets, founded on the natural run of English speech, which led me to adopt the ten-syllable blank verse line as the basic unit of my metres. The advantages of familiarity are obvious, but there is a drawback. I have found it a reasonable working rule that the sense of Horace's Latin can normally be adequately reproduced in an equal number of English syllables. But the basic units of Horace's frequent metres have eleven or twelve syllables. This has meant that I have been working in restricted space. On the whole I believe this is salutary. It is good for the language to have to work hard in a verse translation. But where Horace's meaning is densely packed I have sometimes had to leave some elements out. Mostly I have been able to do this without regret because his topical allusions can often be shortened or omitted today without injury to the essential sense. Nevertheless there are places where I have felt uncomfortable about forced omissions, and although these will not trouble the inexpert, I regret the annoyance to the expert.

Proper Names

My policy has been to leave all names as they stand, with a few exceptions which are readily understood (e.g. Jove for Jupiter), or which have familiar English equivalents (e.g. Horace himself, Virgil, Mercury). I have also preserved their scansion, or at any rate the number of syllables, which means that the scansion of my own verse depends on recognising the number of syllables correctly. This is not simple: anyone could be forgiven for failing to realise that Asterie has four syllables, and modern media usage is liable to obscure the fact that Theseus has only two. I have therefore provided a numerical key in the Notes where it seems necessary, and made use of the diaeresis in the English text. For this intrusive pedantry I apologise to those who do not need it. Where relevant the Notes also record discernible Greek meanings hidden in fictional names.

Names which appear in the English text will, unless they are Horace's fictional acquaintances (Pyrrha, Telephus etc.), be explained so far as necessary either in the Notes or in the Glossary of Names at the end. The Index of Opening Words in Appendix 5 lists also the addressee of each ode (if any) and, in brackets, any fictional names featured.

3. The Notes

The Notes are entirely in English, and all lead words are taken from the English text. They are designed to steer inexpert readers through the labyrinth of allusions, whether mythical, historical or contemporary, and the obliquities of Horace's train of thought. There is no learning on Horace's sources, prosody, grammar or text, topics which can, if desired, be approached through works listed in Appendix 4. Here and there I have offered interpretations of Horace's intentions which are my own, and not necessarily orthodox. They do not have to be believed, but they may help the interested reader to form an independent view. So far as the experts are concerned, my advice is not to trouble with the Notes. The information they will have already, and the comments they will not need.

4. The Text

Since this is not a learned edition, and the Latin text I have used is there for all to see, I need say little about it. Usually it is the Oxford Classical Text (Wickham, ed. Garrod, 1912), as modified by West (for Books 1-3). But occasionally I have for personal reasons preferred some variant from another source. Only once have I ventured a personal emendation: in the last stanza of the Cleopatra ode (1.37, *Nunc est bibendum*) I have postponed a comma in order to adopt a sense which its received positioning has denied at least since the time of Bentley (1711). This audacity I have briefly explained in the Notes, and I hope to justify it at greater length in the future.

The newcomer needs to understand that Books 1-3 form a complete collection, that Book 4 was an afterthought, and that between them came the Secular Hymn. This explains the three sections into which the text is divided, and the need for the short introductory note to each of them.

5. Glossary and Appendices

After the Notes the following further material will be found.

Glossary of Names

This gives a very brief explanation of unfamiliar names which occur in the English text, but are not mentioned in the Notes.

Appendices

1. Chronology
A chronological framework of the most important events in Horace's life and the major historical events relevant to the Odes.

2. Metres
A more detailed account of my metrical practice.

3. Augustan Policies
A skeleton list of the most important policies of Augustus. These are relevant to understanding all the Odes, and essential for the Roman Odes at the beginning of Book 3.

4. Further Reading
A list of helpful material for the inexpert reader who wishes to know more.

5. Index of Opening Words
The Odes are usually identified by their opening words. This index enables them to be found. It names the addressee (if any) of each ode, and the fictional characters mentioned in it, so that these can also be traced.

The First Collection: Books 1-3

Book 1

Books 1-3 were published as a single collection in 23 BC. Horace had already published two books of Satires (in hexameters) and one of Epodes (in largely iambic metres). They are early works, comparatively unpolished and conversational. But the Odes represented something much more important to Horace. They were his original literary project, the importation to Roman letters of the subjects, metres, styles and methods of the Greek lyric poets, in particular of Alcaeus, Sappho and Pindar. The first and last poems in this collection proclaim his ambition to be ranked as their equal, and ultimately his sense of having achieved it.

The order in which the odes appear is generally considered to be that ordained by Horace himself. In this Book there is some perceptible logic to it. The first eleven odes introduce ten of the twelve metres used in this collection (and are sometimes called the Parade Odes for this reason). Pride of place among the addressees goes to Maecenas, whose name is the very first word, and who is also addressed in the first ode in the second half of the Book (20). There follow Augustus (2), a ship carrying Virgil (3), the consul of the year of publication (4), a lighter interlude (5), Augustus' right-hand general (6) and a prominent beneficiary of Augustus' policy of clemency (7). Neighbouring odes are sometimes clearly related (e.g. 16 and 17). The climax is the great Cleopatra ode (37), but the last word, by way of contrast, is given to a lighter miniature (38). This Book contains the largest number of odes, but with the shortest average length (5.76 stanzas). It is a curious fact that this average increases with each succeeding Book (2 – 7.15, 3 – 8.36, 4 – 9.7).

To the reader new to Horace it may well be discouraging to tackle the poems in the order presented, since several of the Parade Odes are dry or difficult, and will be better appreciated after the more accessible aspects of Horace have been enjoyed. It may be more rewarding to start with 5, then 8 and then move on through the Book. Particularly indigestible to the newcomer in this Book, and probably best reserved to a second reading, are 2, 7, 12, 15, 18, 28 and 35.

1.1

Maecenas atavis edite regibus,
o et praesidium et dulce decus meum:
sunt quos curriculo pulverem Olympicum
collegisse iuvat, metaque fervidis

evitata rotis palmaque nobilis
terrarum dominos evehit ad deos;
hunc, si mobilium turba Quiritium
certat tergeminis tollere honoribus;

illum, si proprio condidit horreo
quidquid de Libycis verritur areis.   10
gaudentem patrios findere sarculo
agros Attalicis condicionibus

numquam demoveas ut trabe Cypria
Myrtoum pavidus nauta secet mare.
luctantem Icariis fluctibus Africum
mercator metuens otium et oppidi

laudat rura sui; mox reficit ratis
quassas, indocilis pauperiem pati.
est qui nec veteris pocula Massici
nec partem solido demere de die   20

spernit, nunc viridi membra sub arbuto
stratus, nunc ad aquae lene caput sacrae.
multos castra iuvant et lituo tubae
permixtus sonitus bellaque matribus

detestata. manet sub Iove frigido
venator tenerae coniugis immemor,
seu visa est catulis cerva fidelibus,
seu rupit teretes Marsus aper plagas.

me doctarum hederae praemia frontium
dis miscent superis, me gelidum nemus   30
nympharumque leves cum Satyris chori
secernunt populo, si neque tibias

1.1

Maecenas, from an ancient royal line
descended, o my fortress, pride and friend,
some people love the dust collected by
Olympic racing chariots, the bend

just grazed by scorching wheels; them victory
exalts above all mortals to the skies.
To one a full career in politics
as champion of the people is the prize;

another longs to cram his granary
with every sweeping of the Libyan trade.
The yeoman proudly breaking with his pick
ancestral fields you never will persuade,

whatever your munificence, to face
in timbers frail the terrors of the sea.
The merchant, fearful of the clash of wind
and wave, extols the rural harmony

of his home town, but soon enough, unused
to poor returns, his damaged fleet repairs.
Then there's the man who values decent wine,
who does not grudge the time from daily cares

to stretch at ease beneath an arbutus
or by a gentle river's sacred head.
Some relish a campaign, discord of fife
and bugle, even battle, that worst dread

of every mother. Shivering through the night
the hunter with his faithful hounds forgets
his tender bride, intent on deer or on
the Marsian boar that tore his fine-spun nets.

But me the honoured poet's ivy crown
lifts to the gods, and my remote domain
is that cool glade where nymphs and satyrs dance,
provided that my Muses don't refrain

Euterpe cohibet nec Polyhymnia
Lesboum refugit tendere barbiton.
quodsi me lyricis vatibus inseres,
sublimi feriam sidera vertice.

1.2

Iam satis terris nivis atque dirae
grandinis misit Pater et rubente
dextera sacras iaculatus arces
    terruit urbem,

terruit gentis, grave ne rediret
saeculum Pyrrhae nova monstra questae
omne cum Proteus pecus egit altos
    visere montis,

piscium et summa genus haesit ulmo
nota quae sedes fuerat columbis,   10
et superiecto pavidae natarunt
    aequore dammae.

vidimus flavum Tiberim retortis
litore Etrusco violenter undis
ire deiectum monumenta regis
    templaque Vestae,

Iliae dum se nimium querenti
iactat ultorem, vagus et sinistra
labitur ripa Iove non probante u-
    xorius amnis.   20

audiet civis acuisse ferrum
quo graves Persae melius perirent,
audiet pugnas vitio parentum
    rara iuventus.

quem vocet divum populus ruentis
imperi rebus? prece qua fatigent
virgines sanctae minus audientem
    carmina Vestam?

from granting inspiration in the flute
and lyre of Lesbos. And if you rank me
an equal of the lyricists of Greece,
my head shall strike the stars in ecstasy.

1.2

Enough of snow and hail inflicted by
the father of the gods, whose fiery-red
right hand has struck the citadels, in Rome
    inspiring dread –

dread nationwide – lest Pyrrha's age return,
a time of novel and prodigious sights
when Proteus shepherded his seals upon
    the mountain heights,

and shoals of fish were stranded in tree-tops,
where lately turtle-doves had raised a brood,
and frantic hinds were forced to swim the sea's
    invading flood.

We've seen the yellow Tiber's waves thrown back
from his Etruscan bank with violence
to cast down Vesta's shrine and Numa's king-
    ly monuments;

vowing unbridled vengeance for his wife,
indignant Ilia, her river-mate
against Jove's wish his left bank overflowed
    in headlong spate.

The tale of weapons forged for civil war,
more fit for use against the foreign foe,
our children's generation, by that crime
    reduced, shall know.

What god should be invoked as saviour of
an empire poised on ruin's brink? What prayer
should Vesta's holy virgins pour in her
    reluctant ear?

cui dabit partis scelus expiandi
Iuppiter? tandem venias precamur 30
nube candentis umeros amictus,
    augur Apollo;

sive tu mavis, Erycina ridens,
quam Iocus circum volat et Cupido;
sive neglectum genus et nepotes
    respicis auctor,

heu nimis longo satiate ludo,
quem iuvat clamor galeaeque leves
acer et Marsi peditis cruentum
    vultus in hostem; 40

sive mutata iuvenem figura
ales in terris imitaris almae
filius Maiae patiens vocari
    Caesaris ultor:

serus in caelum redeas diuque
laetus intersis populo Quirini,
neve te nostris vitiis iniquum
    ocior aura

tollat; hic magnos potius triumphos,
hic ames dici pater atque princeps, 50
neu sinas Medos equitare inultos
    te duce, Caesar.

1.3

Sic te diva potens Cypri,
sic fratres Helenae, lucida sidera,
    ventorumque regat pater
obstrictis aliis praeter Iapyga,

    navis, quae tibi creditum
debes Vergilium, finibus Atticis
    reddas incolumem precor,
et serves animae dimidium meae.

Whom will Jove name to cleanse us from our past
pollution? Come in answer to our hymns,
augur Apollo, veiling in a cloud
    your blinding limbs;

or laughing Venus come, escorted by
Humour and Cupid, if it is your will;
or if you still regard your toiling sons,
    and have your fill

of sport prolonged, come founder Mars, whose joy
is in the helmet's flash, the trumpet's bray,
the swordsman snarling at his rival's blood
    ebbing away.

Or flying Mercury, if it is you
whose godhead in a youthful man resides,
applauded for wreaking revenge upon
    the regicides,

put off returning to the skies, among
the Roman people take protracted ease,
bear with our faults and be not tempted by
    the robber breeze

too soon; enjoy your mighty triumphs here,
as Father and as Foremost hailed; no Mede
shall exercise a horse unscathed, if you,
    Caesar, will lead.

1.3

    Goddess of Cyprus, hear me now,
and you, twinned constellation, Helen's brothers,
    and you, the father of the winds:
let loose the western breeze, but stay all others;

    so may the ship entrusted with
Virgil discharge its cargo sound and whole
    upon the shore of Attica,
a precious freight, as dear as half my soul.

illi robur et aes triplex
circa pectus erat, qui fragilem truci 10
commisit pelago ratem
primus, nec timuit praecipitem Africum

decertantem Aquilonibus
nec tristis Hyadas, nec rabiem Noti,
quo non arbiter Hadriae
maior, tollere seu ponere vult freta.

quem mortis timuit gradum,
qui siccis oculis monstra natantia,
qui vidit mare turbidum et
infamis scopulos Acroceraunia? 20

nequiquam deus abscidit
prudens Oceano dissociabili
terras, si tamen impiae
non tangenda rates transiliunt vada.

audax omnia perpeti
gens humana ruit per vetitum nefas.
audax Iapeti genus
ignem fraude mala gentibus intulit.

post ignem aetheria domo
subductum macies et nova febrium 30
terris incubuit cohors,
semotique prius tarda necessitas

leti corripuit gradum.
expertus vacuum Daedalus aera
pennis non homini datis:
perrupit Acheronta Herculeus labor.

nil mortalibus ardui est:
caelum ipsum petimus stultitia, neque
per nostrum patimur scelus
iracunda Iovem ponere fulmina. 40

His heart was oak, no, triple bronze
who first upon the open sea put forth
 his cockleshell, and fearlessly
confronted all the tempests from the north

 brawling with blasts from Africa,
the rainy Hyades and the erratic
 southerly gale, prime arbiter
of storm or stillness in the Adriatic.

 What threat of death could daunt the man
who faced the raging waves without emotion,
 the dread Acroceraunian
headland, the swimming monsters of the ocean?

 God in his wisdom set apart
the continents with barriers of sea –
 in vain if man then plies across
the gulfs in ships, forsaking piety.

 Recklessly daring everything,
to headlong sacrilege man sets his hand.
 Reckless Prometheus to mankind
imported fire, ill-omened contraband;

 and after fire was smuggled in
men suffered from consumption and a brew
 of unknown fevers, and the pace
of death's approach, so measured hitherto,

 accelerated. Daedalus
experimented in the empty air
 on wings unnatural to man,
and Hercules broke into Pluto's lair.

 Our mortal folly knows no bounds,
and heaven itself is not for us too high;
 our crimes demand chastisement; how
can Jove his wrathful thunderbolt put by?

1.4

Solvitur acris hiems grata vice veris et Favoni,
    trahuntque siccas machinae carinas,
ac neque iam stabulis gaudet pecus aut arator igni,
    nec prata canis albicant pruinis.

iam Cytherea choros ducit Venus imminente Luna
    iunctaeque Nymphis Gratiae decentes
alterno terram quatiunt pede, dum gravis Cyclopum
    Vulcanus ardens visit officinas.

nunc decet aut viridi nitidum caput impedire myrto
    aut flore terrae quem ferunt solutae;   10
nunc et in umbrosis Fauno decet immolare lucis,
    seu poscat agna sive malit haedo.

pallida Mors aequo pulsat pede pauperum tabernas
    regumque turris. o beate Sesti,
vitae summa brevis spem nos vetat incohare longam.
    iam te premet nox fabulaeque Manes

et domus exilis Plutonia; quo simul mearis,
    nec regna vini sortiere talis,
nec tenerum Lycidan mirabere, quo calet iuventus
    nunc omnis et mox virgines tepebunt.   20

1.5

Quis multa gracilis te puer in rosa
perfusus liquidis urget odoribus
    grato, Pyrrha, sub antro?
        cui flavam religas comam,

simplex munditiis? heu quotiens fidem
mutatosque deos flebit et aspera
    nigris aequora ventis
        emirabitur insolens,

1.4

Welcome to spring, as harsh winter dissolves before breezes
                                                          from western shores,
　　as dried-out hulls are winched down to the sea;
cattle no longer have need of the byre, nor the ploughman of
                                                          fireside warmth,
　　the fields from hoar-frost's silver shroud are free.

Dancing returns, led by Venus beneath night's superintending light,
　　the comely Graces with alternate feet
trample the ground linking arms with the nymphs, while Vulcan
                                                          inspects the grim
　　workshops of Etna, fuelling their heat.

Now is the time to perfume the head and bind it with green myrtle,
　　or any bloom the quickened soil unfreezes,
time in the shadowy grove to offer in honour of Faunus' name
　　a kid or lamb, whichever better pleases.

Palaces, no less than poor men's hovels, o Sestius fortune's friend,
　　death's bloodless hand indifferently invades;
life's impermanence warns men against ambitious long-term plans.
　　Soon night will crush you and the fabled Shades;

once you arrive at the beggarly dwelling of Pluto, no more playing
　　dice to determine arbiters of wine,
no more admiring young Lycidas, whom all the boys are on fire for now,
　　for whom the girls will soon begin to pine.

1.5

　　What slender suitor slick with scented oils
　　cajoles you, Pyrrha, in your pretty lair,
　　　　for whom among the roses
　　　　　　you preen your golden hair,

　　demure and dainty? At your broken vows,
　　at raging tempests darkening your sea,
　　　　he'll often groan, dumbfounded
　　　　　　in his naivety;

qui nunc te fruitur credulus aurea,
qui semper vacuam, semper amabilem   10
    sperat, nescius aurae
        fallacis! miseri, quibus

intemptata nites. me tabula sacer
votiva paries indicat uvida
    suspendisse potenti
        vestimenta maris deo.

1.6

Scriberis Vario fortis et hostium
victor Maeonii carminis alite,
    qua rem cumque ferox navibus aut equis
        miles te duce gesserit:

nos, Agrippa, neque haec dicere nec gravem
Pelidae stomachum cedere nescii
    nec cursus duplicis per mare Ulixei
        nec saevam Pelopis domum

conamur, tenues grandia, dum pudor
imbellisque lyrae Musa potens vetat   10
    laudes egregii Caesaris et tuas
        culpa deterere ingeni.

quis Martem tunica tectum adamantina
digne scripserit aut pulvere Troico
    nigrum Merionen aut ope Palladis
        Tydiden superis parem?

nos convivia, nos proelia virginum
sectis in iuvenes unguibus acrium
    cantamus vacui, sive quid urimur
        non praeter solitum leves.   20

for trusting in your sunshine he'll not know
how fickle are your breezes, he'll suppose
　　your welcome will be cloudless
　　　　for ever. Woe to those

you dazzle unsuspecting. As for me,
I've offered (as a votive plaque informs)
　　my sodden clothes to Neptune,
　　　　the master of all storms.

1.6

Let Varius, that bird of epic song,
tell of your valour and your glorious
exploits of leadership, alike with horse
　　and ship victorious.

Such themes, Agrippa, I could no more dare
than obstinate Achilles' tantrums, or
two-faced Ulysses' voyage, or Pelops'
　　bloodstained descendants; for

such weight I am too puny; modesty
and my unwarlike Muse forbid me to
demean by want of talent the renown
　　of Caesar and of you.

Whose style can rise to Mars in panoply,
or Meriones with dust of battle grey,
or Diomedes challenging the gods,
　　as Pallas' protégé?

My war-songs are of youths attacked by girls
with sharpened fingernails; in carefree fashion
convivial joys I sing – sometimes with warmth,
　　but always this side passion.

1.7

Laudabunt alii claram Rhodon aut Mytilenen
    aut Epheson bimarisve Corinthi
moenia vel Baccho Thebas vel Apolline Delphos
    insignis aut Thessala Tempe:

sunt quibus unum opus est intactae Palladis urbem
    carmine perpetuo celebrare et
undique decerptam fronti praeponere olivam:
    plurimus in Iunonis honorem

aptum dicet equis Argos ditisque Mycenas:
    me nec tam patiens Lacedaemon   10
nec tam Larisae percussit campus opimae,
    quam domus Albuneae resonantis

et praeceps Anio ac Tiburni lucus et uda
    mobilibus pomaria rivis.
albus ut obscuro deterget nubila caelo
    saepe Notus neque parturit imbris

perpetuo, sic tu sapiens finire memento
    tristitiam vitaeque labores
molli, Plance, mero, seu te fulgentia signis
    castra tenent seu densa tenebit   20

Tiburis umbra tui. Teucer Salamina patremque
    cum fugeret, tamen uda Lyaeo
tempora populea fertur vinxisse corona,
    sic tristis adfatus amicos:

'quo nos cumque feret melior fortuna parente,
    ibimus, o socii comitesque,
nil desperandum Teucro duce et auspice Teucro
    certus enim promisit Apollo

ambiguam tellure nova Salamina futuram.
    o fortes peioraque passi   30
mecum saepe viri, nunc vino pellite curas;
    cras ingens iterabimus aequor.'

1.7

Others may praise Mytilene or Ephesus or the delights
    of Rhodes or of Corinth the queen of two seas,
of Tempe or Thebes, dear to Bacchus, or Delphi, beloved
    of Apollo, but I shall extol none of these;

there are those whose one purpose is Athens, the stronghold of Pallas
    the virgin, in unending verse to acclaim,
and to pluck for their foreheads the olive wherever it grows;
    many another in honour of Juno's name

will tell of the horses of Argos and wealthy Mycenae;
    but I am less struck by the bountiful plain
of Larissa, or disciplined Lacedaemonian lands,
    than by the Albunian Sibyl's domain

and Anio's torrent, the grove of Tiburnus, and orchards
    of apple-trees watered by rippling streams.
Just as the wind often wipes away lowering clouds
    from the sky, which with rain not incessantly teems,

in the same way, if you're wise, you will try to curtail
    low spirits, friend Plancus, and wearisome stress
with mellowing wine, whether camping in military pomp,
    or refreshing yourself in the cooling caress

of your shadowy Tibur. When Teucer from Salamis sailed
    into exile, they say he first wetted his head
with wine, and around it a garland of poplar he bound,
    then to his band of dispirited comrades he said:

'Friends and companions, our fortune will prove less unkind
    than my father; wherever it leads we shall go.
With Teucer as leader and augur let no man despair,
    for Apollo has promised a rival shall grow

in the future for Salamis, founded afresh overseas.
    Many times and far worse, my valiant men,
we have suffered together, now banish all troubles with wine;
    tomorrow we brave the broad ocean again.'

1.8

Lydia, dic, per omnis
te deos oro, Sybarin cur properes amando
    perdere, cur apricum
oderit campum, patiens pulveris atque solis,

    cur neque militaris
inter aequalis equitat, Gallica nec lupatis
    temperat ora frenis?
cur timet flavum Tiberim tangere? cur olivum

    sanguine viperino
cautius vitat neque iam livida gestat armis   10
    bracchia, saepe disco
saepe trans finem iaculo nobilis expedito?

    quid latet, ut marinae
filium dicunt Thetidis sub lacrimosa Troiae
    funera, ne virilis
cultus in caedem et Lycias proriperet catervas?

1.9

Vides ut alta stet nive candidum
Soracte, nec iam sustineant onus
    silvae laborantes, geluque
        flumina constiterint acuto.

dissolve frigus ligna super foco
large reponens atque benignius
    deprome quadrimum Sabina,
        o Thaliarche, merum diota:

permitte divis cetera, qui simul
stravere ventos aequore fervido   10
    deproeliantis, nec cupressi
        nec veteres agitantur orni.

1.8

Tell, I beg you, Lydia,
why this urgency to ruin Sybaris with deadly charm?
    why the sunlit training ground
does he now despise, though neither dust nor heat will do him harm?

    Why does he not exercise
with the cavalry cadets, nor join in learning to restrain
    Gaulish colts with jagged bits?
Why has he withdrawn from yellow Tiber? Why does he disdain

    wrestler's oil like viper's blood?
How is it his arms no longer bear the warrior's bruises dark,
    he who has a champion's
skill at hurling spear and discus often far beyond the mark?

    Why is he malingering,
like the son of Thetis on the eve of Troy's grievous demise,
    lest, by man's attire betrayed,
he should be to battle drafted with Troy's Lycian allies?

1.9

Look at Soracte mantled deep in white,
the groaning woods can scarcely bear the press
    of such a fall of snow, the rivers
        stand arrested, icebound, motionless.

Come, Thaliarchus, banish winter's chill,
pile high the logs upon the fire, spare not;
    relent, and fetch the fourth-year Sabine
        vintage in the double-handled pot.

Trust all else to the gods, at whose command
storm-blasts at war above a raging sea,
    and creaking mountain-ash and cypress,
        all subside into serenity.

quid sit futurum cras fuge quaerere et
quem Fors dierum cumque dabit lucro
   appone, nec dulcis amores
     sperne puer neque tu choreas,

donec virenti canities abest
morosa. nunc et campus et areae
   lenesque sub noctem susurri
     composita repetantur hora,   20

nunc et latentis proditor intimo
gratus puellae risus ab angulo
   pignusque dereptum lacertis
     aut digito male pertinaci.

1.10

Mercuri, facunde nepos Atlantis,
qui feros cultus hominum recentum
   voce formasti catus et decorae
     more palaestrae,

te canam, magni Iovis et deorum
nuntium curvaeque lyrae parentem,
   callidum quidquid placuit iocoso
     condere furto.

te, boves olim nisi reddidisses
per dolum amotas, puerum minaci   10
voce dum terret, viduus pharetra
   risit Apollo.

quin et Atridas duce te superbos
Ilio dives Priamus relicto
Thessalosque ignis et iniqua Troiae
   castra fefellit.

tu pias laetis animas reponis
sedibus virgaque levem coerces
aurea turbam, superis deorum
   gratus et imis.   20

Don't fret at what tomorrow holds, account
as profit every day allowed by chance,
  give time to dancing and indulging,
    you too, in the sweetness of romance,

while youth is green, hair glossy, temper mild.
Now is your time for healthy recreation,
  for sauntering, for soft endearments
    whispered at the twilit assignation;

time for the lure of laughter that betrays
the girl in some inmost recess concealed,
  and then the token snatched away from
    fingers that resist, yet partly yield.

1.10

Mercury, seed of Atlas, silver-tongued,
whose art to primitive mankind did teach
more cultivated ways, through wrestling and
  the gift of speech,

messenger of great Jove and all the gods,
the first to tune the curving lyre's sweet string,
patron astute of every playful theft,
  of you I sing.

Apollo, fulminating to regain
his cows, purloined by your precocious guile,
noticed his quiver missing, and could not
  suppress a smile.

Past Atreus' sons, past Myrmidon watch-fires,
from Troy king Priam journeyed undetected,
eluding the besiegers' hostile ranks,
  by you protected.

Guide of the golden wand, to righteous souls
in ghostly throng their resting place you show,
respected equally by gods above
  and gods below.

1.11

Tu ne quaesieris, scire nefas, quem mihi quem tibi
finem di dederint, Leuconoe, nec Babylonios
temptaris numeros. ut melius, quidquid erit, pati,
seu pluris hiemes seu tribuit Iuppiter ultimam,

quae nunc oppositis debilitat pumicibus mare
Tyrrhenum: sapias, vina liques, et spatio brevi
spem longam reseces. dum loquimur, fugerit invida
aetas: carpe diem, quam minimum credula postero.

1.12

Quem virum aut heroa lyra vel acri
    tibia sumis celebrare, Clio?
quem deum? cuius recinet iocosa
        nomen imago

aut in umbrosis Heliconis oris
aut super Pindo gelidove in Haemo
unde vocalem temere insecutae
        Orphea silvae

arte materna rapidos morantem
fluminum lapsus celerisque ventos,   10
blandum et auritas fidibus canoris
        ducere quercus?

quid prius dicam solitis parentis
laudibus, qui res hominum ac deorum,
qui mare et terras variisque mundum
        temperat horis?

unde nil maius generatur ipso,
nec viget quicquam simile aut secundum:
proximos illi tamen occupavit
        Pallas honores,   20

1.11

What the end the gods ordain for you and me, Leuconoë,
ask not, such designs are secret; don't consult astrology
or Chaldean incantations; better far your fate to bear,
whether you have many winters, or this is your final year

now with sullen shingle beaches wearing out the Tuscan sea.
Practise wisdom; filter wine, and prune back to life's brevity
long ambition; as we argue spiteful minutes steal away;
don't rely upon tomorrow's harvest, gather in today.

1.12

What man, what demigod, do you select,
Clio, on lyre or piercing flute to greet?
What god, whose name the mountain echo will
   in play repeat

upon the shady slope of Helicon,
or Pindus' height, or Haemus' chilly fell,
from which the woods by Orpheus' melodies
   were drawn pell-mell,

as by his mother's art he checked the flow
of rushing rivers and the flying breeze,
and with the sweetness of his music charmed
   the listening trees?

Before the Father whom could I presume
to praise, who over gods and mankind reigns,
who land and sea controls, and seasons of
   the sky ordains?

From him comes nothing greater than himself,
nothing to equal, nothing to compare;
the honour of the second place to him
   Pallas shall bear,

proeliis audax; neque te silebo,
Liber, et saevis inimica Virgo
beluis, nec te, metuende certa
    Phoebe sagitta.

dicam et Alciden puerosque Ledae,
hunc equis, illum superare pugnis
nobilem; quorum simul alba nautis
    stella refulsit,

defluit saxis agitatus umor,
concidunt venti fugiuntque nubes,   30
et minax, quod sic voluere, ponto
    unda recumbit.

Romulum post hos prius an quietum
Pompili regnum memorem an superbos
Tarquini fascis, dubito, an Catonis
    nobile letum.

Regulum et Scauros animaeque magnae
prodigum Paulum superante Poeno
gratus insigni referam Camena
    Fabriciumque.   40

hunc et incomptis Curium capillis
utilem bello tulit et Camillum
saeva paupertas et avitus apto
    cum lare fundus.

crescit occulto velut arbor aevo
fama Marcelli; micat inter omnis
Iulium sidus velut inter ignis
    luna minores.

gentis humanae pater atque custos,
orte Saturno, tibi cura magni   50
Caesaris fatis data: tu secundo
    Caesare regnes.

doughty in battle; nor shall I forget
you, Bacchus, nor Diana, enemy
of predators, nor Phoebus, deadly in
    your archery.

I'll sing of Hercules and Leda's twins,
one for his riding, one for boxing known,
whose brilliant star to sailors brings relief
    as soon as shown,

for then the tempest dies, the driven spray
drains off the rocks, they bid the storm-clouds black
to scatter, and the swelling waves into
    the deep fall back.

Who's next, Camena? Romulus perhaps,
peace under Numa, Tarquin's fabled pride,
the noble suicide of Cato, how
    can I decide?

Then Regulus, the Scauri, and Paulus
who gave his life at Cannae selflessly,
Fabricius too, all these I'll single out
    for eulogy.

Camillus and the bearded Curius
to military usefulness were bred
by frugal life in an ancestral farm's
    narrow homestead.

Marcellan fame expands unnoticed, like
a tree; and as the moon outshines by far
the lesser lights, all others fade beside
    the Julian star.

O Father, seed of Saturn, guardian of
mankind, the care of Caesar, by decree
of fate, is yours; rule on with Caesar as
    your deputy.

ille seu Parthos Latio imminentis
egerit iusto domitos triumpho,
sive subiectos Orientis orae
   Seras et Indos,

te minor laetum reget aequus orbem;
tu gravi curru quaties Olympum,
tu parum castis inimica mittes
   fulmina lucis.   60

1.13

   Cum tu, Lydia, Telephi
cervicem roseam, cerea Telephi
   laudas bracchia, vae meum
fervens difficili bile tumet iecur.

   tum nec mens mihi nec color
certa sede manent, umor et in genas
   furtim labitur, arguens
quam lentis penitus macerer ignibus.

   uror, seu tibi candidos
turparunt umeros immodicae mero   10
   rixae, sive puer furens
impressit memorem dente labris notam.

   non, si me satis audias,
speres perpetuum dulcia barbare
   laedentem oscula quae Venus
quinta parte sui nectaris imbuit.

   felices ter et amplius
quos irrupta tenet copula nec malis
   divulsus querimoniis
suprema citius solvet amor die.   20

However many of Rome's enemies
he leads in triumph, whether Parthian bands
or Indians or Chinamen who throng
    the eastern lands,

below you shall his glad dominion be;
yours is the power that shall Olympus jolt,
you shall assail polluted evil with
    the thunderbolt.

1.13

When you extol your Telephus
(*smooth arms and rosy neck of Telephus*)
    by heaven, Lydia, I seethe,
my liver swells and boils in bitter juice.

My temper and my colour rise
beyond control; see furtive moisture slide
    along my cheeks, betraying how
deep-seated flames are simmering inside,

which flare when drunken violence
erupts and blemishes your shoulders white,
    and when that oaf implants upon
your mouth his tell-tale mark with frenzied bite.

Take heed, fidelity you can't
expect from one who viciously abuses
    those honeyed lips, which Venus with
quintessence of ambrosia infuses.

Thrice blessed, and more, are couples whose
uniting bond holds fast, whose love, unshaken
    by mutual complaints, endures
till by the final parting overtaken.

1.14

O navis, referent in mare te novi
fluctus! o quid agis? fortiter occupa
    portum! nonne vides ut
      nudum remigio latus,

et malus celeri saucius Africo,
antennaeque gemant, ac sine funibus
    vix durare carinae
      possint imperiosius

aequor? non tibi sunt integra lintea,
non di quos iterum pressa voces malo.   10
    quamvis Pontica pinus,
      silvae filia nobilis,

iactes et genus et nomen inutile,
nil pictis timidus navita puppibus
    fidit. tu, nisi ventis
      debes ludibrium, cave.

nuper sollicitum quae mihi taedium,
nunc desiderium curaque non levis,
    interfusa nitentis
      vites aequora Cycladas.   20

1.15

Pastor cum traheret per freta navibus
Idaeis Helenen perfidus hospitam,
ingrato celeris obruit otio
    ventos, ut caneret fera

Nereus fata: 'mala ducis avi domum,
quam multo repetet Graecia milite,
coniurata tuas rumpere nuptias
    et regnum Priami vetus.

1.14

The rising waves will force you back to sea,
stout ship. Take action; fight your way steadfast
    to harbour. Your whole broadside
      is stripped of oars; your mast

and yards are groaning painfully before
the tearing southerly; unfrapped your hull
    can scarcely hold against the
      maelstrom's tyrannical

onslaught. Your sails are all in shreds; your gods
are gone, no more to answer to your need.
    Your timbers may be Pontic,
      the forest's proudest seed,

but sailors put no trust in gilded poops,
vain is your boast of names and pedigrees.
    Beware, lest you're reduced to
      the sport of every breeze.

The wearisome unease I felt for you
has now become the lover's desperate yearning;
    avoid the tempting straits of
      the Cyclades, returning.

1.15

As the false shepherd in his Phrygian ship
carried his host's wife Helen overseas,
Nereus imposed unwelcome calm upon
    the winds, to utter these

dire words: 'Ill-omened is the freight you bear,
in quest of whom all Greece a force will send
sworn to destroy your union with her,
    and Priam's reign to end.

heu heu, quantus equis, quantus adest viris
sudor! quanta moves funera Dardanae   10
genti! iam galeam Pallas et aegida
    currusque et rabiem parat.

nequiquam Veneris praesidio ferox
pectes caesariem grataque feminis
imbelli cithara carmina divides,
    nequiquam thalamo gravis

hastas et calami spicula Gnosii
vitabis strepitumque et celerem sequi
Aiacem; tamen heu serus adulteros
    crinis pulvere collines.   20

non Laertiaden, exitium tuae
gentis, non Pylium Nestora respicis?
urgent impavidi te Salaminius
    Teucer, te Sthenelus sciens

pugnae, sive opus est imperitare equis,
non auriga piger. Merionen quoque
nosces. ecce furit te reperire atrox
    Tydides melior patre,

quem tu, cervus uti vallis in altera
visum parte lupum graminis immemor,   30
sublimi fugies mollis anhelitu,
    non hoc pollicitus tuae.

iracunda diem proferet Ilio
matronisque Phrygum classis Achillei;
post certas hiemes uret Achaicus
    ignis Iliacas domos.'

1.16

O matre pulchra filia pulchrior,
quem criminosis cumque voles modum
    pones iambis, sive flamma
      sive mari libet Hadriano.

Alas, alas, what sweat is here for horse
and man, what carnage for the Trojan realm!
Already brooding Pallas burnishes
    her aegis and her helm.

In vain, by Venus shielded, you will strut,
and preen your curls, and tune those mincing airs
that women love; in vain the boudoir you
    will haunt, to hide your fears

of deadly missiles, shafts of Cretan reed,
the battle-clamour, and the swift pursuit
of Ajax, for the dust shall in the end
    your lustful locks pollute.

Have you no thought of Pylian Nestor,
or of your nation's scourge, Laertes' son?
Teucer is on your heels and Sthenelus,
    in arms a champion,

and expert with the chariot-team at need.
You'll learn of Meriones, and taste the fire
of one who means to find you, Tydeus' son,
    superior to his sire,

whom you, as when a deer, which sights afar
a wolf, forgets its grazing, in distress
gasping for breath will flee – belying all
    your boasts to your mistress.

Achilles' furious detachment will
the day of reckoning for Troy adjourn;
after the fated span Achaean fire
    the Trojan homes shall burn.'

1.16

Of lovely mother daughter lovelier still,
condemn those scurrilous lampoons to fire
   or fling them in the Adriatic
    sea, whichever sentence you desire.

non Dindymene, non adytis quatit
mentem sacerdotum incola Pythius,
   non Liber aeque, non acuta
     sic geminant Corybantes aera,

tristes ut irae, quas neque Noricus
deterret ensis nec mare naufragum   10
   nec saevus ignis nec tremendo
     Iuppiter ipse ruens tumultu.

fertur Prometheus addere principi
limo coactus particulam undique
   desectam et insani leonis
     vim stomacho apposuisse nostro.

irae Thyesten exitio gravi
stravere et altis urbibus ultimae
   stetere causae cur perirent
     funditus imprimeretque muris   20

hostile aratrum exercitus insolens.
compesce mentem: me quoque pectoris
   temptavit in dulci iuventa
     fervor et in celeris iambos

misit furentem: nunc ego mitibus
mutare quaero tristia, dum mihi
   fias recantatis amica
     opprobriis animumque reddas.

1.17

Velox amoenum saepe Lucretilem
mutat Lycaeo Faunus et igneam
   defendit aestatem capellis
     usque meis pluviosque ventos.

impune tutum per nemus arbutos
quaerunt latentis et thyma deviae
   olentis uxores mariti,
     nec viridis metuunt colubras

Nothing unseats the mind – not Cybele,
not Bacchus, not the Pythian within
  his holy shrine, not Corybantes
    clashing out their brazen cymbal-din –

like vengeful anger, which is not deterred
by crafted steel, by ship-devouring sea,
  by conflagration, even by the
    awful power of Jove in panoply.

They say Prometheus, fashioning man's clay
with elements from every creature snatched,
  the violence of a raging lion
    to the human temperament attached.

By anger was Thyestes cruelly
brought low, and anger is the reason why
  high cities have succumbed to utter
    ruin, with their walls ploughed under by

implacable invaders. Come, restrain
your indignation. I too in the heat
  of careless youth was tempted to the
    folly of composing indiscreet

lampoons, but now I hope to cultivate
forgiveness, not revenge. I'll make a start
  if only you'll relent and, all harsh
    words recanted, give me back your heart.

1.17

From Arcady to fair Lucretilis
swift-footed Faunus often comes, whose power
  unfailingly protects my goats from
    torrid heat alike and gusty shower.

Unharmed the consorts and the offspring of
their evil-smelling lord explore the brake
  in search of hidden berries and of
    thyme, untroubled by the gaudy snake

nec Martialis haediliae lupos,
utcumque dulci, Tyndari, fistula   10
  valles et Vsticae cubantis
    levia personuere saxa.

di me tuentur, dis pietas mea
et musa cordi est. hic tibi copia
  manabit ad plenum benigno
    ruris honorum opulenta cornu:

hic in reducta valle Caniculae
vitabis aestus et fide Teia
  dices laborantis in uno
    Penelopen vitreamque Circen: 20

hic innocentis pocula Lesbii
duces sub umbra, nec Semeleius
  cum Marte confundet Thyoneus
    proelia, nec metues protervum

suspecta Cyrum, ne male dispari
incontinentis iniciat manus
  et scindat haerentem coronam
    crinibus immeritamque vestem.

1.18

Nullam, Vare, sacra vite prius severis arborem
circa mite solum Tiburis et moenia Catili.
siccis omnia nam dura deus proposuit, neque
mordaces aliter diffugiunt sollicitudines.

quis post vina gravem militiam aut pauperiem crepat?
quis non te potius, Bacche pater, teque, decens Venus?
ac ne quis modici transiliat munera Liberi,
Centaurea monet cum Lapithis rixa super mero

debellata, monet Sithoniis non levis Euhius,
cum fas atque nefas exiguo fine libidinum   10
discernunt avidi. non ego te, candide Bassareu,
invitum quatiam, nec variis obsita frondibus

or by marauding wolf, whenever his
sweet pan-pipe, Tyndaris, re-echoes round
   Ustica's sunken valley-floor and
     saturates the rocks with reedy sound.

The gods protect me here, my piety
and verses gratify them; ready here
   you'll find a lavish store of kindness
     and abundance of rich country fare.

In this sequestered vale you can escape
midsummer's heat; in Teian style you can
   sing of Penelope and glass-green
     Circe vying for a single man.

Once here you shall enjoy beneath the shade
the gentle wine of Lesbos; you shall see
   no brawls inflamed by Bacchus; you shall
     not be troubled by the jealousy

of that hot-tempered bully Cyrus, nor
shall he lay brutal hands on you, nor tear
   the garland on your forehead, nor the
     unoffending garments that you wear.

1.18

First the sacred vine, friend Varus, plant your vineyard first of all,
as you sow the gentle meadows near to Tibur's city wall;
god imposes endless hardships on the man who's always dry,
wine alone can chase away the gnawing of adversity.

After wine who harps on crushing poverty or war's alarms,
rather than the praise of father Bacchus and of Venus' charms?
But don't overstep the moderate bounds of Liber's rites; recall
Centaurs done to death by Lapiths in intoxicated brawl,

and Sithonians chastised by Euhius, when they by light
of their appetites had ventured to distinguish wrong from right.
I shall not against your wishes rouse you, comely Bassareus,
nor your hidden emblems rashly to the daylight introduce.

sub divum rapiam. saeva tene cum Berecyntio
cornu tympana, quae subsequitur caecus Amor sui
et tollens vacuum plus nimio Gloria verticem
arcanique Fides prodiga, perlucidior vitro.

1.19

Mater saeva Cupidinum
Thebanaeque iubet me Semelae puer
    et lasciva Licentia
finitis animum reddere amoribus.

urit me Glycerae nitor
splendentis Pario marmore purius:
    urit grata protervitas
et vultus nimium lubricus aspici.

in me tota ruens Venus
Cyprum deseruit, nec patitur Scythas   10
    et versis animosum equis
Parthum dicere nec quae nihil attinent.

hic vivum mihi caespitem, hic
verbenas, pueri, ponite turaque
    bimi cum patera meri:
mactata veniet lenior hostia.

1.20

Vile potabis modicis Sabinum
cantharis, Graeca quod ego ipse testa
conditum levi, datus in theatro
   cum tibi plausus,

clare Maecenas eques, ut paterni
fluminis ripae simul et iocosa
redderet laudes tibi Vaticani
   montis imago.

But restrain your wildly blaring horn and frenzied drum, behind
which in riot come complacent Love of self, completely blind,
boastful Glory rearing up an empty head absurdly high,
and Discretion blabbing secrets, glasslike in transparency.

1.19

> The cruel mother of desires,
> and Bacchus, son of Theban Semele,
>   and wanton Licence, force me to
> revive a heart long dead to ecstasy.

> Afire for Glycera's bright skin,
> outshining purest marble, I'm afire
>   for her enchanting impudence
> and for her glamour, perilous to admire.

> Total onslaught by Venus drives
> my thoughts away from trivialities,
>   from Scythia, or the Parthian,
> aggressive when he wheels his horse and flees.

> Heap fresh turf for an altar, boys,
> bring greenery and frankincense and bring
>   a bowl of unmixed wine; she'll come
> more gently if I make an offering.

1.20

Rough Sabine you will quaff from modest cups
drawn from a jar that I myself was sealing
that very day the audience's cheers
   for you were pealing,

until ancestral Tiber shouted with
applause for you, Maecenas, noble knight,
and joyful echoes bore your praises from
   Vatican's height.

Caecubum et prelo domitam Caleno
tu bibes uvam: mea nec Falernae
    temperant vites neque Formiani
        pocula colles.

10

1.21

Dianam tenerae dicite virgines,
intonsum, pueri, dicite Cynthium
    Latonamque supremo
        dilectam penitus Iovi.

vos laetam fluviis et nemorum coma,
quaecumque aut gelido prominet Algido
    nigris aut Erymanthi
        silvis aut viridis Gragi.

vos Tempe totidem tollite laudibus
natalemque, mares, Delon Apollinis,
    insignemque pharetra
        fraternaque umerum lyra.

10

hic bellum lacrimosum, hic miseram famem
pestemque a populo et principe Caesare in
    Persas atque Britannos
        vestra motus aget prece.

1.22

Integer vitae scelerisque purus
non eget Mauris iaculis neque arcu
nec venenatis gravida sagittis,
   Fusce, pharetra,

sive per Syrtis iter aestuosas
sive facturus per inhospitalem
Caucasum vel quae loca fabulosus
   lambit Hydaspes.

Your cellar offers you Calenian
and Caecuban; my wine is from my area,
no choice Falernian or Formian,
   nothing superior.

1.21

Come, gentle maidens, sing Diana's praise,
and of unshorn Apollo sing, you boys,
   Latona honour also,
      who Jove's deep love enjoys.

Tell of Diana's love of streams and all
the leaves that on cold Algidus are seen,
   on Erymanthus darker,
      on Gragus lighter green.

Exalt as warmly Tempe and Delos,
Apollo's place of birth, you male-voice choir,
   his famous quiver too, and
      his brother's gift, the lyre.

From Rome and Caesar he'll divert disease,
famine and war, those harbingers of tears,
   to Persia and to Britain,
      persuaded by your prayers.

1.22

The man of upright life, unstained by crime,
needs no Moroccan javelin to throw,
no quiver, Fuscus, full of poisoned barbs,
   nor any bow,

whether he purposes to travel through
forbidding Caucasus, or fabled lands
washed by Hydaspes, or the sweltering
   Syrtes quicksands.

namque me silva lupus in Sabina,
dum meam canto Lalagen et ultra 10
terminum curis vagor expeditis,
   fugit inermem,

quale portentum neque militaris
Daunias latis alit aesculetis
nec Iubae tellus generat, leonum
   arida nutrix.

pone me pigris ubi nulla campis
arbor aestiva recreatur aura,
quod latus mundi nebulae malusque
   Iuppiter urget; 20

pone sub curru nimium propinqui
solis in terra domibus negata:
dulce ridentem Lalagen amabo,
   dulce loquentem.

1.23

Vitas inuleo me similis, Chloe,
quaerenti pavidam montibus aviis
   matrem non sine vano
     aurarum et siluae metu.

nam seu mobilibus vepris inhorruit
ad ventum foliis seu virides rubum
   dimovere lacertae,
     et corde et genibus tremit.

atqui non ego te tigris ut aspera
Gaetulusve leo frangere persequor: 10
   tandem desine matrem
     tempestiva sequi viro.

For while I strayed too far in Sabine woods,
intent on Lalage, remote from stress,
a wolf turned tail and fled from me, though I
    was weaponless,

a monster such as warlike Daunia
in all its forest lairs could never nourish,
nor could Numidia's parched wilderness
    where lions flourish.

Transport me to the tundra desolate
where never tree enjoys a summer breeze,
a region of the world where clouds oppress
    and blizzards freeze,

or to the tropics where the sun's too close
for man to make his home, my shield shall be –
my sweetly laughing, sweetly speaking love,
    my Lalage.

1.23

You shun me, Chloë, like a baby fawn
whose mother in the trackless hills has strayed;
    she starts in needless panic
        at every shift and shade,

and if a lizard flickers on the thorn
or a breeze among the thistles in the brake
    flutters the leaves, her heart leaps,
        her knees in terror quake.

But I'm no brutish predator, no wolf
to chase and tear you ruthlessly; my dear,
    forget about your mother,
        your time for love is here.

1.24

Quis desiderio sit pudor aut modus
tam cari capitis? praecipe lugubris
cantus, Melpomene, cui liquidam pater
    vocem cum cithara dedit.

ergo Quintilium perpetuus sopor
urget! cui Pudor et Iustitiae soror,
incorrupta Fides, nudaque Veritas
    quando ullum inveniet parem?   10

multis ille bonis flebilis occidit,
nulli flebilior quam tibi, Vergili.
tu frustra pius heu non ita creditum
    poscis Quintilium deos.

quid si Threicio blandius Orpheo
auditam moderere arboribus fidem,
num vanae redeat sanguis imagini,
    quam virga semel horrida,   20

non lenis precibus fata recludere,
nigro compulerit Mercurius gregi?
durum: sed levius fit patientia
    quidquid corrigere est nefas.

1.25

Parcius iunctas quatiunt fenestras
iactibus crebris iuvenes protervi,
nec tibi somnos adimunt, amatque
    ianua limen,

quae prius multum facilis movebat
cardines; audis minus et minus iam
'me tuo longas pereunte noctes,
    Lydia, dormis?'

1.24

Why should restraint curtail our longing for
a friend so dearly loved? Lend me your lyre,
Melpomene, and limpid voice; in me
    a requiem inspire.

And so Quintilius has gone to his
long sleep; his equal shall we ever see
in modesty, just dealing, truthfulness,
    unswerving loyalty?

His death is mourned by many honest men,
and you have mourned him, Virgil, most of all,
but piety can't rectify life's terms;
    he's past your prayers' recall.

What if, surpassing Orpheus, you could charm
the very trees to hearken to your song?
Could that restore the lifeblood to his shade,
    once to the lightless throng

he has been herded by the fateful wand
of Mercury, whom no appeals deflect?
It's hard, but time alone can ease the pain
    which nothing can correct.

1.25

Less often do young men fling pebbles at
your shuttered windows, Lydia, almost
they leave your sleep untroubled; your front door
   cleaves to its post,

which used to exercise so readily
its hinges; now the cry comes less and less:
'How can you sleep all night, oblivious
   of my distress?'

invicem moechos anus arrogantis
flebis in solo levis angiportu,   10
Thracio bacchante magis sub inter-
   lunia vento,

cum tibi flagrans amor et libido
quae solet matres furiare equorum,
saeviet circa iecur ulcerosum,
   non sine questu

laeta quod pubes hedera virenti
gaudeat pulla magis atque myrto,
aridas frondis hiemis sodali
   dedicet Euro.   20

1.26

Musis amicus tristitiam et metus
tradam protervis in mare Creticum
   portare ventis, quis sub Arcto
     rex gelidae metuatur orae,

quid Tiridaten terreat unice
securus. o quae fontibus integris
   gaudes, apricos necte flores,
     necte meo Lamiae coronam

Piplei dulcis! nil sine te mei
prosunt honores: hunc fidibus novis,   10
   hunc Lesbio sacrare plectro
     teque tuasque decet sorores.

1.27

Natis in usum laetitiae scyphis
pugnare Thracum est: tollite barbarum
   morem, verecundumque Bacchum
     sanguineis prohibete rixis.

Age brings your turn to taste the slights of love,
made light of, lonely, on the street outcast,
exposed before the north wind's frenzied glee,
    its moonless blast,

but still tormented by the animal
concupiscence that maddens mares on heat,
and stews within your ulcerous entrails,
    until you bleat

that ivy's tender green and myrtle dark
are all young studs will deign to lay a hand on,
while dry leaves they to winter's henchman, the
    east wind, abandon.

1.26

Befriended by the Muses, I can scorn
rebellions in the frozen north; complete
    is my indifference to trembling
        Tiridates; I banish to Crete

upon the boisterous breeze my discontent
and tensions. Lover of fresh waters, twist
    a crown for Lamia my friend, a
        worthy crown of blossom summer-kissed,

Piplean Muse. Without you praise from me
is worthless; he deserves the restrung lyre
    of Lesbos to exalt him, tuned by
        you and by the whole Pierian choir.

1.27

Wine cups are meant as instruments of joy,
their use as missiles would degrade a Thracian.
    Where are your manners? Spare good-tempered
        Bacchus a barbaric altercation.

vino et lucernis Medus acinaces
immane quantum discrepat: impium
   lenite clamorem, sodales,
      et cubito remanete presso.

vultis severi me quoque sumere
partem Falerni? dicat Opuntiae   10
   frater Megillae quo beatus
      vulnere, qua pereat sagitta.

cessat voluntas? non alia bibam
mercede. quae te cumque domat Venus,
   non erubescendis adurit
      ignibus, ingenuoque semper

amore peccas. quidquid habes, age
depone tutis auribus. a! miser,
   quanta laborabas Charybdi,
      digne puer meliore flamma.   20

quae saga, quis te solvere Thessalis
magus venenis, quis poterit deus?
   vix illigatum te triformi
      Pegasus expediet Chimaera.

1.28

Te maris et terrae numeroque carentis harenae
   mensorem cohibent, Archyta,
pulveris exigui prope litus parva Matinum
   munera, nec quicquam tibi prodest

aerias temptasse domos animoque rotundum
   percurrisse polum morituro.
occidit et Pelopis genitor, conviva deorum,
   Tithonusque remotus in auras,

et Iovis arcanis Minos admissus, habentque
   Tartara Panthoiden iterum Orco   10
demissum, quamvis clipeo Troiana refixo
   tempora testatus nihil ultra

What's this? a Persian dagger waved about?
What a grotesque affront to lamplit dining!
   Come, stifle this unholy uproar,
      partygoers, and remain reclining.

My turn, you think, to taste the sterner wine?
Then first Megilla's brother must explain
   whose arrow in his heart has caused such
      blissful but excruciating pain.

No answer? Then, I warn you, I won't drink.
Whatever flame has brought you to this pass
   I'm sure it won't disgrace you, since your
      preference is for a decent class

of mistress. Look, you know your secret's safe
with me, just whisper it. Ye gods above!
   Poor boy, you're toiling in Charybdis,
      you who merited a better love!

What witch, what wizard with Thessalian spells
can save you now, what god can set you free?
   Not even Pegasus could rescue
      you from that three-faced monstrosity.

1.28

Though you measured the sea and the earth and the numberless sands,
   Archytas, you narrowly now are constrained
by a handful of dust offered near the Apulian shore,
   nor in the end have you any advantage attained

by your mental assault on the aerial realms, or exploring
   heaven's expanse, for still to the grave you were borne.
Death carried Tantalus off, who dined with Olympian gods,
   and Tithonus at last, though he dwelt in the dawn,

Minos as well, though privy to secrets of Jove. Acheron
   hems in Euphorbus, the second time thither removed,
who, by unhooking his shield, which after the downfall of Troy
   had been hung in the temple, conclusively proved

nervos atque cutem morti concesserat atrae,
iudice te non sordidus auctor
naturae verique. sed omnis una manet nox
et calcanda semel via leti.

dant alios Furiae torvo spectacula Marti;
exitio est avidum mare nautis;
mixta senum ac iuvenum densentur funera; nullum
saeva caput Proserpina fugit.   20

me quoque devexi rapidus comes Orionis
Illyricis Notus obruit undis.
at tu, nauta, vagae ne parce malignus harenae
ossibus et capiti inhumato

particulam dare: sic, quodcumque minabitur Eurus
fluctibus Hesperiis, Venusinae
plectantur silvae te sospite, multaque merces
unde potest tibi defluat aequo

ab Iove Neptunoque sacri custode Tarenti.
neglegis immeritis nocituram   30
postmodo te natis fraudem committere? fors et
debita iura vicesque superbae

te maneant ipsum: precibus non linquar inultis,
teque piacula nulla resolvent.
quamquam festinas, non est mora longa; licebit
iniecto ter pulvere curras.

1.29

Icci, beatis nunc Arabum invides
gazis, et acrem militiam paras
non ante devictis Sabaeae
regibus, horribilique Medo   .

nectis catenas? quae tibi virginum
sponso necato barbara serviet?
puer quis ex aula capillis
ad cyathum statuetur unctis,

that his sinews and bones were all he had yielded to death –
  and you judged his teaching shed brilliant light
upon nature and truth. But for all men the path must be walked
  only once to the single, perpetual night.

Some by the Fates are condemned as the playthings of pitiless Mars;
  mariners often succumb to the ravening waves;
young men and old to their deaths are crowded indifferently;
  Proserpine ruthlessly draws one and all to their graves.

I myself met with my end in the hostile Illyrian sea,
  swept overboard by a wild equinoctial storm.
But, fellow sailor, I beg of you, grudge not a measure of sand,
  pity my bones and my skull, my unburied form;

sprinkle a pinch as you pass; then when skies threaten squalls from the east,
  let the woods of Venusia suffer the blow,
and may you be unscathed, and from every available source
  may riches upon you abundantly flow

from Jove and from Neptune, who holy Tarentum protects.
  Can you not see you are risking that harm may ensue
for your innocent future descendants? Perhaps you will find
  that denial of rights is in store for you too

and a fall for your pride; if you leave me, my curse will avenge;
  no penance will put matters right; you will pay.
Though your journey is urgent, there's no need to linger for long;
  just scatter three handfuls, then hasten away.

1.29

  So, Iccius, you're sizing up the loot
  of Araby, devising total war
    against the hitherto unconquered
      Sheban princelings, forging shackles for

    the dreaded Medes? What dusky maiden will
    become your slave, a newly-widowed bride?
      What royal page with perfumed hair will
        tend your wine-cup stationed at your side,

doctus sagittas tendere Sericas
arcu paterno? quis neget arduis   10
    pronos relabi posse rivos
        montibus et Tiberim reverti,

cum tu coemptos undique nobilis
libros Panaeti Socraticam et domum
    mutare loricis Hiberis,
        pollicitus meliora, tendis?

1.30

O Venus, regina Cnidi Paphique,
sperne dilectam Cypron et vocantis
ture te multo Glycerae decoram
    transfer in aedem.

fervidus tecum puer et solutis
Gratiae zonis properentque Nymphae
et parum comis sine te Iuventas
    Mercuriusque.

1.31

Quid dedicatum poscit Apollinem
vates? quid orat de patera novum
    fundens liquorem? non opimae
        Sardiniae segetes feraces,

non aestuosae grata Calabriae
armenta, non aurum aut ebur Indicum
    non rura quae Liris quieta
        mordet aqua taciturnus amnis.

premant Calenam falce quibus dedit
fortuna vitem, dives et aureis   10
    mercator exsiccet culillis
        vina Syra reparata merce,

more skilled in serving his ancestral bow
with Chinese arrows? Who would now deny
   that Tiber could turn round, and rivers
      flow back up the mountains to the sky,

when you, who promised better things, propose
to dump the noble books you've brought together –
   your Stoics and your Platonists – in
      favour of waistcoats of Spanish leather?

1.30

Come, Venus, queen of eastern shrines, desert
Cyprus and switch to Glycera's fine home,
who summons you with clouds of incense to
   transfer to Rome.

Make haste to bring with you your amorous boy,
your Nymphs, the Graces with their girdles free,
and Youth so drab without you, and not least
   bring Mercury.

1.31

What does the poet ask Apollo for
on dedication day, as he libates
   new liquor from the bowl? Not bumper
      crops from rich Sardinian estates,

not herds from hot Calabria, not gold
and ivory from India collected,
   not country vineyards by the gentle
      stream of Liris noiselessly bisected.

No, let the lucky owner of the vine
see to the pruning; let the millionaire
   swill down his wine from golden goblets
      traded for imported Syrian ware

dis carus ipsis, quippe ter et quater
anno revisens aequor Atlanticum
   impune. me pascunt olivae,
     me cichorea levesque malvae.

frui paratis et valido mihi,
Latoe, dones, et, precor, integra
   cum mente, nec turpem senectam
     degere nec cithara carentem.   20

1.32

Poscimus si quid vacui sub umbra
lusimus tecum, quod et hunc in annum
vivat et pluris, age dic Latinum,
   barbite, carmen,

Lesbio primo modulate civi,
qui ferox bello, tamen inter arma
sive iactatam religarat udo
   litore navim,

Liberum et Musas Veneremque et illi
semper haerentem puerum canebat   10
et Lycum nigris oculis nigroque
   crine decorum.

o decus Phoebi et dapibus supremi
grata testudo Iovis, o laborum
dulce lenimen, mihi cumque salve
   rite vocanti.

1.33

Albi, ne doleas plus nimio memor
immitis Glycerae neu miserabilis
decantes elegos, cur tibi iunior
   laesa praeniteat fide.

(dear to the very gods he'll visit the
Atlantic seaboard thrice a year at least
   unscathed).To me a dish of olives,
      chicory and mallow makes a feast.

I pray for health to savour what I have
and faculties intact, and grant to me,
   Apollo, undegraded closing
      years, still graced by joy in poetry.

1.32

If ever strumming with you in the shade
I've played a tune that hearers may applaud
this year and next, my lyre, strike now, I beg,
   a Latin chord.

Your sound the citizen of Lesbos first
refined, who, steadfast in the midst of war,
or fresh from making fast his bruised ship to
   the storm-wet shore,

would sing of Bacchus and the Muses nine,
of Venus and of Cupid at her side,
of Lycus too, his comely black-haired boy
   and jet-black-eyed.

Apollo's pride, guest at the feasts of Jove,
sweet lightener of toil, o tortoiseshell,
aid me whenever I in proper form
   invoke your spell.

1.33

Enough of moping verses, Albius,
on heartless Glycera; obliterate
her broken promises, her preference for
   a younger candidate.

insignem tenui fronte Lycorida
Cyri torret amor, Cyrus in asperam
declinat Pholoen; sed prius Apulis
    iungentur capreae lupis,

quam turpi Pholoe peccet adultero.
sic visum Veneri, cui placet impares   10
formas atque animos sub iuga aenea
    saevo mittere cum ioco.

ipsum me melior cum peteret Venus,
grata detinuit compede Myrtale
libertina, fretis acrior Hadriae
    curvantis Calabros sinus.

1.34

Parcus deorum cultor et infrequens
insanientis dum sapientiae
    consultus erro, nunc retrorsum
        vela dare atque iterare cursus

cogor relictos: namque Diespiter,
igni corusco nubila dividens
    plerumque, per purum tonantis
        egit equos volucremque currum

quo bruta tellus et vaga flumina,
quo Styx et invisi horrida Taenari   10
    sedes Atlanteusque finis
        concutitur. valet ima summis

mutare et insignem attenuat deus,
obscura promens; hinc apicem rapax
    fortuna cum stridore acuto
        sustulit, hic posuisse gaudet.

Fine-boned Lycoris burns with passion for
Cyrus, while he strays after Pholoë;
but sooner will she-goats with wolves be joined
    than that stern miss will be

drawn into an adulterous affair.
So Venus wills, who loves to clamp her yoke
of bronze on ill-assorted couples, and
    enjoys the cruel joke.

I too, though better love was offered, once
succumbed – a victim willingly unmanned –
to Myrtale, more wayward than the waves
    that scour the hollowed land.

1.34

A grudging, rare, adherent of the gods
I used to stray, professing an insane
    philosophy, but now I find I'm
        forced to go about and sail again

abandoned courses: for Diespiter
who normally from stormclouds darts his beam
    of lightning, through a cloudless heaven
        drove his chariot and thunder-team,

a shock to solid earth and flowing rivers,
convulsing Styx and the abyss unholy
    of Taenarus and Ocean's utmost
        margins. God can interchange the lowly

and mighty; he puts down the glorious
exalting the unknown. Fortune now seizes
    the crown from one with strident cry, now
        drops it on another as she pleases.

1.35

O diva, gratum quae regis Antium,
praesens vel imo tollere de gradu
   mortale corpus vel superbos
     vertere funeribus triumphos,

te pauper ambit sollicita prece
ruris colonus, te dominam aequoris
   quicumque Bithyna lacessit
     Carpathium pelagus carina.

te Dacus asper, te profugi Scythae,
urbesque gentesque et Latium ferox   10
   regumque matres barbarorum et
     purpurei metuunt tyranni,

iniurioso ne pede proruas
stantem columnam, neu populus frequens
   ad arma cessantis, ad arma
     concitet imperiumque frangat.

te semper anteit serva Necessitas,
clavos trabalis et cuneos manu
   gestans aena, nec severus
     uncus abest liquidumque plumbum.   20

te Spes et albo rara Fides colit
velata panno, nec comitem abnegat,
   utcumque mutata potentis
     veste domos inimica linquis.

at vulgus infidum et meretrix retro
periura cedit, diffugiunt cadis
   cum faece siccatis amici
     ferre iugum pariter dolosi.

serves iturum Caesarem in ultimos
orbis Britannos et iuvenum recens   30
   examen Eois timendum
     partibus Oceanoque rubro.

1.35

Goddess and queen revered in Antium,
whose might can mortal man's estate reverse
    to high from humble, or reduce a
        proud triumphal chariot to a hearse,

to you the needy smallholder repeats
his prayers, to you as mistress of the waves
    the anxious trader, whose fine-timbered
        merchantman the Cretan ocean braves;

the distant tribes, the city-states and peoples,
as well as Latium, all hold you in dread,
    so do barbarian matriarchs and
        chiefs, and tyrants in the purple bred,

for fear you may capriciously kick down
their palaces, and give the mob its hour
    to congregate and raise the cry *To*
        arms, to arms, and overthrow their power.

Before you, holding wedges and beam-nails
in brazen gauntlet, stalks your grim handmaid,
    Necessity, with iron hook and
        molten lead forbiddingly arrayed;

with you go Hope and white-gloved Loyalty,
who from your company do not withdraw
    when you change coat and, in the guise of
        enemy, desert a great man's door;

while fickle crowd and courtesan foresworn
shrink back, and former friends, once they've made free
    with every drop of wine, decamp, too
        treacherous to share adversity.

Keep Caesar safe, who is about to make
his way to Britain, earth's remotest shore,
    and our young swarm of heroes, who the
        East and the Red Sea will overawe.

eheu, cicatricum et sceleris pudet
fratrumque. quid nos dura refugimus
    aetas? quid intactum nefasti
       liquimus? unde manum iuventus

metu deorum continuit? quibus
pepercit aris? o utinam nova
    incude diffingas retusum in
       Massagetas Arabasque ferrum!   40

1.36

Et ture et fidibus iuvat
placare et vituli sanguine debito
    custodes Numidae deos,
qui nunc Hesperia sospes ab ultima

    caris multa sodalibus,
nulli plura tamen dividit oscula
    quam dulci Lamiae, memor
actae non alio rege puertiae

    mutataeque simul togae.
Cressa ne careat pulchra dies nota,   10
    neu promptae modus amphorae,
neu morem in Salium sit requies pedum,

    neu multi Damalis meri
Bassum Threicia vincat amystide,
    neu desint epulis rosae
neu vivax apium neu breve lilium.

    omnes in Damalin putris
deponent oculos, nec Damalis novo
    divelletur adultero
lascivis hederis ambitiosior.   20

Our age is shamed by scars from brothers got.
From what iniquity have we refrained?
   What sacrilege have we not dared? From
      what misdeed has fear of god restrained

our youth? What sacred shrine is undefiled?
Upon your anvil, Goddess, would that you,
   for use against our nation's foreign
      enemies, would forge our swords anew.

1.36

   With incense, lyric music and
a bull-calf's blood let us discharge the vow
     to guardian gods of Numida,
who safe from furthest Spain has come back now,

   showering kisses left and right
among his friends, and most of all upon
     his well remembered Lamia,
his boyhood exemplar and paragon,

   his peer in taking manhood's robe.
For celebration chalk this day in white:
     no limit on the flow of wine,
from acrobatic dancing no respite;

   let thirsty Damalis allow
Bassus to win the drinking victory;
     let roses grace the feast and short-
lived lilies and robuster celery.

   On Damalis all melting eyes
will fasten, nor will anyone unclasp
     the arms she folds round Numida,
more clinging than the wanton ivy's grasp.

1.37

Nunc est bibendum, nunc pede libero
pulsanda tellus, nunc Saliaribus
   ornare pulvinar deorum
      tempus erat dapibus, sodales.

antehac nefas depromere Caecubum
cellis avitis, dum Capitolio
   regina dementis ruinas
      funus et imperio parabat

contaminato cum grege turpium
morbo virorum, quidlibet impotens   10
   sperare fortunaque dulci
      ebria. sed minuit furorem

vix una sospes navis ab ignibus,
mentemque lymphatam Mareotico
   redegit in veros timores
      Caesar ab Italia volantem

remis adurgens, accipiter velut
mollis columbas aut leporem citus
   venator in campis nivalis
      Haemoniae, daret ut catenis   20

fatale monstrum; quae generosius
perire quaerens nec muliebriter
   expavit ensem, nec latentis
      classe cita reparavit oras;

ausa et iacentem visere regiam
vultu sereno, fortis et asperas
   tractare serpentis, ut atrum
      corpore combiberet venenum,

deliberata morte ferocior
saevis Liburnis, scilicet invidens   30
   privata deduci superbo
      non humilis mulier triumpho.

1.37

Now is the time to drink, to stamp the ground
without restraint, my friends, to deck with feasts
    the tables of the gods, to set them
        banquets worthy of the Salian priests.

Till now it was unfitting to fetch down
the treasured vintage from its dusty home,
    while that demented queen was plotting
        rack and ruin for the might of Rome,

abetted by her vice-polluted crew
of semi-men, with luck intoxicated
    and blind with limitless ambition,
        till her folly was at last deflated

by scarce one ship escaping from the flames,
and then her mind, awash with eastern wine,
    was jolted into sober dread by
        Caesar bearing down upon her line

of flight from Roman waters – as a hawk
stoops on a dove, or as upon the plains
    of Thessaly the hunter courses
        down the hare – meaning to put in chains

the deadly fiend; but she, seeking a death
more noble, neither womanishly quailed
    before the sword, nor headlong with her
        galleys to some secret refuge sailed,

but bore to look upon her fallen walls
with face unmoved, and found the hardihood
    to grasp the scaly serpent, so its
        venom could be drunk into her blood;

once set on death she was more ruthless than
the fierce Liburnians, her high disdain
    refused to countenance the public
        degradation of the triumph-train.

1.38

Persicos odi, puer, apparatus,
displicent nexae philyra coronae;
mitte sectari, rosa quo locorum
    sera moretur.

simplici myrto nihil allabores
sedulus curo: neque te ministrum
dedecet myrtus neque me sub arta
    vite bibentem.

1.38

Away with fancy woven garlands, boy,
I can't abide such oriental show;
don't trouble to go seeking corners where
   late roses blow.

Use myrtle, I insist on nothing more
elaborate: plain myrtle suits my wine,
you serving and me drinking it, beneath
   my shady vine.

Book 2

Book 2 is the most homogeneous of Books 1-3. Out of twenty odes none is longer than ten stanzas and none shorter than five; twelve are Alcaics and six are Sapphics, so that there is much less variety of metre; thirteen are addressed to living individuals, including three, all in the second half of the Book, addressed to Maecenas. Between the resounding 1, addressed to the distinguished figure of Pollio (who earned respect even from Syme), and the surreal vision of 20 are found some of the best loved and most characteristic odes: on the shortness of life (14) and the need to enjoy it (3), on loving a slave girl (4), on his favourite places (6), on welcoming an old comrade in arms (7) and on the pestilential tree which nearly brained him (13). It is the most accessible of the four books.

Candidates for deferment to the second reading are 2, 15, 18.

2.1

Motum ex Metello consule civicum
bellique causas et vitia et modos
   ludumque Fortunae gravisque
      principum amicitias et arma

nondum expiatis uncta cruoribus,
periculosae plenum opus aleae,
   tractas, et incedis per ignis
      suppositos cineri doloso.

paulum severae Musa tragoediae
desit theatris: mox ubi publicas   10
   res ordinaris, grande munus
      Cecropio repetes cothurno,

insigne maestis praesidium reis
et consulenti, Pollio, curiae,
   cui laurus aeternos honores
      Delmatico peperit triumpho.

iam nunc minaci murmure cornuum
perstringis auris, iam litui strepunt,
   iam fulgor armorum fugaces
      terret equos equitumque vultus.   20

audire magnos iam videor duces
non indecoro pulvere sordidos,
   et cuncta terrarum subacta
      praeter atrocem animum Catonis.

Iuno et deorum quisquis amicior
Afris inulta cesserat impotens
   tellure victorum nepotes
      rettulit inferias Iugurthae.

quis non Latino sanguine pinguior
campus sepulcris impia proelia   30
   testatur auditumque Medis
      Hesperiae sonitum ruinae?

2.1

Civil unrest sown in Metellus' year,
the causes, crimes and ways of war, the twists
   of Fortune's mocking game, the fateful
     treaties made between protagonists,

the taint of blood still unredeemed – all these
you handle, hazarding a dangerous throw,
   tiptoeing over ashes, under
     which live embers treacherously glow.

Let theatres miss your tragedies awhile,
set history in order first, and then
   turn your attention to your major
     work, Athenian drama, once again,

friend Pollio, distinguished champion
in court and senatorial debate,
   whose glory, won by your Dalmatian
     triumph, time will not eradicate.

Now, now with deep discordance of war-horns
you stun the ears, now bugles screech and blare,
   now horse and rider turn and fly, in
     terror of the armour's blinding glare.

And now I seem to hear a meeting of
great leaders honourably by dust defiled,
   masters of all the world, except for
     Cato, to the last unreconciled.

Pro-African Juno, once forced to leave
that country unavenged, has now betrayed
   the conquerors' descendants, as a
     blood-price to placate Jugurtha's shade.

In foreign fields enriched by Latin dead
grave-mounds our fratricidal strife attest,
   and, echoing among the Medes like
     thunder, devastation in the West.

qui gurges aut quae flumina lugubris
ignara belli? quod mare Dauniae
   non decoloravere caedes?
      quae caret ora cruore nostro?

sed ne relictis, Musa procax, iocis
Ceae retractes munera neniae,
   mecum Dionaeo sub antro
      quaere modos leviore plectro.   40

2.2

Nullus argento color est avaris
abdito terris, inimice lamnae
   Crispe Sallusti, nisi temperato
      splendeat usu.

vivet extento Proculeius aevo
notus in fratres animi paterni;
   illum aget penna metuente solvi
      Fama superstes.

latius regnes avidum domando
spiritum, quam si Libyam remotis   10
   Gadibus iungas et uterque Poenus
      serviat uni.

crescit indulgens sibi dirus hydrops
nec sitim pellit, nisi causa morbi
   fugerit venis et aquosus albo
      corpore languor.

redditum Cyri solio Phraaten
dissidens plebi numero beatorum
eximit Virtus, populumque falsis
   dedocet uti   20

vocibus, regnum et diadema tutum
deferens uni propriamque laurum,
quisquis ingentis oculo irretorto
   spectat acervos.

What sea, what strait has not experienced
our melancholy wars? What ocean's flood
   is not with Daunian slaughter stained? Has
     any shore not gorged upon our blood?

But tales of woe are wearisome, my Muse;
remember they need spicing with a smile.
   Come to some haunt of Venus, where we'll
     cultivate a lighter-hearted style.

2.2

Silver is colourless when buried in
the grasping earth, Sallust; it needs to be
burnished by moderate use – you've said as much
   repeatedly.

The generosity of Proculeius
towards his brothers lasting fame shall bring;
renown shall bear his name to future years
   on tireless wing.

By taming greed you'd rule more widely than
if you both Punic lands could integrate
from Libya to remote Cadiz, one vast
   client estate.

To banish dropsy's bloated lethargy
its cause the pallid sufferer must first
expel; indulgence stimulates, not stems,
   the deadly thirst.

The restoration of Phraätes to
his throne forbids misuse of words, for he
despite the popular belief would not
   by Virtue be

called blessed, for kingship's crown and accolade
belong to him alone who can pass by
a heaped-up hoard of gold, and not cast back
   a wistful eye.

2.3

Aequam memento rebus in arduis
servare mentem, non secus in bonis
    ab insolenti temperatam
      laetitia, moriture Delli,

seu maestus omni tempore vixeris,
seu te in remoto gramine per dies
    festos reclinatum bearis
      interiore nota Falerni.

quo pinus ingens albaque populus
umbram hospitalem consociare amant   10
    ramis? quid obliquo laborat
      lympha fugax trepidare rivo?

huc vina et unguenta et nimium brevis
flores amoenae ferre iube rosae,
    dum res et aetas et sororum
      fila trium patiuntur atra.

cedes coemptis saltibus et domo
villaque flavus quam Tiberis lavit;
    cedes, et exstructis in altum
      divitiis potietur heres.   20

divesne prisco natus ab Inacho
nil interest an pauper et infima
    de gente sub divo moreris,
      victima nil miserantis Orci.

omnes eodem cogimur, omnium
versatur urna serius ocius
    sors exitura et nos in aeternum
      exsilium impositura cumbae.

2.3

Maintain a level head when times are hard,
and equally, when fortune is your friend,
   restrain extravagant elation,
      Dellius; remember life will end,

whether you pass your days a prey to gloom,
or spend each feast-day savouring your best
   Falernian, on some secluded
      bank stretched out, indulgently at rest.

See how these lofty pines and poplars white
conspire to weave their branches overhead
   in friendly shade; see how this bustling
      river skips along its twisting bed.

Call forth, then, wine and perfume and the blooms
of lovely roses that too soon will drop,
   while chance and age allow, and that black
      thread the Sisters Three have yet to crop.

You'll leave your purchased woodlands, your town-house,
your villa which the Tiber passes by,
   you'll leave them, and your heir will pocket
      all the riches you have stacked so high.

You may be wealthy and of royal blood,
or homeless, penniless, of mean descent;
   it matters not, you are a victim
      owed to Orcus, who does not relent.

Each man the same fate summons, late or soon
the lot of each revolving in the urn
   is shaken out and lands him in the
      ferry for the shore of no return.

2.4

Ne sit ancillae tibi amor pudori,
Xanthia Phoceu, prius insolentem
serva Briseis niveo colore
    movit Achillem;

movit Aiacem Telamone natum
forma captivae dominum Tecmessae;
arsit Atrides medio in triumpho
    virgine rapta,

barbarae postquam cecidere turmae
Thessalo victore et ademptus Hector   10
tradidit fessis leviora tolli
    Pergama Grais.

nescias an te generum beati
Phyllidis flavae decorent parentes:
regium certe genus et penatis
    maeret iniquos.

crede non illam tibi de scelesta
plebe delectam, neque sic fidelem,
sic lucro aversam potuisse nasci
    matre pudenda.   20

bracchia et vultum teretesque suras
integer laudo; fuge suspicari
cuius octavum trepidavit aetas
    claudere lustrum.

2.5

Nondum subacta ferre iugum valet
cervice, nondum munia comparis
    aequare nec tauri ruentis
        in venerem tolerare pondus.

2.4

Your passion for a slave-girl, Xanthias,
is no disgrace; the proud Achilles gave
his love to snowy-armed Briseïs, who
 was just a slave;

Ajax the son of Telamon was by
Tecmessa, his bondmaiden, captivated;
Atrides with a ravished girl became
 infatuated

in triumph's hour, when the Thessalian's
success in battle and Hector's demise
delivered Troy to weary Argive arms,
 a crippled prize.

Your fair-haired Phyllis' parents may be rich,
a source of honour to their son in law;
her gloom is for her royal line's eclipse,
 you may be sure.

You picked her – not from vicious stock, not you;
such scorn of wealth, such loyal circumspection,
believe me, could not possibly spring from
 a base connection.

Her arms, her face, her pretty ankles, I
impartially admire – all quite delicious;
relax, I'm over forty now, no need
 to be suspicious.

2.5

Unbroken to the yoke, she has not yet
the strength to give a ploughing-partner full
 support, nor yet to bear the weight of
  sexual aggression from a bull.

circa virentis est animus tuae
campos iuvencae, nunc fluviis gravem
   solantis aestum, nunc in udo
     ludere cum vitulis salicto

praegestientis. tolle cupidinem
immitis uvae: iam tibi lividos   10
   distinguet Autumnus racemos
     purpureo varius colore.

iam te sequetur: currit enim ferox
aetas et illi quos tibi dempserit
   apponet annos; iam proterva
     fronte petet Lalage maritum,

dilecta quantum non Pholoe fugax,
non Chloris albo sic umero nitens
   ut pura nocturno renidet
     luna mari, Cnidiusve Gyges,   20

quem si puellarum insereres choro,
mire sagaces falleret hospites
   discrimen obscurum solutis
     crinibus ambiguoque vultu.

2.6

Septimi, Gadis aditure mecum et
Cantabrum indoctum iuga ferre nostrum et
barbaras Syrtis, ubi Maura semper
   aestuat unda,

Tibur Argeo positum colono
sit meae sedes utinam senectae,
sit modus lasso maris et viarum
   militiaeque.

unde si Parcae prohibent iniquae,
dulce pellitis ovibus Galaesi   10
flumen et regnata petam Laconi
   rura Phalantho.

Your heifer's inclination leads her to
lush watermeadows; now in rivers she
   escapes oppressive heat, now in the
      osier-beds she longs precociously

to flirt with bull-calves. Curb your craving for
the unripe grape; quite soon enough for you
   will autumn's changing palette darken
      light green clusters with a purple hue.

The passing years diminish you, but are
enhancing her; soon she'll be the pursuer,
   soon Lalage will learn the playful
      butting moves which mark the bovine wooer.

You'll love her more than flighty Pholoë
or Chloris whose skin emulates the sheen
   of flawless moonbeams smiling on the
      midnight ocean, or than epicene

Gyges from Cnidos, who, if you were to
slip him into a line of dancing girls,
   would fool the shrewdest diner with his
      feminine good looks and floating curls.

2.6

Septimius, who'd face Cadiz with me,
or Cantabri who from our yoke recoil,
or cruel Syrtes where the Moorish waves
   forever boil,

as home for my old age I choose Tibur,
established by the Argive pioneer,
a place to rest from toils by land and sea
   and old warfare.

If fate denies the first, the country round
Spartan Tarentum is my second dream,
where leather-coated sheep are watered at
   Galaesus' stream.

ille terrarum mihi praeter omnis
angulus ridet, ubi non Hymetto
mella decedunt viridique certat
   baca Venafro,

ver ubi longum tepidasque praebet
Iuppiter brumas, et amicus Aulon
fertili Baccho minimum Falernis
   invidet uvis.   20

ille te mecum locus et beatae
postulant arces; ibi tu calentem
debita sparges lacrima favillam
   vatis amici.

2.7

O saepe mecum tempus in ultimum
deducte Bruto militiae duce,
   quis te redonavit Quiritem
      dis patriis Italoque caelo,

Pompei, meorum prime sodalium?
cum quo morantem saepe diem mero
   fregi coronatus nitentis
      malobathro Syrio capillos.

tecum Philippos et celerem fugam
sensi relicta non bene parmula,   10
   cum fracta virtus, et minaces
      turpe solum tetigere mento.

sed me per hostis Mercurius celer
denso paventem sustulit aere;
   te rursus in bellum resorbens
      unda fretis tulit aestuosis.

ergo obligatam redde Iovi dapem
longaque fessum militia latus
   depone sub lauru mea, nec
      parce cadis tibi destinatis.   20

That corner of the world delights me more
than any other, where the olive betters
Venafrum's and the honey challenges
    that of Hymettus,

where spring comes early, winter's not too cold,
and Aulon's terraces, by Bacchus blessed,
produce a wine that has no envy of
    the very best.

That place, those happy citadels, invite
us both; there shall you offer at the end
a tear upon the still-warm ashes of
    your poet-friend.

2.7

Pompey, how often under Brutus's
command you marched at crisis-time with me;
    who now has brought you back, a Roman
        citizen again, to Italy?

To drown in wine the lagging day with you,
my foremost comrade, often I rejoiced,
    my brow arrayed with garlands, and my
        hair with scented Syrian lotion moist.

With you I shared Philippi's rout, when I
regrettably mislaid my pretty shield,
    when courage crumbled and ambition
        in the mire dishonourably kneeled.

Me in my panic nimble Mercury
concealed with mist and rescued from the foe,
    but you the seething tide of battle
        sucked back in with deadly undertow.

So now do justice to the waiting casks
laid down for you, and in my laurel grove
    relax your limbs fatigued by warfare;
        dedicate the feast you owe to Jove.

oblivioso levia Massico
ciboria exple; funde capacibus
  unguenta de conchis. quis udo
    deproperare apio coronas

curatve myrto? quem Venus arbitrum
dicet bibendi? non ego sanius
  bacchabor Edonis: recepto
    dulce mihi furere est amico.

2.8

Ulla si iuris tibi peierati
poena, Barine, nocuisset umquam,
dente si nigro fieres vel uno
    turpior ungui,

crederem. sed tu, simul obligasti
perfidum votis caput, enitescis
pulchrior multo iuvenumque prodis
    publica cura.

expedit matris cineres opertos
fallere et toto taciturna noctis   10
signa cum caelo gelidaque divos
    morte carentis.

ridet hoc, inquam, Venus ipsa, rident
simplices Nymphae, ferus et Cupido,
semper ardentis acuens sagittas
    cote cruenta.

adde quod pubes tibi crescit omnis,
servitus crescit nova, nec priores
impiae tectum dominae relinquunt,
    saepe minati.   20

te suis matres metuunt iuvencis,
te senes parci, miseraeque nuper
virgines nuptae, tua ne retardet
    aura maritos.

Come, polish up the cups and fill them high
with Massic wine, that brings forgetfulness.
   Pour perfume by the jugful! Hurry!
     Who will freshen up some sprigs of cress

or myrtle for the wreathes? Who's Venus' choice
to rule the drinking? I begin to burn
   with Bacchic frenzy! There is joy in
     going mad to greet a friend's return.

2.8

Barine, if I'd ever seen you pay
the smallest price for perjury – bewail
discolouration of a tooth or just
   one fingernail –

I might believe you. But you dazzle all
the more once you have sworn some new untruth,
parading forth, a public peril to
   adoring youth.

You cheat for profit – now your mother's grave,
and now the constellations and the still
night sky, and now the very gods whom death
   can never chill.

I tell you Venus mocks your lies, so do
her artless nymphs, and Cupid as he hones
on bloody stone the scorching darts which sear
   your lovers' bones.

What's worse the young now swell your following,
a second wave of bondage, while the first,
for all their promises, cannot escape
   your chains accursed.

All dread you: mothers for their bull-calves, old
men for their pockets: virgin brides lament
lest bridegrooms stay out late, distracted by
   your wafted scent.

2.9

Non semper imbres nubibus hispidos
manant in agros aut mare Caspium
    vexant inaequales procellae
        usque, nec Armeniis in oris,

amice Valgi, stat glacies iners
mensis per omnis aut Aquilonibus
    querqueta Gargani laborant
        et foliis viduantur orni:

tu semper urges flebilibus modis
Mysten ademptum, nec tibi Vespero   10
    surgente decedunt amores
        nec rapidum fugiente solem.

at non ter aevo functus amabilem
ploravit omnis Antilochum senex
    annos, nec impubem parentes
        Troilon aut Phrygiae sorores

flevere semper, desine mollium
tandem querelarum, et potius nova
    cantemus Augusti tropaea
        Caesaris et rigidum Niphaten,   20

Medumque flumen gentibus additum
victis minores volvere vertices,
    intraque praescriptum Gelonos
        exiguis equitare campis.

2.10

Rectius vives, Licini, neque altum
semper urgendo neque, dum procellas
cautus horrescis, nimium premendo
    litus iniquum.

2.9

Not always does the rain pour down upon
the bristling fields, nor does the squalling wind
    incessantly arouse the northern
        sea, nor does the ice of winter bind

Armenian shores, friend Valgius, throughout
the year, nor autumn's tempests always grieve
    the oaken groves of Garganus and
        rowans of their foliage bereave.

You're always harping on the loss of your
Mystes in mournful elegies; lovelorn
    you greet the evening star, not stopping
        when it's overtaken by the dawn.

Did Nestor spend his triple span of life
bewailing his adored Antilochus?
    Did Priam and his daughters mourn the
        prematurely slaughtered Troïlus

forever? Check at last these womanish
complaints; let us join forces to extol
    Caesar's new triumphs in annexing
        stark Niphates to the empire's roll,

and in compelling Persian Euphrates
to moderate its waves, till now so proud,
    and the Geloni to confine their
        horses to the narrow space allowed.

2.10

You'll steer aright, Licinius, if you
don't always head for deeper waters, nor
in fear of squalls bear down too close upon
    the leeward shore.

auream quisquis mediocritatem
diligit, tutus caret obsoleti
sordibus tecti, caret invidenda
    sobrius aula.

saepius ventis agitatur ingens
pinus et celsae graviore casu
decidunt turres feriuntque summos
    fulgura montis.

10

sperat infestis, metuit secundis
alteram sortem bene praeparatum
pectus. informis hiemes reducit
    Iuppiter, idem

summovet. non, si male nunc, et olim
sic erit: quondam cithara tacentem
suscitat Musam neque semper arcum
    tendit Apollo.

20

rebus angustis animosus atque
fortis appare; sapienter idem
contrahes vento nimium secundo
    turgida vela.

2.11

Quid bellicosus Cantaber et Scythes,
Hirpine Quincti, cogitet Hadria
    divisus obiecto, remittas
        quaerere, nec trepides in usum

poscentis aevi pauca: fugit retro
levis iuventas et decor, arida
    pellente lascivos amores
        canitie facilemque somnum.

non semper idem floribus est honor
vernis, neque uno Luna rubens nitet
    vultu: quid aeternis minorem
        consiliis animum fatigas?

10

The man who cultivates the golden mean
is safe, too sober for a hearth disgraced
by squalor, or the ostentation of
   palatial taste.

It is the topmost peaks are targeted
by lightning; to the wind the tallest ash
bends most; the highest tower collapses with
   the loudest crash.

The wisely-ordered mind anticipates,
in evil times with hope, in good with dread,
fortune's reversal; Jove brings winter back,
   and Jove instead

gives spring. If now your luck is out, it will
return; Apollo does not always use
his arrows, sometimes with his lyre he wakes
   the sleeping Muse.

In narrow straits you must be spirited
and resolute, but with a following gale
be circumspect, take in your sheet and trim
   your too-full sail.

2.11

The warlike Cantabri and Scythians
aren't on your doorstep; what they mean to do
   need not concern you Quinctius, don't
     bother asking; life's demands are few,

don't fret about them. Bloom and grace of youth
have slipped away from us, grey hairs have chased
   away light-hearted love affairs, and
     slumber once so easily embraced.

The springtime glory of the blossom will
recede; the stormy moon will not blush red
   unchanged; why overtax your waning
     faculties by planning far ahead?

cur non sub alta vel platano vel hac
pinu iacentes sic temere et rosa
   canos odorati capillos,
     dum licet, Assyriaque nardo

potamus uncti? dissipat Euhius
curas edaces. quis puer ocius
   restinguet ardentis Falerni
     pocula praetereunte lympha?   20

quis devium scortum eliciet domo
Lyden? eburna dic age cum lyra
   maturet incomptum Lacaenae
     more comas religata nodum.

2.12

Nolis longa ferae bella Numantiae
nec durum Hannibalem nec Siculum mare
Poeno purpureum sanguine mollibus
   aptari citharae modis,

nec saevos Lapithas et nimium mero
Hylaeum domitosque Herculea manu
Telluris iuvenes, unde periculum
   fulgens contremuit domus

Saturni veteris; tuque pedestribus
dices historiis proelia Caesaris,   10
Maecenas, melius ductaque per vias
   regum colla minacium.

me dulces dominae Musa Licymniae
cantus, me voluit dicere lucidum
fulgentis oculos et bene mutuis
   fidum pectus amoribus,

quam nec ferre pedem dedecuit choris
nec certare ioco nec dare bracchia
ludentem nitidis virginibus sacro
   Dianae celebris die.   20

Why don't we here and now while time permits
scent these grey locks with spikenard and rose,
stretch out beneath this plane-tree or this
lofty pine in casual repose,

and drink together? Bacchus will disperse
anxieties. A boy is needed fast
to moderate your heady wine with
water from this brook that's flowing past.

Who'll coax call-girl Lyde from her retreat?
Make sure she brings her lyre, the ivory one,
at once – no pause to titivate her
hair, it's perfect in a simple bun.

2.12

You wouldn't wish the fierce Numantine wars,
the hardships of the Hannibal campaigns,
or Mylae's crimsoned waves to be demeaned
by tender lyric strains,

nor drunken brawls of Lapith and Centaur,
nor Hercules reducing to defeat
the earthborn Giants, who by their assault
had rocked the glittering seat

of Saturn; so, Maecenas, the account
of Caesar's victories, and bellicose
princelings in chains paraded, will be far
more suited to your prose.

My Muse steers me to your Licymnia,
her charming voice, her glance's lightning-learned
directness, and her loyal commitment to
a love so well returned,

who joined, and graced, the line of dancers and
the trial of wit, and linked her arms in play
with white-clad maidens celebrating on
Diana's sacred day.

num tu quae tenuit dives Achaemenes
aut pinguis Phrygiae Mygdonias opes
    permutare velis crine Licymniae,
        plenas aut Arabum domos,

cum flagrantia detorquet ad oscula
cervicem aut facili saevitia negat,
    quae poscente magis gaudeat eripi,
        interdum rapere occupet?

2.13

Ille et nefasto te posuit die
quicumque primum, et sacrilega manu
    produxit, arbos, in nepotum
        perniciem opprobriumque pagi;

illum et parentis crediderim sui
fregisse cervicem et penetralia
    sparsisse nocturno cruore
        hospitis; ille venena Colcha

et quidquid usquam concipitur nefas
tractavit, agro qui statuit meo   10
    te triste lignum, te caducum
        in domini caput immerentis.

quid quisque vitet numquam homini satis
cautum est in horas: navita Bosphorum
    Poenus perhorrescit neque ultra
        caeca timet aliunde fata;

miles sagittas et celerem fugam
Parthi, catenas Parthus et Italum
    robur; sed improvisa leti
        vis rapuit rapietque gentis.   20

quam paene furvae regna Proserpinae
et iudicantem vidimus Aeacum
    sedesque descriptas piorum et
        Aeoliis fidibus querentem

If you were offered all king Croesus' gold,
or Phrygian Midas' treasure, would you care
to barter for them even a single strand
    of your Licymnia's hair,

when she to your impassioned lips inclines
her neck, or teasingly perverse refuses,
a friend to stolen kisses, who at times
    the role of robber chooses?

2.13

It was a godless man who planted you
upon a lawless day, pernicious tree,
    bequeathing ruin to his offspring,
      infamy to this locality;

I swear he was the sort of ruffian
to break his mother's neck, or stain at night
    with blood of some defenceless guest his
      household shrine; a criminal who might

traffic in poisons and all other kinds
of vice was he who placed you, fateful tree,
    in my domain, to fall upon your
      owner passing inoffensively.

Watch as he will, a man can't be on guard
at every moment; sailors dread the straits
    of Bosphorus, unmindful of the
      hidden fate that round the headland waits;

the soldier fears the backward arrow of
the Parthian, the Parthian fears to go
    in chains to Rome, but what is always
      fatal is the unexpected blow.

How near I came to seeing that dark realm
of Proserpine, and Aeacus unfolding
    judgment, the region of the blessed, and
      Sappho in Aeolian lyrics scolding

Sappho puellis de popularibus,
et te sonantem plenius aureo,
   Alcaee, plectro dura navis,
      dura fugae mala, dura belli!

utrumque sacro digna silentio
mirantur umbrae dicere; sed magis   30
   pugnas et exactos tyrannos
      densum umeris bibit aure vulgus.

quid mirum, ubi illis carminibus stupens
demittit atras belua centiceps
   auris et intorti capillis
      Eumenidum recreantur angues?

quin et Prometheus et Pelopis parens
dulci laborem decipitur sono,
   nec curat Orion leones
      aut timidos agitare lyncas.   40

2.14

Eheu fugaces, Postume, Postume,
labuntur anni nec pietas moram
   rugis et instanti senectae
      adferet indomitaeque morti:

non si trecenis quotquot eunt dies,
amice, places illacrimabilem
   Plutona tauris, qui ter amplum
      Geryonen Tityonque tristi

compescit unda, scilicet omnibus,
quicumque terrae munere vescimur,   10
   enaviganda, sive reges
      sive inopes erimus coloni.

frustra cruento Marte carebimus
fractisque rauci fluctibus Hadriae,
   frustra per autumnos nocentem
      corporibus metuemus Austrum:

her countrywomen, and, Alcaeus, you,
with golden touch and in robuster style
   portraying the relentless hardships
      faced in warfare, naval life, exile.

They both command a wondering silence from
the listening shades, but most the triumph-song
   of strife and tyranny expelled is
      drunk in by the densely pressing throng; –

no wonder when that magic sound can charm
the hundred-headed hound to droop his ears
   bewitched, and all the snakes to sway in
      pleasure twined among the Furies' hairs;

the music even cheats the torment of
Prometheus, lending him a breathing space,
   and rests the wary lynx and lion
      while Orion pauses in the chase.

2.14

Alas, my friend, alas, the years retreat
and vanish, nor can piety delay
   the onward march of wrinkles and old
      age and death itself, that none can stay.

Not with three hecatombs of bulls a day,
my Postumus, could you appease impassive
   Pluto, whose gloomy stream imprisons
      Tityos and Geryon's thrice-massive

carcase – that stream which every one of us
who on the fruits of nature's bounty feed
   must navigate, no matter whether
      potentate or peasant pinched by need.

In vain we turn aside from bloodshed, and
the clamour of the Adriatic sea;
   in vain against the south wind's autumn
      blast we wrap our bodies timidly.

visendus ater flumine languido
Cocytos errans et Danai genus
   infame damnatusque longi
      Sisyphus Aeolides laboris: 20

linquenda tellus et domus et placens
uxor, neque harum quas colis arborum
   te praeter invisas cupressos
      ulla brevem dominum sequetur:

absumet heres Caecuba dignior
servata centum clavibus et mero
   tinget pavimentum superbo,
      pontificum potiore cenis.

2.15

Iam pauca aratro iugera regiae
moles relinquent, undique latius
   extenta visentur Lucrino
      stagna lacu, platanusque caelebs

evincet ulmos; tum violaria et
myrtus et omnis copia narium
   spargent olivetis odorem
      fertilibus domino priori;

tum spissa ramis laurea fervidos
excludet ictus, non ita Romuli   10
   praescriptum et intonsi Catonis
      auspiciis veterumque norma.

privatus illis census erat brevis,
commune magnum: nulla decempedis
   metata privatis opacam
      porticus excipiebat Arcton,

nec fortuitum spernere caespitem
leges sinebant, oppida publico
   sumptu iubentes et deorum
      templa novo decorare saxo.   20

We all must journey to the black morass
of sinuous Cocytus, to that brood
   of wicked brides, to Sisyphus in
      sentence of eternal servitude.

You too must leave your land, your home, the wife
you love, and of the trees that you have sown
   which will attend their short-lived master's
      parting? Hated cypress-wood alone.

Your worthier heir will down the Caecuban
which you behind a hundred locks have stored,
   and stain your tessellated floors with
      wine that even priests could not afford.

2.15

Palatial piles will soon leave little space
for ploughland, private fishponds everywhere
   will dwarf the Lucrine lake itself, and
      unproductive plane-trees overbear

the elms; then gilly-flowers and myrtle shrubs
and hosts of nose-beguiling blooms will shed
   their cloying scent where formerly the
      fertile olive groves were husbanded,

and interwoven laurel boughs will screen
from sunburn. Things in Romulus's reign
   were different, nor did ancient ways or
      bearded Cato's precepts so ordain.

Then private wealth was small, the common stock
was great; no closely measured colonnade
   designed for private residents could
      capture all the northern-facing shade;

the law prohibited the casual waste
of turf, and out of public funds required
   the towns and temples of the gods with
      handsome new-cut stone to be attired.

2.16

Otium divos rogat in patenti
prensus Aegaeo, simul atra nubes
condidit lunam neque certa fulgent
    sidera nautis;

otium bello furiosa Thrace,
otium Medi pharetra decori,
Grosphe, non gemmis neque purpura ve-
    nale nec auro.

non enim gazae neque consularis
summovet lictor miseros tumultus   10
mentis et curas laqueata circum
    tecta volantis.

vivitur parvo bene, cui paternum
splendet in mensa tenui salinum
nec levis somnos timor aut cupido
    sordidus aufert.

quid brevi fortes iaculamur aevo
multa? quid terras alio calentis
sole mutamus? patriae quis exsul
    se quoque fugit?   20

scandit aeratas vitiosa navis
Cura nec turmas equitum relinquit,
ocior cervis et agente nimbos
    ocior Euro.

laetus in praesens animus quod ultra est
oderit curare et amara lento
temperet risu; nihil est ab omni
    parte beatum.

abstulit clarum cita mors Achillem,
longa Tithonum minuit senectus,   30
et mihi forsan, tibi quod negarit,
    porriget hora.

2.16

Peace is the merchant's prayer, when caught by squalls
far out in the Aegean sea, as soon
as guiding stars are dimmed and dark clouds ride
    across the moon;

for peace the Persian in his gaudy gear,
for peace the Thracian prays, by war distraught,
but, Grosphus, not by purple, gold or gems
    can peace be bought.

For neither hoarded bullion nor a troop
of consular lictors can ever halt
the mind's ferment, the cares that flitter through
    the coffered vault.

Scant goods bring ample comfort to the man
whose table with a father's salt-pot gleams,
who suffers neither fear nor greed to mar
    his easy dreams.

Life is so short, why do we set our sights
so high? Why do we seek a different sun?
What fugitive from homeland ever has
    himself outrun?

Corroding care will board the bronze-clad yacht,
and mount among the Knights' parading swarm,
swifter than deer, yes, swifter than the blast
    that drives the storm.

The heart that values present happiness
should scorn to press for more, should face the test
of setbacks with a smile; no portion is
    completely blessed.

By sudden death Achilles was cut short,
by age Tithonus was relentlessly
worn down; what life denies to you, it may
    bestow on me.

te greges centum Siculaeque circum
mugiunt vaccae, tibi tollit hinnitum
apta quadrigis equa, te bis Afro
    murice tinctae

vestiunt lanae: mihi parva rura et
spiritum Graiae tenuem Camenae
Parca non mendax dedit et malignum
    spernere vulgus.   40

2.17

Cur me querelis exanimas tuis?
nec dis amicum est nec mihi te prius
    obire, Maecenas, mearum
        grande decus columenque rerum.

a! te meae si partem animae rapit
maturior vis, quid moror altera,
    nec carus aeque nec superstes
        integer? ille dies utramque

ducet ruinam. non ego perfidum
dixi sacramentum: ibimus, ibimus,   10
    utcumque praecedes, supremum
        carpere iter comites parati.

me nec Chimaerae spiritus igneae
nec, si resurgat, centimanus Gyges
    divellet umquam: sic potenti
        Iustitiae placitumque Parcis.

seu Libra seu me Scorpios aspicit
formidolosus, pars violentior
    natalis horae, seu tyrannus
        Hesperiae Capricornus undae,   20

utrumque nostrum incredibili modo
consentit astrum: te Iovis impio
    tutela Saturno refulgens
        eripuit volucrisque Fati

Round you a hundred flocks, and herds of cows
from Sicily, give tongue, your whinnying mare
is ready for the racing chariot,
    the robes you wear

are twice-dipped purple, while my little lot
is narrow land, from Greece a slender vein
of inspiration, and, for those who live
    by spite, disdain.

2.17

Don't scare me so, Maecenas, you who are
my greatest pride and buttress; neither I
    nor any god would welcome it if
        you should be the first of us to die.

Your early death would ravage half my soul,
and then for the surviving half what point
    in living could remain, bereaved and
        blighted? No, that day must mark our joint

quietus. I have sworn this solemn vow:
whenever you lead I shall go; that trip,
    that final trip, we'll take together,
        friends in long-ordained companionship.

Not hundred-handed Gyges, should he wake,
nor the Chimaera's flames could sever me
    from this resolve; of all-controlling
        Fate and Justice such is the decree.

Let Libra or let dreadful Scorpio
observe me from my birth-hour's grimmest quarters,
    or Capricorn who exercises
        strict dominion over western waters,

our stars still march in startling harmony;
for Jove blazed forth at Saturn's base intent
    and snatched you to security by
        reining to a halt the winged descent

tardavit alas, cum populus frequens
laetum theatris ter crepuit sonum:
   me truncus illapsus cerebro
      sustulerat, nisi Faunus ictum

dextra levasset, Mercurialium
custos virorum. reddere victimas   30
   aedemque votivam memento:
      nos humilem feriemus agnam.

2.18

   Non ebur neque aureum
mea renidet in domo lacunar,
   non trabes Hymettiae
premunt columnas ultima recisas

   Africa, neque Attali
ignotus heres regiam occupavi,
   nec Laconicas mihi
trahunt honestae purpuras clientae:

   at fides et ingeni
benigna vena est, pauperemque dives   10
   me petit: nihil supra
deos lacesso nec potentem amicum

   largiora flagito,
satis beatus unicis Sabinis.
   truditur dies die,
novaeque pergunt interire lunae:

   tu secanda marmora
locas sub ipsum funus et sepulcri
   immemor struis domos
marisque Bais obstrepentis urges   20

   summovere litora,
parum locuples continente ripa.
   quid quod usque proximos
revellis agri terminos et ultra

of fate, that day the theatre audience
close-packed three times in glad applause erupted;
   while me that falling tree-branch would have
    brained had not its blow been interrupted

by Faunus' arm, the bulwark of all men
who follow Mercury. Be sure to keep
   your promise of a shrine and worthy
    victims; I shall smite a modest sheep.

2.18

   No ivory or gold
in my house from a panelled ceiling gleams,
   no columns hewn afar
in Africa support expensive beams

   of marble, nor have I
acquired a palace by remote bequest,
   nor am I honoured by
distinguished women in rich purple dressed.

   But I'm discreet, and tap
a vein of talent; rich men, though I'm poor,
   befriend me; from the gods
or from a patron I need nothing more,

   nor ask it, being with
my patch of Sabine country satisfied.
   Day aside by day
is thrust, the crescent moon will soon have died;

   at death's door you proceed
to order stone, not thinking of your grave
   but planning houses, and
you strain to push back the protesting wave

   from Baiae's beach, deeming
dry land too mean for your magnificence.
   And at the same time you
are pulling up your neighbour's boundary fence

limites clientium
salis avarus? pellitur paternos
   in sinu ferens deos
    et uxor et vir sordidosque natos.

   nulla certior tamen
rapacis Orci fine destinata
   aula divitem manet
    erum. quid ultra tendis? aequa tellus

   pauperi recluditur
regumque pueris, nec satelles Orci
   callidum Promethea
    revinxit auro captus. hic superbum

   Tantalum atque Tantali
genus coercet, hic levare functum
   pauperem laboribus
    vocatus atque non vocatus audit.

30

40

2.19

Bacchum in remotis carmina rupibus
vidi docentem – credite posteri –
   Nymphasque discentes et aures
    capripedum Satyrorum acutas.

Euhoe, recenti mens trepidat metu
plenoque Bacchi pectore turbidum
   laetatur: Euhoe, parce Liber,
    parce gravi metuende thyrso!

fas pervicaces est mihi Thyiadas
vinique fontem lactis et uberes
   cantare rivos atque truncis
    lapsa cavis iterare mella:

fas et beatae coniugis additum
stellis honorem tectaque Penthei
   disiecta non leni ruina
    Thracis et exitium Lycurgi.

10

and grabbing greedily
dependants' land; your client, dispossessed,
    with wife and household gods
retreats, his shabby sons clasped to his breast.

    But even for the rich
the fated destination is the hall
    of Orcus; what's to seek
beyond? Impartial earth a place for all

    provides, for princes and
for paupers; proffered gold did not induce
    the escort of the dead
to cut the bonds of wily Prometheus.

    The haughty Tantalids
he hampers, but the man whose straitened lot
    of toil is over he
relieves, attentive whether called or not.

2.19

I've sighted Bacchus on a lonely crag
holding a music master-class (believe it
    posterity) with audience of
      Nymphs and Satyrs eager to receive it.

Aiee! Possession by the god inspires
a sudden rush of dread and joy. Aiee!
    God of the dreadful thyrsus, pity,
      god of liberation, pity me!

So may I tell of riotous maenads,
of fountains spouting wine, of rivers filled
    with frothing milk, and rightly tell of
      honey out of hollow trees distilled,

may tell of Ariadne honoured by
a constellation, or the broadcast strewing
    of Pentheus' ruined palace, and the
      Thracian king Lycurgus's undoing.

tu flectis amnis, tu mare barbarum,
tu separatis uvidus in iugis
  nodo coerces viperino
    Bistonidum sine fraude crinis: 20

tu cum parentis regna per arduum
cohors Gigantum scanderet impia,
  Rhoetum retorsisti leonis
    unguibus horribilique mala;

quamquam choreis aptior et iocis
ludoque dictus non sat idoneus
  pugnae ferebaris: sed idem
    pacis eras mediusque belli.

te vidit insons Cerberus aureo
cornu decorum leniter atterens   30
  caudam et recedentis trilingui
    ore pedes tetigitque crura.

2.20

Non usitata nec tenui ferar
penna biformis per liquidum aethera
  vates, neque in terris morabor
    longius, invidiaque maior

urbis relinquam. non ego pauperum
sanguis parentum, non ego quem vocas,
  dilecte Maecenas, obibo
    nec Stygia cohibebor unda.

iam iam residunt cruribus asperae
pelles, et album mutor in alitem   10
  superne, nascunturque leves
    per digitos umerosque plumae.

iam Daedaleo notior Icaro
visam gementis litora Bosphori
  Syrtisque Gaetulas canorus
    ales Hyperboreosque campos.

You divert rivers, tame the savage sea,
on far-flung mountain tops, in wine new-bathed,
   you interweave the vipers worn by
      Bacchanals among their locks unscathed.

And when the impious troop of Giants scaled
the heights, imperilling your father's cause,
   in lion's shape you hurled back mighty
      Rhoetus with your fearsome teeth and claws.

Although less fit for warfare than the arts
of dance and comedy (so ran your fame),
   yet in the thick of battle, as in
      peace, your mighty presence proved the same.

In all your golden glory Cerberus
eyed you submissively, and meekly flicked
   his tail, and as you passed back up, your
      ankles with his triple tongue he licked.

2.20

A poet in mid-metamorphosis,
upon no commonplace or paltry wing
   I'll soar, earthbound no longer, through the
      empyrean, far above the sting

of urban backbiting. For I, a child
of poor and humble parentage, and I,
   your creature, dear Maecenas, shall not
      be confined by Styx – I shall not die.

Rough scales are even now enveloping
my legs, now to a bird's my upper parts
   are changing, from my shoulders to my
      finger-ends the snowy plumage starts.

More famous now than Icarus himself
I'll visit the resounding Dardanelles,
   the Syrtes too, and carol forth my
      swansong to the Hyperborean fells.

me Colchus et qui dissimulat metum
Marsae cohortis Dacus et ultimi
   noscent Geloni, me peritus
      discet Hiber Rhodanique potor.   20

absint inani funere neniae
luctusque turpes et querimoniae;
   compesce clamorem ac sepulcri
      mitte supervacuos honores.

My works the furthest tribesmen – Colchians,
Geloni, Dacians – all will recognise,
   while connoisseurs who dwell beside the
      Ebro and the Rhone will memorise.

My grave shall be a cenotaph; for dirge
and lamentation there shall be no room;
   repress all sordid grief, and please no
      empty honours for the empty tomb

Book 3

This Book is the climax of Horace's project, and its principal focus is at the beginning. The first six odes, known as the 'Roman Odes', form a unique group. They are all long, all in Alcaics and all devoted to the praise of Augustus, express and implied, and the propagation of his political programme. They cannot be properly appreciated without at least a rudimentary grasp of the policies comprised in that programme, which form themes and sub-themes in all the Roman Odes. A brief summary of the most important topics will be found in Appendix 3, and the Notes will assume familiarity with the numbering there. The Roman Odes are not the most digestible, they lack the lightness of touch that is so attractive in Horace's more personal poetry, but of their kind they are supreme. They are deeply felt. From his youth Horace had lived in a society racked by civil war. At the age of twenty-two he fought on the losing side at Philippi (42 BC), and it was as a beneficiary of the policy of clemency that he was able to reinstate himself. It was not until after the victory of Actium (31 BC) and the subsequent mopping up that civil peace supervened. It is no wonder that he was profoundly grateful to Augustus for restoring order and security. If the full flavour of the Odes is to be tasted, any temptation to skip the Roman Odes should be resisted.

The last ode is a triumphant assertion of the immortality of his achievement. Apart from that the second half of the Book is framed by two important odes (16 and 29) addressed to Maecenas. Without overstepping the bounds of the friendship attested by the earlier odes addressed to his patron, Horace is concerned to insist on his essential independence; he is his own man, and he can stand on his own feet, if necessary.

Candidates for deferment are 2 (though it contains what was once the most quoted, and is now the most hated, line in the Odes), 11, 14, 16, 24 and 27.

3.1

Odi profanum vulgus et arceo;
favete linguis; carmina non prius
    audita Musarum sacerdos
        virginibus puerisque canto.

regum timendorum in proprios greges,
reges in ipsos imperium est Iovis,
    clari Giganteo triumpho
        cuncta supercilio moventis.

est ut viro vir latius ordinet
arbusta sulcis, hic generosior   10
    descendat in Campum petitor,
        moribus hic meliorque fama

contendat, illi turba clientium
sit maior: aequa lege Necessitas
    sortitur insignis et imos;
        omne capax movet urna nomen.

destrictus ensis cui super impia
cervice pendet, non Siculae dapes
    dulcem elaborabunt saporem,
        non avium citharaeque cantus   20

somnum reducent: somnus agrestium
lenis virorum non humilis domos
    fastidit umbrosamque ripam,
        non Zephyris agitata Tempe.

desiderantem quod satis est neque
tumultuosum sollicitat mare
    nec saevus Arcturi cadentis
        impetus aut orientis Haedi,

non verberatae grandine vineae
fundusque mendax, arbore nunc aquas   30
    culpante, nunc torrentia agros
        sidera, nunc hiemes iniquas.

3.1

Stand back, the uninitiated crowd,
in silence, I address the Roman young;
   as high priest of the Muses I shall
      sing of matters hitherto unsung.

Dread kings control their subject populace,
but Jupiter himself controls the kings;
   he overthrew the Giants, and his
      eyebrow orders all created things.

One man may boast more vineyards than the next;
one candidate for office may rely
   on noble ancestry, another
      on upright morality and high

repute, a third may lead the largest claque
of clients; fate will handle each the same –
   the lots of high and low are tumbled
      round the urn which carries every name.

The guilty man above whose neck there hangs
a naked sword no banquet can allure,
   however lavish, nor can sweetest
      sound of instrument or birdsong cure

his sleeplessness: but sleep does not deny
to country labourers its soothing balm
   on shady bank, in gently wind-kissed
      valley, or in unpretentious farm.

The man who wants no more than is enough
fears no alarms, not tempests out at sea,
   nor angry setting of Arcturus,
      nor the rising Kid's ferocity,

nor tender vineshoots battered by the hail,
nor harvests disappointing spring's forecast,
   betrayed by deluge, or by sullen
      summer's blaze, or winter's wicked blast.

contracta pisces aequora sentiunt
iactis in altum molibus; huc frequens
   caementa demittit redemptor
      cum famulis dominusque terrae

fastidiosus: sed Timor et Minae
scandunt eodem quo dominus, neque
   decedit aerata triremi et
      post equitem sedet atra Cura.   40

quodsi dolentem nec Phrygius lapis
nec purpurarum sidere clarior
   delenit usus nec Falerna
      vitis Achaemeniumque costum,

cur invidendis postibus et novo
sublime ritu moliar atrium?
   cur valle permutem Sabina
      divitias operosiores?

3.2

Angustam amice pauperiem pati
robustus acri militia puer
   condiscat et Parthos feroces
      vexet eques metuendus hasta

vitamque sub divo et trepidis agat
in rebus. illum ex moenibus hosticis
   matrona bellantis tyranni
      prospiciens et adulta virgo

suspiret, eheu, ne rudis agminum
sponsus lacessat regius asperum   10
   tactu leonem, quem cruenta
      per medias rapit ira caedis.

dulce et decorum est pro patria mori:
mors et fugacem persequitur virum,
   nec parcit imbellis iuventae
      poplitibus timidove tergo.

Fish find the sea diminished now that piles
are forced into the deep, and rubble poured
    by teeming workforce and contractor,
        even by the restless owner, bored

with solid earth; yet fear and foreboding
will climb as high as he; they will not spare
    the brazen pleasure-boat; behind the
        most distinguished horseman sits black care.

But since no gemstone mined in Phrygia,
no glorious purple dye, no finest wine,
    no perfume of Arabia can
        soothe away the smallest pain of mine,

why should I build myself a lofty hall
with entrance grand, a fashionable address?
    Why should I trade my Sabine vale for
        riches that will bring me only stress?

3.2

A boy should be toughened by discipline
and schooled to welcome poverty, to chase
    and terrify with horse and spear the
        savage Parthians, and to embrace

life in the open and the presence of
real danger. Royal women, stationed high
    on hostile walls, the bride-to-be and
        queen, on catching sight of him should sigh

in horror lest the bridegroom-prince below,
as yet unskilled in battle, should waylay
    that furious lion they see slicing
        murderously through the bloody fray.

A patriotic death earns sweet renown;
fleeing won't save a man from death's attack;
    the runaway will end hamstrung, or
        with a coward's death-wound in his back.

Virtus repulsae nescia sordidae
intaminatis fulget honoribus,
   nec sumit aut ponit securis
      arbitrio popularis aurae.   20

Virtus, recludens immeritis mori
caelum, negata temptat iter via,
   coetusque vulgaris et udam
      spernit humum fugiente penna.

est et fideli tuta silentio
merces: vetabo, qui Cereris sacrum
   vulgarit arcanae, sub isdem
      sit trabibus fragilemque mecum

solvat phaselon: saepe Diespiter
neglectus incesto addidit integrum: 30
   raro antecedentem scelestum
      deseruit pede Poena claudo.

3.3

Iustum et tenacem propositi virum
non civium ardor prava iubentium,
   non vultus instantis tyranni,
      mente quatit solida neque Auster,

dux inquietae turbidus Hadriae,
nec fulminantis magna manus Iovis:
   si fractus illabatur orbis,
      impavidum ferient ruinae.

hac arte Pollux et vagus Hercules
enisus arces attigit igneas,   10
   quos inter Augustus recumbens
      purpureo bibet ore nectar.

hac te merentem, Bacche pater, tuae
vexere tigres indocili iugum
   collo trahentes; hac Quirinus
      Martis equis Acheronta fugit,

Virtue disdains political rebuff
and shines with an unblemished reputation,
   and neither takes nor gives up office
      at the shifts of public adulation.

Virtue to those whose merit transcends death
offers a private route to heaven's height,
   soaring above the vulgar throng and
      humid earth in liberating flight.

Loyal discretion also finds a sure
reward; the man who blabs the mystery
   of Ceres I shall not permit to
      share my lodging nor to launch with me

a fragile pinnace. Often angry Jove
the blameless with the culpable will break;
   though crime may steal a march, club-footed
      vengeance seldom fails to overtake.

3.3

The man of steadfast purpose and good faith
no clamour of the crowd on evil bent,
   no frowning tyrant's menaces can
      shake from his resolve, no violent

sou'wester rousing Adriatic swells,
nor lightning-bolt by Jove's own hand displayed;
   let the whole firmament collapse in
      fragments, he will face it undismayed.

Thus Pollux and much-travelled Hercules
by labours reached the fiery upper air,
   with whom Augustus shall recline and
      purple-stained the draft of nectar share.

Thus, father Bacchus, you deserved your ride
drawn thither by your tigers, angrily
   chafing the yoke; and thus Quirinus,
      horsed by Mars, the underworld could flee,

gratum elocuta consiliantibus
Iunone divis: 'Ilion, Ilion
   fatalis incestusque iudex
      et mulier peregrina vertit   20

in pulverem, ex quo destituit deos
mercede pacta Laomedon, mihi
   castaeque damnatum Minervae
      cum populo et duce fraudulento.

iam nec Lacaenae splendet adulterae
famosus hospes nec Priami domus
   periura pugnaces Achivos
      Hectoreis opibus refringit,

nostrisque ductum seditionibus
bellum resedit. protinus et gravis   30
   iras et invisum nepotem,
      Troica quem peperit sacerdos,

Marti redonabo; illum ego lucidas
inire sedes, ducere nectaris
   sucos et adscribi quietis
      ordinibus patiar deorum.

dum longus inter saeviat Ilion
Romamque pontus, qualibet exsules
   in parte regnanto beati;
      dum Priami Paridisque busto   40

insultet armentum et catulos ferae
celent inultae, stet Capitolium
   fulgens triumphatisque possit
      Roma ferox dare iura Medis.

horrenda late nomen in ultimas
extendat oras, qua medius liquor
   secernit Europen ab Afro,
      qua tumidus rigat arva Nilus,

after the gods in conclave had approved
this speech by Juno: 'Troy by an unchaste
   and deadly judge and by a foreign
      woman has been utterly laid waste;

yes Troy, which, when the gods were cheated of
due payment by Laomedon the thief,
   was forfeit to Minerva chaste and
      me, with Trojans and that swindling chief.

But no more does her infamous house-guest
dazzle the Spartan harlot; as protector
   against invading Greeks no more does
      Priam's faithless house rely on Hector.

The war protracted by our quarrelling
has died away. My bitter anger I
   hereby relent and I release to
      Mars my hated grandson, mothered by

the Trojan priestess. Him I shall permit
to gain the realms of light, to sample sweet
   nectar, and to enrol among the
      gods, recruited to their calm retreat.

As long as Rome and Troy are severed by
the ocean, let the outcasts spread their sway
   as widely as they please; while cattle
      freely trample and young beasts can play

untroubled on the graves of Priam and
Paris, the Capitol may radiate
   its glory, and by right of conquest
      Rome may for the Medes new laws dictate.

Let Rome's name be a terror known in all
remotest lands, from where the narrow straits
   part Africa from Europe to the
      land which Nile's abundance irrigates;

aurum irrepertum et sic melius situm,
cum terra celat, spernere fortior   50
   quam cogere humanos in usus
     omne sacrum rapiente dextra.

quicumque mundo terminus obstitit,
hunc tanget armis, visere gestiens,
   qua parte debacchentur ignes,
     qua nebulae pluviique rores.

sed bellicosis fata Quiritibus
hac lege dico, ne nimium pii
   rebusque fidentes avitae
     tecta velint reparare Troiae.   60

Troiae renascens alite lugubri
fortuna tristi clade iterabitur,
   ducente victrices catervas
     coniuge me Iovis et sorore.

ter si resurgat murus aeneus
auctore Phoebo, ter pereat meis
   excisus Argivis, ter uxor
     capta virum puerosque ploret.'

non hoc iocosae conveniet lyrae:
quo, Musa, tendis? desine pervicax   70
   referre sermones deorum et
     magna modis tenuare parvis.

3.4

Descende caelo et dic age tibia
regina longum Calliope melos,
   seu voce nunc mavis acuta,
     seu fidibus citharave Phoebi.

auditis? an me ludit amabilis
insania? audire et videor pios
   errare per lucos, amoenae
     quos et aquae subeunt et aurae.

the unmined gold, much better placed when in
the ground concealed, let her be resolute
   to spurn, not shape to human use, for
      greedy aims which decency pollute.

To every limit of the world her arms
shall penetrate in her desire to view
   the wildest ecstasies of climate,
      torrid heat or clouds of drenching dew.

But this condition I impose upon
the warrior Romans: let them not rebuild
   the ancient walls of Troy, with misplaced
      piety and false ambition filled.

Ill-omened would that rebirth be, bringing
to Troy a second sorry overthrow,
   for I, Jove's sister and his wife, to
      lead my troops in victory would go.

If thrice by Phoebus' aid the brazen wall
should rise again, then thrice would my Argives
   destroy it, thrice would sons and husbands
      be lamented by their captive wives.'

But what is this, my Muse? Such matters are
too weighty for my lyre; no more rehearse
   the discourse of the gods, for noble
      themes are trivialised by slender verse.

3.4

Descend from heaven and upon the flute
perform, my queen, a full-length melody,
   or sing if you prefer, or tune the
      Greek or Latin lyre, Calliope.

You hear her? Or is this a fancy which
enchants me? For I seem to hear, and stray
   through hallowed woodlands, where beguiling
      breezes over rippling waters play.

me fabulosae Vulture in Apulo
nutricis extra limen Apuliae   10
   ludo fatigatumque somno
      fronde nova puerum palumbes

texere, mirum quod foret omnibus,
quicumque celsae nidum Aceruntiae
   saltusque Bantinos et arvum
      pingue tenent humilis Ferenti

ut tuto ab atris corpore viperis
dormirem et ursis, ut premerer sacra
   lauroque collataque myrto,
      non sine dis animosus infans.   20

vester, Camenae, vester in arduos
tollor Sabinos, seu mihi frigidum
   Praeneste seu Tibur supinum
      seu liquidae placuere Baiae.

vestris amicum fontibus et choris
non me Philippis versa acies retro,
   devota non exstinxit arbos,
      nec Sicula Palinurus unda.

utcumque mecum vos eritis, libens
insanientem navita Bosphorum   30
   temptabo et urentis harenas
      litoris Assyrii viator,

visam Britannos hospitibus feros
et laetum equino sanguine Concanum,
   visam pharetratos Gelonos
      et Scythicum inviolatus amnem.

vos Caesarem altum, militia simul
fessas cohortis abdidit oppidis,
   finire quaerentem labores
      Pierio recreatis antro.   40

It's told that in my childhood, on Vultur,
when I outside Apulia's bounds was lost,
   worn out by games, asleep, on me a
     coverlet of leaves wood pigeons tossed

(a miracle to the inhabitants
of Aceruntia, where eagles soar,
   or Bantine forests, or Ferentum's
     fertile farmland on the valley floor),

to guard my slumber, save my infant limbs
from vipers black and roving bears unharmed,
   with sacred laurel strewn and myrtle,
     by a numinous afflatus warmed.

I'm yours, Camenae, yours whether I climb
the Sabine hills, or am diverted by
   Praeneste cool or Tibur's gently
     sloping site or Baiae's limpid sky.

Thanks to my welcome at your holy springs
Philippi's chaos did not finish me,
   nor that accursed branch, nor yet the
     waves of Palinurus' promontory.

With you at hand, by sea I'll gladly dare
the maelstrom of the Bosphorus, by land
   as far as the Assyrian gulf I'll
     venture, bordered by its burning sand;

unharmed I'll visit Britain, hostile to
strangers, Geloni skilled with bow and quiver,
   Concani, who delight to drink the
     blood of horses, and the Scythian river.

High Caesar, who, as soon as he dismissed
to local life his troops wearied by war,
   was seeking to conclude his labours,
     you in your Pierian cave restore.

vos lene consilium et datis et dato
gaudetis almae. scimus ut impios
   Titanas immanemque turbam
     fulmine sustulerit caduco,

qui terram inertem, qui mare temperat
ventosum, et umbras regnaque tristia
   divosque mortalisque turmas
     imperio regit unus aequo.

magnum illa terrorem intulerat Iovi
fidens iuventus horrida bracchiis   50
   fratresque tendentes opaco
     Pelion imposuisse Olympo.

sed quid Typhoeus et validus Mimas,
aut quid minaci Porphyrion statu,
   quid Rhoetus evulsisque truncis
     Enceladus iaculator audax

contra sonantem Palladis aegida
possent ruentes? hinc avidus stetit
   Vulcanus, hinc matrona Iuno et
     numquam umeris positurus arcum,   60

qui rore puro Castalia lavit
crinis solutos, qui Lyciae tenet
   dumeta natalemque silvam,
     Delius et Patareus Apollo.

vis consili expers mole ruit sua:
vim temperatam di quoque provehunt
   in maius; idem odere viris
     omne nefas animo moventis.

testis mearum centimanus Gyges
sententiarum, notus et integrae   70
   temptator Orion Dianae,
     virginea domitus sagitta.

Gentle advice you give, and you rejoice
in the result. We know the overgrown
   and brazen band of Titans was by
      means of crashing thunderbolts thrown down

by him who governs all things that exist –
the earth unmoving and the restless sea,
   the underworld, all gods and men – with
      absolute and just authority.

No small alarm in Jove himself they roused,
that gang which bristled with a thousand fists,
   those brothers who strove Pelion to
      pile upon Olympus veiled in mists.

But what could Typhon or huge Mimas do,
or what Porphyrion with his towering stance,
   or Rhoetus or Enceladus, who
      hurled uprooted tree trunks like a lance?

How could their onset dent the aegis of
Minerva? Here stood Vulcan smouldering,
   there mother Juno, and beside her
      he who had no time for shouldering

his bow, who bathes in pure Castalian dew
his loosened hair, who loves the countryside
   around his special shrines, Apollo,
      Patareus, in Delos glorified.

Force uncontrolled implodes by its own mass;
judicious force the gods themselves enhance,
   but they detest the violence which
      strives all kinds of evil to advance.

Witness the hundred-handed Gyges, and
Orion who notoriously assailed
   Diana's spotless virtue – but the
      virgin's deadly archery prevailed.

iniecta monstris Terra dolet suis
maeretque partus fulmine luridum
    missos ad Orcum; nec peredit
        impositam celer ignis Aetnen,

incontinentis nec Tityi iecur
reliquit ales, nequitiae additus
    custos; amatorem trecentae
        Pirithoum cohibent catenae.   80

3.5

Caelo tonantem credidimus Iovem
regnare: praesens divus habebitur
    Augustus adiectis Britannis
        imperio gravibusque Persis.

milesne Crassi coniuge barbara
turpis maritus vixit et hostium –
    pro curia inversique mores! –
        consenuit socerorum in armis

sub rege Medo Marsus et Apulus,
anciliorum et nominis et togae   10
    oblitus aeternaeque Vestae,
        incolumi Iove et urbe Roma?

hoc caverat mens provida Reguli
dissentientis condicionibus
    foedis et exemplo trahentis
        perniciem veniens in aevum,

si non periret immiserabilis
captiva pubes. 'signa ego Punicis
    adfixa delubris et arma
        militibus sine caede' dixit   20

'derepta vidi; vidi ego civium
retorta tergo bracchia libero
    portasque non clausas et arva
        Marte coli populata nostro.

Spread over them the Earth laments her brood
of monsters, felled by lightning to the gloom
    of Orcus; Etna's crushing weight is
        not diminished by its lava-spume,

nor has the vulture, sent to persecute
the wicked lust of Tityos, decamped,
    but gnaws him still; by countless chains the
        ravisher Pirithous is cramped.

3.5

The thunderclap proclaims Jove rules the skies;
when Britons and dread Parthians to the fold
    of empire are coerced, Augustus
        as a god on earth will be extolled.

Have Crassus' Marsians and Apulians
serving the Parthian king prolonged their lives,
    and grown old bearing arms beside our
        foes, the fathers of their alien wives,

forgetting Vesta's flame, the sacred shields,
their dress, their names – and all with Rome still free
    and Jove's precinct still safe? Alas for
        Rome's inaction and degeneracy.

All this the prudent Regulus foresaw
when he rejected shameful stipulations,
    which would have offered an example
        ruinous to future generations,

if those unpitiable prisoners
had been recovered. 'I have seen' he said
    'our standards nailed in Punic temples,
        armour snatched away, with no blood shed,

from Romans; I have seen free citizens
with elbows twisted back being frogmarched,
    and gates reopened, fields reseeded
        which our victories had lately parched.

auro repensus scilicet acrior
miles redibit. flagitio additis
    damnum: neque amissos colores
        lana refert medicata fuco,

nec vera virtus, cum semel excidit,
curat reponi deterioribus.   30
    si pugnat extricata densis
        cerva plagis, erit ille fortis

qui perfidis se credidit hostibus,
et Marte Poenos proteret altero,
    qui lora restrictis lacertis
        sensit iners timuitque mortem.

hic, unde vitam sumeret inscius,
pacem duello miscuit. o pudor!
    o magna Carthago, probrosis
        altior Italiae ruinis!'   40

fertur pudicae coniugis osculum
parvosque natos ut capitis minor
    ab se removisse et virilem
        torvus humi posuisse vultum,

donec labantis consilio patres
firmaret auctor numquam alias dato,
    interque maerentis amicos
        egregius properaret exsul.

atqui sciebat quae sibi barbarus
tortor pararet; non aliter tamen   50
    dimovit obstantis propinquos
        et populum reditus morantem

quam si clientum longa negotia
diiudicata lite relinqueret,
    tendens Venafranos in agros
        aut Lacedaemonium Tarentum.

Will any ransomed soldier come back home
bolder? You're merely adding wasteful cost
   to infamy; wool stained with colour
     never will retrieve the whiteness lost,

and native courage, fallen low, does not
rekindle readily the coward's heart.
   When fawns, escaped from nets, will turn and
     fight, then he may play the hero's part

who has surrendered to a faithless foe,
and he will reavenge our Punic wrongs
   who, fearing death yet unresisting,
     let his pinioned arms be bound by thongs,

who, in blind desperation to preserve
his life, confounded peace with war. O shame,
   that mighty Carthage should stand taller
     by Rome's turpitude and tarnished name!'

They say that, like one stripped of civil rights,
he turned aside his loving wife's embrace
   and his young family, and grimly
     fixed upon the ground his steadfast face,

until the hesitating Senate with
unprecedented counsel he had swayed,
   then through his grieving friends he started
     out on noble exile undelayed.

Full well he knew what cruel torture was
in store for him; as calmly nonetheless
   he parted his protesting kinsmen
     and the crowd impeding his progress,

as if, his clients' weary business done
and judgment handed down, he was intent on
   recuperating in Venafran
     meadows or Laconian Tarentum.

3.6

Delicta maiorum immeritus lues,
Romane, donec templa refeceris
   aedesque labentis deorum et
      foeda nigro simulacra fumo.

dis te minorem quod geris, imperas:
hinc omne principium, huc refer exitum:
   di multa neglecti dederunt
      Hesperiae mala luctuosae.

iam bis Monaeses et Pacori manus
non auspicatos contudit impetus   10
   nostros et adiecisse praedam
      torquibus exiguis renidet.

paene occupatam seditionibus
delevit urbem Dacus et Aethiops,
   hic classe formidatus, ille
      missilibus melior sagittis.

fecunda culpae saecula nuptias
primum inquinavere et genus et domos;
   hoc fonte derivata clades
      in patriam populumque fluxit.   20

motus doceri gaudet Ionicos
matura virgo et fingitur artibus
   iam nunc et incestos amores
      de tenero meditatur ungui;

mox iuniores quaerit adulteros
inter mariti vina, neque eligit
   cui donet impermissa raptim
      gaudia luminibus remotis,

sed iussa coram non sine conscio
surgit marito, seu vocat institor   30
   seu navis Hispanae magister,
      dedecorum pretiosus emptor.

3.6

Though guiltless, Roman, you shall expiate
your parents' sins until you have repaired
   the gods' collapsing temples and their
     images with filthy soot besmeared.

You rule the world because the gods rule you;
from them begin, and in them always end.
   Neglected gods a multitude of
     pains to groaning Italy portend.

Twice with Pacorus has Monaeses now
confounded our unsacramented blows;
   to add our plunder to his tawdry
     finery triumphantly he crows.

Preoccupied by insurrection, Rome
almost fell victim to the restless Dacians,
   those expert bowmen, and Egyptians
     skilful in their naval operations.

Past centuries, fertile in vice, marriage,
the family, the home contaminated;
   soon, channelled from that source, corruption
     through our land and people percolated.

Today the growing girl longs to be taught
lascivious dance, and revels in the art,
   already dwelling on illicit
     passions with the whole of her young heart;

soon she is eyeing younger lovers while
her husband drinks, but cannot choose to whom
   she metes out her forbidden favours
     hastily and in a darkened room,

for beckoned openly, in full view of
her husband, she gets up to meet the hire
   of huckster or of Spanish merchant-
     captain, of her shame the lavish buyer.

non his iuventus orta parentibus
infecit aequor sanguine Punico,
   Pyrrhumque et ingentem cecidit
     Antiochum Hannibalemque dirum,

sed rusticorum mascula militum
proles, Sabellis docta ligonibus
   versare glebas et severae
     matris ad arbitrium recisos   40

portare fustis, sol ubi montium
mutaret umbras et iuga demeret
   bobus fatigatis, amicum
     tempus agens abeunte curru.

damnosa quid non imminuit dies?
aetas parentum peior avis tulit
   nos nequiores, mox daturos
     progeniem vitiosiorem.

3.7

Quid fles, Asterie, quem tibi candidi
primo restituent vere Favonii
   Thyna merce beatum,
     constantis iuvenem fide

Gygen? ille Notis actus ad Oricum
post insana Caprae sidera frigidas
   noctes non sine multis
     insomnis lacrimis agit.

atqui sollicitae nuntius hospitae,
suspirare Chloen et miseram tuis   10
   dicens ignibus uri,
     temptat mille vafer modis.

ut Proetum mulier perfida credulum
falsis impulerit criminibus nimis
   casto Bellerophontae
     maturare necem refert:

From different parents sprang the young men who
with Punic blood the seas incarnadined,
   and Pyrrhus, great Antiochus and
     Hannibal repaid in deadly kind,

the manly stock of stalwart countrymen,
accustomed to the Samnite mattock, deft
   to dig the turf and, governed by an
     austere matriarch, to chop and heft

the firewood, while the setting sun drew down
the mountain shadows, and at last unyoked
   the weary oxen, ushering the
     welcome hour of rest, in twilight cloaked.

What does not crumble under time's assault?
Our fathers, worse than theirs, to baser ill
   begot us, in our turn to spawn a
     generation more degraded still.

3.7

Don't weep for your Gyges, Asterië;
the first fair wind of spring will carry him
   back home your loyal suitor
     and loaded to the brim

with merchandise. The stormy south wind drove
him to the port of Oricum, where he
   is passing winter's evenings
     in grieving wakefully.

His hostess tempts him through a go-between;
with hints of ardent longing he beguiles,
   deceitfully deploying
     a thousand subtle wiles.

He tells of puritan Bellerophon
mendaciously traduced by Proetus' wife,
   until the king contrived an
     attempt against his life;

narrat paene datum Pelea Tartaro,
Magnessam Hippolyten dum fugit abstinens;
    et peccare docentis
        fallax historias movet.   20

frustra: nam scopulis surdior Icari
voces audit adhuc integer. at tibi
    ne vicinus Enipeus
        plus iusto placeat cave;

quamvis non alius flectere equum sciens
aeque conspicitur gramine Martio,
    nec quisquam citus aeque
        Tusco denatat alveo.

prima nocte domum claude neque in vias
sub cantu querulae despice tibiae,   30
    et te saepe vocanti
        duram difficilis mane.

3.8

Martiis caelebs quid agam Kalendis,
quid velint flores et acerra turis
plena miraris positusque carbo in
    caespite vivo,

docte sermones utriusque linguae?
voveram dulcis epulas et album
Libero caprum prope funeratus
    arboris ictu.

hic dies anno redeunte festus
corticem adstrictum pice dimovebit   10
amphorae fumum bibere institutae
    consule Tullo.

sume, Maecenas, cyathos amici
sospitis centum et vigiles lucernas
perfer in lucem: procul omnis esto
    clamor et ira.

he adds how Peleus barely cheated death
when he rejected false Hippolyte.
    With such tales he inveigles
        to immorality.

In vain: for deaf as granite Gyges hears
such tales, as yet unheeding. But take care
    yourself that young Enipeus
        does not approach too near;

among the cavalry cadets, it's true,
he takes the eye, in horsemanship supreme,
    and none can match his speed through
        the Tiber's Tuscan stream;

but in the evening bolt your door, don't peep
at sounds of serenading down below;
    and when he calls you cruel
        be obdurate; say no.

3.8

With all your learning in the rituals
of Greece and Rome, are you perplexed to see
a grassy altar, garlands, incense, coals,
   arranged for me,

a bachelor – and this All-Matrons' day?
When Bacchus foiled that homicidal bough,
a feast of milk-white goat I promised him,
   a solemn vow.

This is the anniversary; today
I'll draw a cork by seal of pitch secured,
and pour a wine, since Tullus' consulate
   in smoke matured.

So drink a hundred toasts, Maecenas, to
your friend's escape; with evening's lamps see in
the dawn's return; there'll be no quarrels or
   unruly din.

mitte civilis super urbe curas:
occidit Daci Cotisonis agmen,
Medus infestus sibi luctuosis
    dissidet armis,   20

servit Hispanae vetus hostis orae
Cantaber sera domitus catena,
iam Scythae laxo meditantur arcu
    cedere campis.

neglegens ne qua populus laboret
parce privatus nimium cavere et
dona praesentis cape laetus horae ac
    linque severa.

3.9

    'Donec gratus eram tibi
nec quisquam potior bracchia candidae
    cervici iuvenis dabat,
Persarum vigui rege beatior.'

    'donec non alia magis
arsisti neque erat Lydia post Chloen,
    multi Lydia nominis
Romana vigui clarior Ilia.'

    'me nunc Thraessa Chloe regit,
dulcis docta modos et citharae sciens,   10
    pro qua non metuam mori,
si parcent animae fata superstiti.'

    'me torret face mutua
Thurini Calais filius Ornyti,
    pro quo bis patiar mori,
si parcent puero fata superstiti.'

    'quid si prisca redit Venus
diductosque iugo cogit aeneo,
    si flava excutitur Chloe
reiectaeque patet ianua Lydiae?'   20

Forget your labours for the good of Rome:
the host of Dacian Cotiso's destroyed,
the forces of the Medes are all against
   themselves deployed,

those ancient foes the Cantabri at last
are tasting servitude in Spanish chains,
with bows unstrung the Scythians plan to leave
   the ravaged plains.

Once more a private citizen, let go
your public role, anxiety-oppressed;
accept the pleasures offered by today,
   give cares a rest.

3.9

'While I was still your favourite, and
no rival round your snowy neck could fling
   his arms, my fortune prospered more
than all the treasure of the Persian king.'

'While you loved no one more than me,
and Lydia's overshadowed Chloë's name,
   my reputation prospered more
than even Roman Ilia's acclaim.'

'Now Thracian Chloë is my queen,
an expert in sweet verses and the lyre;
   to save her life I shall not shrink
from death myself, if so the Fates require.'

'For Calaïs from Thurii
with well-requited passion I'm on fire;
   to save his life I shall embrace
my death twice over, if the Fates require.'

'What if the former love returns,
to link the sundered pair with brazen chain?
   If fair-haired Chloë is shut out,
and jilted Lydia free to call again?'

'quamquam sidere pulchrior
ille est, tu levior cortice et improbo
    iracundior Hadria,
tecum vivere amem, tecum obeam libens.'

3.10

Extremum Tanain si biberes, Lyce,
saevo nupta viro, me tamen asperas
porrectum ante fores obicere incolis
    plorares Aquilonibus.

audis quo strepitu ianua, quo nemus
inter pulchra satum tecta remugiat
ventis, et positas ut glaciet nives
    puro numine Iuppiter?

ingratam Veneri pone superbiam,
ne currente retro funis eat rota.   10
non te Penelopen difficilem procis
    Tyrrhenus genuit parens.

o quamvis neque te munera nec preces
nec tinctus viola pallor amantium
nec vir Pieria paelice saucius
    curvat, supplicibus tuis

parcas, nec rigida mollior aesculo
nec Mauris animum mitior anguibus.
non hoc semper erit liminis aut aquae
    caelestis patiens latus.   20

3.11

Mercuri – nam te docilis magistro
movit Amphion lapides canendo –
tuque testudo resonare septem
   callida nervis,

'Though he is handsome as a star,
and you as sullen as a stormy sky
    and fickle as a bobbing cork,
with you I'd gladly live and gladly die.'

3.10

Were you a Scythian, Lyce, wedded to
a savage, you would flinch to see my plight,
stretched out on this hard doorstep, victim of
    the local north wind's bite.

Your gate is creaking and within your fine
courtyard the trees are groaning, can you hear?
Outside the drifted snow is freezing in
    the cloudless atmosphere.

Venus condemns your arrogance; you lose
the bucket if the rope escapes – you'll see;
your Tuscan father never meant you for
    a stern Penelope.

Though nothing softens you, not gifts nor pleas
nor lovers' pallor chilling into blue,
nor husband panting for his paramour,
    yet show some mercy to

your suppliants. You're callous as a snake,
and more unbending than an old oak tree.
This backside won't put up with drenchings at
    your door indefinitely.

3.11

Come, Mercury, from whom Amphion learned
how music can move mountains by its spell,
and you, so resonant on seven strings,
  come, tortoiseshell,

nec loquax olim neque grata, nunc et
divitum mensis et amica templis,
dic modos, Lyde quibus obstinatas
    applicet auris,

quae velut latis equa trima campis
ludit exsultim metuitque tangi,   10
nuptiarum expers et adhuc protervo
    cruda marito.

tu potes tigris comitesque silvas
ducere et rivos celeris morari;
cessit immanis tibi blandienti
    ianitor aulae,

Cerberus, quamvis furiale centum
muniant angues caput eius atque
spiritus taeter saniesque manet
    ore trilingui.   20

quin et Ixion Tityosque vultu
risit invito, stetit urna paulum
sicca, dum grato Danai puellas
    carmine mulces.

audiat Lyde scelus atque notas
virginum poenas et inane lymphae
dolium fundo pereuntis imo,
    seraque fata,

quae manent culpas etiam sub Orco.
impiae – nam quid potuere maius? –   30
impiae sponsos potuere duro
    perdere ferro.

una de multis face nuptiali
digna periurum fuit in parentem
splendide mendax et in omne virgo
    nobilis aevum,

unfavoured once and dumb, but now at feasts
of wealthy men and gods a welcome friend,
sing now a song to make rebellious
   Lyde attend;

she, like a three-year filly roaming free,
too skittish to be ridden, frisks at will,
unmated and to conjugal contact
   unbroken still.

You lead the tiger and the woodland tree,
you pacify the torrent in full spate;
and Cerberus you charmed, the watchdog of
   the desolate

abode, though Fury-like a hundred snakes
entwine his head, and from his three-tongued maw
there issues a repulsive stench and gouts
   of slobbered gore.

Despite himself Ixion had to smile
and Tityos, the Danaïds stood by
enraptured at your tune, and for a space
   their urn was dry.

Let Lyde hear the crime and punishment
of those young brides, of precious water lost
by leakage emptying the jar, and of
   the fated cost

of crime, exacted in the underworld.
Unrighteously (for what worse could they do?)
unrighteously each took a dagger and
   her bridegroom slew.

One only, worthy of her marriage vows,
her promise to her father false forswore,
faithfully faithless, honourably famed
   for evermore.

'surge' quae dixit iuveni marito,
'surge, ne longus tibi somnus, unde
non times, detur; socerum et scelestas
    falle sorores,   40

quae velut nactae vitulos leaenae
singulos eheu lacerant: ego illis
mollior nec te feriam neque intra
    claustra tenebo.

me pater saevis oneret catenis,
quod viro clemens misero peperci:
me vel extremos Numidarum in agros
    classe releget.

i pedes quo te rapiunt et aurae,
dum favet nox et Venus, i secundo   50
omine et nostri memorem sepulcro
    scalpe querelam.'

3.12

Miserarum est neque amori
dare ludum neque dulci
mala vino lavere aut exanimari metuentis
patruae verbera linguae.

tibi qualum Cythereae
puer ales, tibi telas
operosaeque Minervae studium aufert, Neobule,
Liparaei nitor Hebri,

simul unctos Tiberinis
umeros lavit in undis,   10
eques ipso melior Bellerophonte, neque pugno
neque segni pede victus:

catus idem per apertum
fugientis agitato
grege cervos iaculari et celer arto latitantem
fruticeto excipere aprum.

'Get up', she hissed to her young husband, 'up,
lest long sleep from a quarter unexpected
descend; past sire and sisters criminal
   slip undetected,

who like a pride of lionesses each
her captive calf is butchering; but I
am soft, and shall not kill you, nor constrain
   you if you fly.

So let my father load me down with chains
for failing to betray my hapless man,
or overseas exile me, to become
   Numidian.

Go under guard of night and Venus, let
you own feet speed you and the friendly gale,
go with good luck, and on my gravestone scratch
   my sorry tale.'

3.12

Wretched the girl with no chance to enjoy
daydreams of love, or with liquor to wash
troubles away at the risk of a swoon, yes of heart-failure, from
fright at the verbal avuncular cosh.

Cupid from you, Neobule, your wool-
basket has stolen; from weaving and loom
Hebrus distracts you, from all of Minerva's activities – that
boy from the south with his radiant bloom –

once he has washed in the Tiber his oiled
shoulders, a horseman who would have surpassed
even Bellerophon, one who in tournaments never has been
conquered, with fist and with foot he's so fast;

skilled in the open, whenever the herd
scatters, to bring down a stag with his spear;
equally swift at close quarters to flush out and finish the wild
boar from the thicket's well camouflaged lair.

3.13

O fons Bandusiae splendidior vitro
dulci digne mero non sine floribus,
    cras donaberis haedo,
        cui frons turgida cornibus

primis et venerem et proelia destinat
frustra: nam gelidos inficiet tibi
    rubro sanguine rivos
        lascivi suboles gregis.

te flagrantis atrox hora Caniculae
nescit tangere, tu frigus amabile   10
    fessis vomere tauris
        praebes et pecori vago.

fies nobilium tu quoque fontium,
me dicente cavis impositam ilicem
    saxis, unde loquaces
        lymphae desiliunt tuae.

3.14

Herculis ritu modo dictus, o plebs,
morte venalem petiisse laurum
Caesar Hispana repetit Penatis
    victor ab ora.

unico gaudens mulier marito
prodeat iustis operata divis,
et soror cari ducis et decorae
    supplice vitta

virginum matres iuvenumque nuper
sospitum. vos, o pueri, et puellae   10
iam virum expertae, male ominatis
    parcite verbis.

3.13

Bandusian spring, more glittering than glass,
deserving roses and sweet wine, you shall
    be honoured with a kid in
      tomorrow's festival,

whose budding horns presage the wars of love
but uselessly, since now his crimson blood,
    for all his lusty birthright,
      shall stain your icy flood.

You bring delicious chill to roaming flocks
and weary beasts exhausted by the yoke,
    beyond the reach of blazing
      midsummer's cruel stroke.

You too shall be a spring renowned in song,
as my words celebrate the ilex tall
    which dominates the rocks whence
      your chattering waters fall.

3.14

Romans, we lately heard that Caesar had
for laurels risked his life, but here from Spain
like Hercules victorious he comes
   back home again.

His wife, rejoicing in her only lord,
attentive to the gods shall forth process,
his loving sister too, and handsome in
   formal headdress,

mothers of virgins and of youthful sons
just now restored to safety. Hush, you boys
and newly married brides, refrain from all
   ill-omened noise.

hic dies vere mihi festus atras
eximet curas; ego nec tumultum
nec mori per vim metuam tenente
    Caesare terras.

i pete unguentum, puer, et coronas
et cadum Marsi memorem duelli,
Spartacum si qua potuit vagantem
    fallere testa.   20

dic et argutae properet Neaerae
murreum nodo cohibere crinem;
si per invisum mora ianitorem
    fiet, abito.

lenit albescens animos capillus
litium et rixae cupidos protervae;
non ego hoc ferrem calidus iuventa
    consule Planco.

3.15

    Uxor pauperis Ibyci,
tandem nequitiae fige modum tuae
    famosisque laboribus:
maturo propior desine funeri

    inter ludere virgines
et stellis nebulam spargere candidis.
    non, si quid Pholoen satis,
et te, Chlori, decet: filia rectius

    expugnat iuvenum domos,
pulso Thyias uti concita tympano.   10
    illam cogit amor Nothi
lascivae similem ludere capreae;

    te lanae prope nobilem
tonsae Luceriam, non citharae decent
    nec flos purpureus rosae
nec poti vetulam faece tenus cadi.

Truly this joyful day will rid me of
my black anxieties; I shall not fear
civil unrest or death by violence
    with Caesar here.

Run, boy, for scent and garlands, and to find
a magnum that recalls the Marsian war;
see if marauding Spartacus has missed
    some skulking jar.

Invite sweet-voiced Neaera: tell her to
make haste to knot her fragrant hair for us –
come back if her obnoxious porter starts
    to make a fuss.

One's taste for quarrels as a boisterous game
diminishes as hair declines to grey;
I'd not have stood it in my headstrong youth,
    in Plancus' day.

3.15

    Enough of public scandal, wife
of needy Ibycus, learn to behave
      with less outrageousness, give up
at last your frolics with the girls; the grave

      is looming over you, and casts
a cloud across their starlike brilliancy.
    Don't think that all your daughter does
is suitable to you: for Pholoë

      may fitly beat a drum and storm
the young men's lodgings like a Bassarid –
    her crush on Nothus goads her to
such escapades, the frisking of a kid.

    But you should mind your spindle and
the local wool, not tuneless harmonies
      nor roses blushing red, you crone,
still less the jorum emptied to the lees.

3.16

Inclusam Danaen turris aenea
robustaeque fores et vigilum canum
tristes excubiae munierant satis
    nocturnis ab adulteris,

si non Acrisium virginis abditae
custodem pavidum Iuppiter et Venus
risisset: fore enim tutum iter et patens
    converso in pretium deo.

aurum per medios ire satellites
et perrumpere amat saxa potentius   10
ictu fulmineo: concidit auguris
    Argivi domus ob lucrum

demersa exitio: diffidit urbium
portas vir Macedo et subruit aemulos
reges muneribus; munera navium
    saevos illaqueant duces.

crescentem sequitur cura pecuniam
maiorumque fames. iure perhorrui
late conspicuum tollere verticem,
    Maecenas, equitum decus.   20

quanto quisque sibi plura negaverit,
ab dis plura feret: nil cupientium
nudus castra peto et transfuga divitum
    partis linquere gestio,

contemptae dominus splendidior rei
quam si quidquid arat impiger Apulus
occultare meis dicerer horreis,
    magnas inter opes inops.

purae rivus aquae silvaque iugerum
paucorum et segetis certa fides meae   30
fulgentem imperio fertilis Africae
    fallit sorte beatior.

3.16

For Danaë immured a brazen tower,
ill-tempered watchdogs and stout oaken doors
would amply have supplied defence against
    nocturnal paramours,

had Jupiter and Venus not contrived
her quaking guard, Acrisius, to mock:
the god, once changed to money, easily
    could bypass any lock.

Gold cleaves a path through sentinels, and with
more impact than a thunderbolt can smash
stone walls; the Greek soothsayer's household was
    engulfed by love of cash

in utter ruin; Philip opened gates
of cities, and opponents undermined,
with bribes; and savage pirates are by snares
    of bribery entwined.

As fortunes grow, care follows and the thirst
for ever greater riches: I was right
to shrink from raising up my head too high,
    Maecenas, noble knight.

The more a man denies himself, the more
god blesses him: I long to leave the side
of riches, and desert to those who with
    their share are satisfied;

I'd rather own my humble farm than be
reputed to have gathered in by stealth
the hard-won grain of all Apulia,
    needy amid great wealth.

A few hectares of woodland, a fresh spring,
and crops that never fail me, make my lot
more happy than the lordly proconsul's,
    although he knows it not.

quamquam nec Calabrae mella ferunt apes
nec Laestrygonia Bacchus in amphora
languescit mihi nec pinguia Gallicis
    crescunt vellera pascuis,

importuna tamen pauperies abest
nec, si plura velim, tu dare deneges.
contracto melius parva cupidine
    vectigalia porrigam,   40

quam si Mygdoniis regnum Alyattei
campis continuem. multa petentibus
desunt multa: bene est, cui deus obtulit
    parca quod satis est manu.

3.17

Aeli vetusto nobilis ab Lamo, –
quando et priores hinc Lamias ferunt
    denominatos et nepotum
        per memores genus omne fastus,

auctore ab illo ducit originem,
qui Formiarum moenia dicitur
    princeps et innantem Maricae
        litoribus tenuisse Lirim

late tyrannus: – cras foliis nemus
multis et alga litus inutili   10
    demissa tempestas ab Euro
        sternet, aquae nisi fallit augur

annosa cornix. dum potes, aridum
compone lignum: cras Genium mero
    curabis et porco bimestri
        cum famulis operum solutis.

For me no storeroom holds maturing jars
of high class wine, no bees prepare prime stocks
of honey, and the Gallic pastures feed
      no fleece-producing flocks,

but searching poverty is far removed,
nor, if I wanted more, would you refuse.
By cutting down my needs I'll better stretch
      my modest revenues

than if I ruled as one the Phrygian
and Persian kingdoms. Those who much demand
lack much: enough is best, though meted out
      by god with frugal hand.

3.17

Distinguished Aelius, descendant of
old Lamus (since it's known your family
    derives its ancient name through all its
      generations from his ancestry,

tracing its origin to him who first
ruled Formiae, as history relates,
    and joined it to those river-lands that
      Liris with its waters inundates,

a broad domain), tomorrow shall a gale
bestrew the woodland floor with fallen leaves
    and all the beach with heaps of useless
      weed, unless the aged crow deceives

in prophesying downpour. While you may,
bring in dry logs: tomorrow you shall feast
    your Genius with wine and sucking
      pig, and servants from their work released.

3.18

Faune, Nympharum fugientum amator,
per meos finis et aprica rura
lenis incedas abeasque parvis
   aequus alumnis,

si tener pleno cadit haedus anno,
larga nec desunt Veneris sodali
vina craterae, vetus ara multo
   fumat odore.

ludit herboso pecus omne campo,
cum tibi Nonae redeunt Decembres;
festus in pratis vacat otioso
   cum bove pagus;

inter audaces lupus errat agnos;
spargit agrestis tibi silva frondis;
gaudet invisam pepulisse fossor
   ter pede terram.

3.19

Quantum distet ab Inacho
Codrus pro patria non timidus mori
   narras et genus Aeaci
et pugnata sacro bella sub Ilio:

quo Chium pretio cadum
mercemur, quis aquam temperet ignibus,
   quo praebente domum et quota
Paelignis caream frigoribus, taces.

da lunae propere novae,
da noctis mediae, da, puer, auguris   10
   Murenae: tribus aut novem
miscentur cyathis pocula commodis.

3.18

Please, Faunus, as you chase the fleeing nymphs,
tread gently on my land and sunlit fields,
bless as you pass the new-born creatures which
  the holding yields,

while each year-end a kid is killed for you,
the vintage, love's companion, overflows
the generous bowl, and redolent with fumes
  your altar glows.

When your December festival comes round,
all beasts are turned into the fields to play;
the country-dwellers, men and oxen, take
  a holiday;

the wolf can stroll through lambs that fear him not;
for you the forest sheds its foliage;
three times the ditcher stamps the hated earth
  in gleeful rage.

3.19

You drone about Greek history
from Inachus to Codrus' martyrdom,
    the progeny of Aeacus
and battles fought round sacred Ilium.

    But what's the price of Chian wine?
Who'll warm the water for it? Whose address
    are we to go to? When can I
thaw out my frozen bones? I'm left to guess.

    Let's toast at once the waxing moon,
and then midnight, and thirdly (boy, make haste)
    Murena's augurate. The blend
is ladles three or nine: to each his taste.

qui Musas amat imparis,
ternos ter cyathos attonitus petet
    vates; tris prohibet supra
rixarum metuens tangere Gratia

    nudis iuncta sororibus.
insanire iuvat: cur Berecyntiae
    cessant flamina tibiae?
cur pendet tacita fistula cum lyra?   20

    parcentis ego dexteras
odi: sparge rosas: audiat invidus
    dementem strepitum Lycus
et vicina seni non habilis Lyco.

    spissa te nitidum coma,
puro te similem, Telephe, Vespero
    tempestiva petit Rhode:
me lentus Glycerae torret amor meae.

3.20

Non vides quanto moveas periclo,
Pyrrhe, Gaetulae catulos leaenae?
dura post paulo fugies inaudax
    proelia raptor,

cum per obstantis iuvenum catervas
ibit insignem repetens Nearchum,
grande certamen, tibi praeda cedat
    maior an illi.

interim, dum tu celeris sagittas
promis, haec dentis acuit timendos,   10
arbiter pugnae posuisse nudo
    sub pede palmam

fertur et leni recreare vento
sparsum odoratis umerum capillis,
qualis aut Nireus fuit aut aquosa
    raptus ab Ida.

Devoted to the Muses nine
I'll take the nine-fold mix, the stronger one;
 adherents of the Graces three
are bound to choose the weaker, and to shun

 all danger of disorder. Now
it's time to welcome madness. Why do I
 not hear the shrilling of the pipe?
The cymbal and the lyre are silent: why?

 Away with stinginess! Toss round
the roses; let the shriek of frenzied flute
 assail ill-natured Lycus and
the younger partner whom he does not suit.

 On cue comes Rhode, Telephus,
drawn by the glossy curls that kiss your shoulders,
 and by your star-like brilliance;
for Glycera my passion slowly smoulders.

3.20

Beware! To snatch the lioness's cub,
friend Pyrrhus, is inviting untold grief;
you'll soon be routed from the field, a mauled
 and humbled thief.

Her onslaught to retrieve Nearchus will
slice through the hero's youthful retinue;
a duel must decide who keeps the prize –
 it's her or you.

But wait, while you collect your swiftest darts,
and she is sharpening her fearsome teeth,
word is the battle's arbiter has placed
 the palm beneath

his naked heel, and now diverts the breeze
with scented curls around his shoulders freed,
as fair as Nireus, fairest of the Greeks,
 or Ganymede.

3.21

O nata mecum consule Manlio,
seu tu querelas sive geris iocos
    seu rixam et insanos amores
        seu facilem, pia testa, somnum,

quocumque lectum nomine Massicum
servas, moveri digna bono die,
    descende, Corvino iubente
        promere languidiora vina.

non ille, quamquam Socraticis madet
sermonibus, te negleget horridus: 10
    narratur et prisci Catonis
        saepe mero caluisse virtus.

tu lene tormentum ingenio admoves
plerumque duro; tu sapientium
    curas et arcanum iocoso
        consilium retegis Lyaeo;

tu spem reducis mentibus anxiis,
virisque et addis cornua pauperi
    post te neque iratos trementi
        regum apices neque militum arma.   20

te Liber et, si laeta aderit, Venus
segnesque nodum solvere Gratiae
    vivaeque producent lucernae,
        dum rediens fugat astra Phoebus.

3.22

Montium custos nemorumque, Virgo,
quae laborantis utero puellas
ter vocata audis adimisque leto,
    diva triformis,

3.21

Brother of my birth-year, purveyor of
moroseness, ready wit, reckless fracas,
   romantic escapades, untroubled
    slumber, o my worshipful wine-jar,

whatever mood your Massic has in store,
now is the special time to break your seal:
   descend, Corvinus is demanding
    liquor with a mellower appeal.

He is not too austere to honour you,
though he is steeped in Greek philosophy
   (why, even Elder Cato used to
    lubricate his fabled probity).

The hardest heads you visit with your brand
of harmless torment; you relax the wise
   with laughter and draw out the secret
    thoughts and tribulations they disguise.

Hope to the troubled spirit you restore,
backbone and courage to the penniless;
   with your support they cringe to neither
    tyrants' wrath nor military duress.

Bacchus will come and joyful Venus too,
perhaps, bringing the slow-unwinding Graces,
   and lamplight shall prolong the night till
    dawn's return the fading stars effaces.

3.22

Virgin protectress of the hills and woods,
deliverer of girls who from the bed
of childbirth call you thrice in fear of death,
   triple godhead,

imminens villae tua pinus esto,
quam per exactos ego laetus annos
verris obliquum meditantis ictum
    sanguine donem.

3.23

Caelo supinas si tuleris manus
nascente Luna, rustica Phidyle,
    si ture placaris et horna
        fruge Lares avidaque porca,

nec pestilentem sentiet Africum
fecunda vitis nec sterilem seges
    robiginem aut dulces alumni
        pomifero grave tempus anno.

nam quae nivali pascitur Algido
devota quercus inter et ilices   10
    aut crescit Albanis in herbis
        victima pontificum securis

cervice tinget: te nihil attinet
temptare multa caede bidentium
    parvos coronantem marino
        rore deos fragilique myrto.

immunis aram si tetigit manus,
non sumptuosa blandior hostia,
    mollivit aversos Penatis
        farre pio et saliente mica.   20

3.24

    Intactis opulentior
thesauris Arabum et divitis Indiae
    caementis licet occupes
Tyrrhenum omne tuis et mare Apulicum,

to you I dedicate the pine which shades
my villa, where I'll gladly sacrifice
 at each year's end a young boar, practising
  his sidelong slice.

3.23

At new moon, country-woman Phidyle,
lift hands to heaven and make good the vow
 to your domestic deities of
  incense, first corn and a greedy sow;

and thus the tender nurselings of your flock
shall all at apple-time disease escape,
 the mildew shall not blight your wheat, nor
  blasts from Africa your swelling grape.

The victim that on snowy Algidus
goes foraging within the oak-tree glade,
 or fattens in the Alban meadows,
  bears a neck destined to stain the blade

of priestly ritual: but not for you
to bribe with scores of slaughtered quadrupeds
 your little gods, just deck with brittle
  myrtle leaves and rosemary their heads.

An empty hand upon the altar placed
can match an ostentatious gift's appeal,
 and pacify the gods by duly
  scattering the pinch of salt and meal.

3.24

 Your fortune may exceed the gems
of India, the gold of Araby,
 your concrete may displace the wide
Tyrrhenian and entire Apulian sea,

si figit adamantinos
summis verticibus dira Necessitas
    clavos, non animum metu,
non mortis laqueis expedies caput.

    campestres melius Scythae,
quorum plaustra vagas rite trahunt domos,   10
    vivunt et rigidi Getae,
immetata quibus iugera liberas

    fruges et Cererem ferunt,
nec cultura placet longior annua,
    defunctumque laboribus
aequali recreat sorte vicarius.

    illic matre carentibus
privignis mulier temperat innocens,
    nec dotata regit virum
coniunx nec nitido fidit adultero.   20

    dos est magna parentium
virtus et metuens alterius viri
    certo foedere castitas;
et peccare nefas aut pretium est mori.

    o quisquis volet impias
caedis et rabiem tollere civicam,
    si quaeret Pater Urbium
subscribi statuis, indomitam audeat

    refrenare licentiam,
clarus postgenitis: quatenus – heu nefas! –   30
    virtutem incolumem odimus,
sublatam ex oculis quaerimus invidi.

    quid tristes querimoniae,
si non supplicio culpa reciditur,
    quid leges sine moribus
vanae proficiunt, si neque fervidis

but if to your roof-tree her nails
of adamant have been attached by Fate,
    your heart from fear, your very life
from death's garrotte you cannot extricate.

    Better the life of Scythians,
whose nomad homes are hauled about in carts,
    or of the primitive Getae,
to whom unlimited grassland imparts

    a common stock of fruit and grain,
who cultivate no longer than a year,
    and when a man can toil no more
a substitute in turn assumes his share;

    whose women don't habitually
ill-treat their motherless stepchildren, nor
    do wives, undowered, tyrannise
their man, nor trust a gilded paramour.

    True virtue is their marriage-gift,
committed faith and chastity, whose eye
    disdains to stray to other men:
for sin is impious – its price: to die.

    Alas, whoever wishes to root out
unholy warfare, fratricide pernicious,
    and see his statue labelled as
'Father of Cities' must rein back all vicious

    permissiveness, and look for praise
in future times, for we, consumed with spite,
    disparage living virtue, but
cry out for it once taken from our sight.

    What use are carping diatribes
if retribution fails to follow crime?
    What use are laws without a change
in habits, if the world's extremes of clime –

pars inclusa caloribus
mundi nec Boreae finitimum latus
    durataeque solo nives
mercatorem abigunt, horrida callidi   40

    vincunt aequora navitae,
magnum pauperies opprobrium iubet
    quidvis et facere et pati
virtutisque viam deserit arduae?

    vel nos in Capitolium,
quo clamor vocat et turba faventium,
    vel nos in mare proximum
gemmas et lapides, aurum et inutile,

    summi materiem mali,
mittamus, scelerum si bene paenitet.   50
    eradenda cupidinis
pravi sunt elementa et tenerae nimis

    mentes asperioribus
formandae studiis. nescit equo rudis
    haerere ingenuus puer
venarique timet, ludere doctior

    seu Graeco iubeas trocho
seu malis vetita legibus alea,
    cum periura patris fides
consortem socium fallat et hospites,   60

    indignoque pecuniam
heredi properet. scilicet improbae
    crescunt divitiae; tamen
curtae nescio quid semper abest rei.

3.25

Quo me, Bacche, rapis tui
plenum? quae nemora aut quos agor in specus
    velox mente nova? quibus
antris egregii Caesaris audiar

whether the parching tropics or
the region near the north wind where the ground
    is always frozen hard with snow –
don't keep the merchant out, and men are found

    with skill to tame the restless sea?
The stain of poverty is now the goad
    to do and suffer anything,
even to bypass virtue's uphill road.

    Our useless gold, our precious stones
and pearls, those instruments of every ill,
    let us on Capitol donate
urged on by public clamour and goodwill,

    or let us cast them in the sea,
if for the past we feel sincere remorse.
    Young people's minds are over-soft
and need some sterner training, if the source

    of our corruption is to be
obliterated. Free-born boys, untaught
    to sit a horse, have not the pluck
for hunting, more adept at childish sport,

    like playing with a Grecian hoop,
or even dicing, an illegal taste;
    no wonder, when the father cheats
his business partner and his guests, in haste

    to rake together money for
his worthless heir. But though they may accrete,
    ill-gotten riches always are
finite, and therefore always incomplete.

3.25

    You whirl me, Bacchus, filled with you,
in sudden transport; in what copse or canyon
    shall I descant on Caesar's fame,
a hymn to elevate him as companion

aeternum meditans decus
stellis inserere et consilio Iovis?
    dicam insigne recens adhuc
indictum ore alio. non secus in iugis

    exsomnis stupet Euhias
Hebrum prospiciens et nive candidam   10
    Thracen ac pede barbaro
lustratam Rhodopen, ut mihi devio

    ripas et vacuum nemus
mirari libet. o Naiadum potens
    Baccharumque valentium
proceras manibus vertere fraxinos,

    nil parvum aut humili modo,
nil mortale loquar. dulce periculum est,
    o Lenaee, sequi deum
cingentem viridi tempora pampino.   20

3.26

Vixi puellis nuper idoneus
et militavi non sine gloria;
    nunc arma defunctumque bello
      barbiton hic paries habebit,

laevum marinae qui Veneris latus
custodit. hic, hic ponite lucida
    funalia et vectis et arcus
      oppositis foribus minaces.

o quae beatam diva tenes Cyprum et
Memphin carentem Sithonia nive,   10
    regina, sublimi flagello
      tange Chloen semel arrogantem.

of heaven's constellations and
of Jupiter himself? My theme shall be
　　arresting, novel, never yet
　　attempted. Like the Bacchant sleeplessly

　　viewing the awe-inspiring sight
of Thracian valleys blanketed with snow,
　　and Rhodope by savage feet
imprinted, I the potent wonder know

　　of roaming riverbanks and glades
unpeopled. Hear me, you who can control
　　the Naiads and the Maenads, though
they rend from earth the tallest ash-tree bole;

　　no mean or humble strain I'll sing,
no mortal music. Perilous but sweet
　　it is to bind my brow with green
vine-shoots, and let you guide my willing feet.

3.26

I've lived my life amenable to women,
oh yes, my share of conquests I've devised,
　　but now upon this wall I'll hang my
　　　weapons and my lyre – demobilised.

My engines of assault on bolted doorways
set down on the left side of Venus' shrine;
　　my coruscating torches here, my
　　　crowbars and my bows I here resign.

O queen of smiling Cyprus and of Memphis
untouched by Thracian winter, I complain
　　of Chloë: lift your whip, I beg, and
　　　flick her once to punish her disdain.

3.27

Impios parrae recinentis omen
ducat et praegnas canis aut ab agro
rava decurrens lupa Lanuvino
    fetaque vulpes:

rumpat et serpens iter institutum
si per obliquum similis sagittae
terruit mannos: ego cui timebo
    providus auspex,

antequam stantis repetat paludes
imbrium divina avis imminentum,   10
oscinem corvum prece suscitabo
    solis ab ortu.

sis licet felix ubicumque mavis,
et memor nostri, Galatea, vivas,
teque nec laevus vetet ire picus
    nec vaga cornix.

sed vides quanto trepidet tumultu
pronus Orion. ego quid sit ater
Hadriae novi sinus et quid albus
    peccet Iapyx.   20

hostium uxores puerique caecos
sentiant motus orientis Austri et
aequoris nigri fremitum et trementis
    verbere ripas.

sic et Europe niveum doloso
credidit tauro latus et scatentem
beluis pontum mediasque fraudes
    palluit audax.

nuper in pratis studiosa florum et
debitae Nymphis opifex coronae,   30
nocte sublustri nihil astra praeter
    vidit et undas.

3.27

Let evil omens greet the wicked man,
a hooting owl, a tawny she-wolf which
runs from the right, a new-whelped vixen, or
    a pregnant bitch,

and let a snake delay him, arrow-like
streaking across, at which his ponies rear.
But I, who for dear friends decode the skies
    with anxious care,

will rouse the raven, harbinger of storms,
before he seeks again the stagnant water,
to utter his prophetic note from the
    propitious quarter.

Remember me through life, my Galatea,
I wish you well wherever you may go;
stay not for inauspicious woodpecker
    nor errant crow.

But see with what unruly turbulence
Orion plunges; too well known to me
are ocean's dirty moods, with skies blown clean
    deceitfully.

The rising wind, the breakers booming on
the beach, the rumour of the roaring seas
are sounds I wish on wives and children of
    my enemies.

Thus did Europa trust her white limbs to
the crafty bull, whose treacherous betrayal
amid the waves and teeming monsters made
    her spirit quail.

One moment she was in the fields, intent
on plaiting for the Nymphs a promised wreath,
next all she dimly saw was stars above
    and waves beneath.

quae simul centum tetigit potentem
oppidis Creten, 'pater, o relictum
filiae nomen, pietasque' dixit
   'victa furore!

unde quo veni? levis una mors est
virginum culpae. vigilansne ploro
turpe commissum, an vitiis carentem
   ludit imago   40

vana, quae porta fugiens eburna
somnium ducit? meliusne fluctus
ire per longos fuit, an recentis
   carpere flores?

si quis infamem mihi nunc iuvencum
dedat iratae, lacerare ferro et
frangere enitar modo multum amati
   cornua monstri.

impudens liqui patrios Penatis,
impudens Orcum moror. o deorum   50
si quis haec audis, utinam inter errem
   nuda leones!

antequam turpis macies decentis
occupet malas teneraeque sucus
defluat praedae, speciosa quaero
   pascere tigris.

"vilis Europe," pater urget absens:
"quid mori cessas? potes hac ab orno
pendulum zona bene te secuta
   laedere collum.   60

sive te rupes et acuta leto
saxa delectant, age te procellae
crede veloci, nisi erile mavis
   carpere pensum

As soon as she had set her foot upon
imperial Crete 'Alas, father,' she cried,
'I've forfeited your name, in folly my
    duty defied.

Whence, whither am I bound? One death's too light
a sentence. Have I something to repent?
Or is it my imagining, and am
    I innocent,

mocked by an empty dream that issued from
the ivory gate? Which would I choose again,
the reckless voyage, or the picnic and
    the daisy-chain?

I loved that wicked bull, but now if I
could lay my hands on him, I'd gladly break
his ugly horns, or seize a sword and slice
    him into steak.

Deserting home was shameful; shameful is
continued life. To any god I pray
who hears me: naked in the lions' den
    I long to stray.

Before decay invades my pretty cheeks,
before the juices of the victim's breast
dry up, I want to be the tigers' meal
    looking my best.

I hear my father's words: "You worthless child,
why hesitate to die? From this stout oak
swing by your girdle, opportunely saved,
    until you choke.

Or if a death on rocks or jagged reefs
attracts you, leap into the raging flood,
for otherwise you'll be dishonouring
    your royal blood

regius sanguis, dominaeque tradi
barbarae paelex." ' aderat querenti
perfidum ridens Venus et remisso
    filius arcu.

mox ubi lusit satis: 'abstineto'
dixit 'irarum calidaeque rixae,   70
cum tibi invisus laceranda reddet
    cornua taurus.

uxor invicti Iovis esse nescis:
mitte singultus, bene ferre magnam
disce fortunam; tua sectus orbis
    nomina ducet.'

3.28

Festo quid potius die
Neptuni faciam? prome reconditum,
    Lyde, strenua Caecubum
munitaeque adhibe vim sapientiae.

inclinare meridiem
sentis ac, veluti stet volucris dies,
    parcis deripere horreo
cessantem Bibuli consulis amphoram.

nos cantabimus invicem
Neptunum et viridis Nereidum comas;   10
    tu curva recines lyra
Latonam et celeris spicula Cynthiae,

summo carmine, quae Cnidon
fulgentisque tenet Cycladas et Paphum
    iunctis visit oloribus;
dicetur merita Nox quoque nenia.

in servile drudgery, a concubine
and bondmaid." ' Close at hand Cupid was lurking
with bow unstrung, and Venus with him stood,
　　unkindly smirking.

Soon having laughed her fill, she snapped 'Refrain
from ranting like an ill-conditioned scold;
that hated bull will bow to you his horns –
　　as yet unpolled.

Know that your lover is unconquered Jove.
Enough self-pity; nerve yourself to face
the claims of high estate; a continent
　　your name shall grace.'

3.28

　　How else to honour Neptune's day,
Lyde? Look lively for a fierce assault
　　　on wisdom's armoury; rouse out
the choicest vintage from the furthest vault.

　　The day does not stand fast but flies,
already noon retreats, why hesitate
　　　to plunder from the store that jar
malingering since Bibulus's date?

　　By turns we'll sing of Neptune and
his green-haired retinue of nymphs; you'll tune
　　　your lyre to tales of Leto and
the swift and deadly goddess of the moon.

　　The final song shall tell of her
who rules the sparkling Cyclades, whose flight
　　　of harnessed swans conveys her to
Paphos; and then a lullaby for Night.

3.29

Tyrrhena regum progenies, tibi
non ante verso lene merum cado
   cum flore, Maecenas, rosarum et
     pressa tuis balanus capillis

iamdudum apud me est. eripe te morae,
nec semper udum Tibur et Aefulae
   declive contempleris arvum et
     Telegoni iuga parricidae.

fastidiosam desere copiam et
molem propinquam nubibus arduis;   10
   omitte mirari beatae
     fumum et opes strepitumque Romae.

plerumque gratae divitibus vices
mundaeque parvo sub lare pauperum
   cenae sine aulaeis et ostro
     sollicitam explicuere frontem.

iam clarus occultum Andromedae pater
ostendit ignem, iam Procyon furit
   et stella vesani Leonis,
     sole dies referente siccos: 20

iam pastor umbras cum grege languido
rivumque fessus quaerit et horridi
   dumeta Silvani, caretque
     ripa vagis taciturna ventis.

tu civitatem quis deceat status
curas et Urbi sollicitus times
   quid Seres et regnata Cyro
     Bactra parent Tanaisque discors.

prudens futuri temporis exitum
caliginosa nocte premit deus,   30
   ridetque si mortalis ultra
     fas trepidat. quod adest memento

3.29

Descendant of Etruscan kings, for you
I have long since prepared an untouched cask
    of mellow wine, Maecenas, with a
        heap of roses and a new-filled flask

of balsam for your hair; procrastinate
no more, stop staring at Praeneste's wide
    downlands, well-watered Tibur, and the
        hills of Circe's son, the parricide.

Abundance will not satisfy; escape
that pile that reaches to the clouds, your home,
    break free from false contentment in the
        smoke and din and moneybags of Rome.

A change is often beneficial to
the rich; a healthy unpretentious meal
    in simple setting, bare of purple
        tapestries, the careworn brow can heal.

Now Cepheus, father of Andromeda,
renews his fire, Procyon blazes out,
    the constellation of the Lion
        rages, and the sun brings summer drought.

The weary shepherd with his panting flock
resorts to shade and water and the ease
    of leafy thickets, while the river
        bank is hushed, deserted by the breeze.

You bend your mind to constitutional
affairs, for Rome is all your anxious care,
    oppressed by what the Chinese and the
        Bactrians and Scythians prepare.

The outcome of the future is concealed
in deepest darkness by god's wise command,
    who laughs at those who strain beyond his
        limits. Mark this: take what is at hand

componere aequus; cetera fluminis
ritu feruntur, nunc medio alveo
    cum pace delabentis Etruscum
        in mare, nunc lapides adesos

stirpesque raptas et pecus et domos
volventis una non sine montium
    clamore vicinaeque silvae,
        cum fera diluvies quietos   40

irritat amnis. ille potens sui
laetusque deget, cui licet in diem
    dixisse 'vixi'. cras vel atra
        nube polum Pater occupato

vel sole puro; non tamen irritum
quodcumque retro est efficiet, neque
    diffinget infectumque reddet
        quod fugiens semel hora vexit.

Fortuna saevo laeta negotio et
ludum insolentem ludere pertinax   50
    transmutat incertos honores,
        nunc mihi, nunc alii benigna.

laudo manentem; si celeris quatit
pennas, resigno quae dedit et mea
    virtute me involvo probamque
        Pauperiem sine dote quaero.

non est meum, si mugiat Africis
malus procellis, ad miseras preces
    decurrere et votis pacisci
        ne Cypriae Tyriaeque merces   60

addant avaro divitias mari.
tunc me biremis praesidio scaphae
    tutum per Aegaeos tumultus
        aura feret geminusque Pollux.

with equanimity; all else flows on
as in a stream, now in mid-channel purling
   unhurriedly to meet the Tuscan
      ocean, now with severed boulders whirling

and torn up roots and cattle and hovels
in chaos, while the mountains resonate
   and forests groan on either bank, for
      thus can calm to cataclysmal spate

be roused. True happiness and self-control
belong to him who can each nightfall say
   'I've lived'. Tomorrow Jupiter can
      send unclouded skies or sullen grey,

it matters not. But one thing even he
will not achieve, he cannot bring to naught
   what's past, nor alter or undo what
      time has in its fleeting passage wrought.

Fortune delights in cruel practices,
humiliating games she grimly savours,
   reversing short-lived honours, granting
      now to others now to me her favours.

Her gifts I value, but if she takes wing
and flits elsewhere, I'll lose them cheerfully,
   enfold myself in virtue's cloak, and
      make a bride of honest penury.

It's not for me, when hurricanes assail
the groaning mast, to fall to abject prayers
   and vows and bargaining to save a
      cargo of exotic eastern wares

from adding to the treasure of the sea.
For I through howling tumult, seated in
   my cockleshell, shall row unscathed to
      land, helped by the breeze and Castor's twin.

3.30

Exegi monumentum aere perennius
regalique situ Pyramidum altius,
quod non imber edax, non Aquilo impotens
possit diruere aut innumerabilis

annorum series et fuga temporum.
non omnis moriar, multaque pars mei
vitabit Libitinam: usque ego postera
crescam laude recens, dum Capitolium

scandet cum tacita virgine pontifex.
dicar, qua violens obstrepit Aufidus   10
et qua pauper aquae Daunus agrestium
regnavit populorum, ex humili potens

princeps Aeolium carmen ad Italos
deduxisse modos. sume superbiam
quaesitam meritis et mihi Delphica
lauro cinge volens, Melpomene, comam.

3.30

It's done, my monument more durable
than bronze and loftier than the Pyramids,
that neither the corroding rain, nor wind
can overthrow, nor yet the fugitive

succession of innumerable years.
I shall not wholly die: great part of me
will cheat the undertaker: I shall thrive
with ever-new acclaim as long as priest

and solemn Vestal climb the Capitol.
They'll speak of me where Aufidus protests,
where Daunus ruled his arid countryside,
as one who rose from low estate to high,

the foremost to import to Italy
the lyric measures of the Greeks. Take pride,
Melpomene, in vindicated praise,
and crown me graciously with Delphic bays.

Secular Hymn

Horace was disappointed with the public reception of Books 1-3. He turned to the conversational hexameters of the first book of Epistles, which was published in 19 BC. Two years later Augustus decided to celebrate the achievements of his regime by reviving the Secular Festival, which was supposed to be held every generation (*saeculum,* an indeterminate period), but had not been held since 146 BC. It involved three successive days (June 1-3) of solemn ceremonial, the principal celebrants being Agrippa and Augustus himself. An original hymn was needed for this outstanding public occasion, and in the absence of Virgil, who had died in 19 BC, the honour of writing it fell to Horace. This assuaged his discontent: it provided the recognition he craved (see 4.3).

Carmen Saeculare

Phoebe silvarumque potens Diana,
lucidum caeli decus, o colendi
semper et culti, date quae precamur
    tempore sacro,

quo Sibyllini monuere versus
virgines lectas puerosque castos
dis, quibus septem placuere colles,
    dicere carmen.

alme Sol, curru nitido diem qui
promis et celas aliusque et idem   10
nasceris, possis nihil urbe Roma
    visere maius.

rite maturos aperire partus
lenis, Ilithyia, tuere matres,
sive tu Lucina probas vocari
    seu Genitalis:

diva, producas subolem, patrumque
prosperes decreta super iugandis
feminis prolisque novae feraci
    lege marita,   20

certus undenos decies per annos
orbis ut cantus referatque ludos
ter die claro totiensque grata
    nocte frequentis.

vosque veraces cecinisse, Parcae,
quod semel dictum stabilis per aevum
terminus servet, bona iam peractis
    iungite fata.

fertilis frugum pecorisque Tellus
spicea donet Cererem corona;
nutriant fetus et aquae salubres
    et Iovis aurae.

Secular Hymn

Diana, queen of woodlands, and Phoebus,
celestial glories to whom men must pray,
and always have done, smile upon our prayers
   this sacred day,

on which the Sibyl's verses have forewarned
that girls and boys, for purity selected,
should hymn the gods who have the seven hills
   of Rome respected.

Warm Sun, whose shining course brings forth, then hides,
the day, changeless through your variety,
maintain Rome as the finest of all sights
   you oversee;

sweet Ilithyia, you who ease the path
of childbirth, keep Rome's mothers in your care,
Lucina or Childbearer (hear the name
   you wish to hear);

cherish our children, goddess, and reward
domestic legislation with success,
promoting marriage and a new desire
   for fruitfulness;

thus each eleventh decade shall bring back
this festival of skill in games and song,
attracting thrice in daytime, thrice by night,
   a hearty throng.

And, Parcae, let the furthest bounds of time
confirm that your predictions are steadfast;
dovetail a fitting future into our
   distinguished past.

Let Earth, in crops and cattle bountiful,
present to Ceres harvest's wheaten wreath;
and let her fruits be nourished by Jove's rain
   and wholesome breath.

condito mitis placidusque telo
supplices audi pueros, Apollo;
siderum regina bicornis, audi,
 Luna, puellas:

Roma si vestrum est opus, Iliaeque
litus Etruscum tenuere turmae,
iussa pars mutare Lares et urbem
 sospite cursu,   40

cui per ardentem sine fraude Troiam
castus Aeneas patriae superstes
liberum munivit iter, daturus
 plura relictis:

di, probos mores docili iuventae,
di, senectuti placidae quietem,
Romulae genti date remque prolemque
 et decus omne.

quaeque vos bubus veneratur albis
clarus Anchisae Venerisque sanguis,   50
impetret, bellante prior, iacentem
 lenis in hostem.

iam mari terraque manus potentis
Medus Albanasque timet securis,
iam Scythae responsa petunt superbi
 nuper et Indi.

iam Fides et Pax et Honos Pudorque
priscus et neglecta redire Virtus
audet, apparetque beata pleno
 Copia cornu.   60

augur et fulgente decorus arcu
Phoebus acceptusque novem Camenis,
qui salutari levat arte fessos
 corporis artus,

Secular Hymn

Sun-god, lay down your arrows and receive
in mild benevolence the young boys' prayer;
Moon-goddess, queen of starlight crescent-horned,
   the maidens hear.

You gods whose work Rome is, who brought from Troy
the pioneers who seized the Tuscan strand,
a remnant destined for safe passage to
   this new-found land,

for whom Aeneas, once he had the flames
and ruin of his fatherland survived
unscathed, the voyage to this wealthier
   landfall contrived,

now grant to youth respectful honest hearts,
to old age dignified serenity,
to Rome itself increase, pre-eminence,
   prosperity,

and grant what with the blood of oxen white
is asked by Venus' and Anchises' heir,
foremost to conquer, and the conquered foe
   foremost to spare.

The Mede now trembles at our strength of arms
on land and sea, and at the lictors' rods;
tribesmen once insolent seek audience
   as if with gods.

Now honour is returning, peace, good faith,
neglected virtue, modesty outworn,
and Plenty comes dispensing riches from
   her well-stocked horn.

Augur Apollo, with his gleaming bow
conspicuous, the Muses' welcome friend,
whose healing art an overburdened limb's
   fatigue can mend,

si Palatinas videt aequus aras,
remque Romanam Latiumque felix
alterum in lustrum meliusque semper
   prorogat aevum.

quaeque Aventinum tenet Algidumque,
quindecim Diana preces virorum   70
curat et votis puerorum amicas
   applicat auris.

haec Iovem sentire deosque cunctos
spem bonam certamque domum reporto,
doctus et Phoebi chorus et Dianae
   dicere laudes.

as sure as he enjoys his altars on
the Palatine, will prosper Rome's affairs
through the next cycle and through endlessly
    improving years;

Diana, who frequents the Aventine,
observes the fifteenfold official prayer,
and to the youthful votaries applies
    a kindly ear.

Our confidence that Jove and all the gods
approve our verses, we, the chorus taught
to honour Phoebus and Diana, shall
    at home report.

The Afterthought: Book 4

According to Suetonius it was Augustus who, wishing to have the military feats of Drusus and Tiberius celebrated, induced Horace to return to lyrics, and to publish this last Book in 13 BC. As if to demonstrate that his old versatility has not deserted him, he proceeds to exhibit no less than eight different metres (including one new one: 7) among only fifteen odes. But this last Book is in several ways noticeably different from the first three. Most conspicuous is the eclipse of Maecenas, who had fallen from grace soon after the publication of the first collection (see Note on 2.12.25-8): he rates only a single mention, though a warm one (11.17-20). Instead the dominant figure is Augustus himself, and inevitably there is some loss of the ease and spontaneity that marked Horace's approaches to his patron: Horace has to feel his way (5). Apart from Drusus and Tiberius (4 and 14), there is more unmediated praise of lesser figures than before (1 and 9). Among Horace's literary models it is now Pindar who takes pride of place (2). And with the public recognition gained from the Secular Hymn, Horace has grown in maturity and self-confidence. The assertiveness of 3.30 is replaced by the fulfilled gratitude of 3, and a measured insistence on the power of poetry to confer immortality (8 and 9). There is less emphasis on frugality, and Horace even hosts a lavish party (11). In the love poems the artificial invitations and final farewells of the forty-year-old are replaced by a new candour from the fifty-year-old: at the end of 1, 11 and 13 and in 10 Horace at last speaks from the heart.

The average length of an ode here reaches nearly ten stanzas. Candidates for deferment are 8, which has suspect elements, and 14.

4.1

Intermissa, Venus, diu
rursus bella moves? parce, precor, precor.
    non sum qualis eram bonae
sub regno Cinarae. desine, dulcium

    mater saeva Cupidinum
circa lustra decem flectere mollibus
    iam durum imperiis: abi
quo blandae iuvenum te revocant preces.

    tempestivius in domum
Pauli purpureis ales oloribus   10
    commissabere Maximi,
si torrere iecur quaeris idoneum:

    namque et nobilis et decens
et pro sollicitis non tacitus reis
    et centum puer artium
late signa feret militiae tuae,

    et, quandoque potentior
largi muneribus riserit aemuli,
    Albanos prope te lacus
ponet marmoream sub trabe citrea.   20

    illic plurima naribus
duces tura, lyraeque et Berecyntiae
    delectabere tibiae
mixtis carminibus non sine fistula;

    illic bis pueri die
numen cum teneris virginibus tuum
    laudantes pede candido
in morem Salium ter quatient humum.

    me nec femina nec puer
iam nec spes animi credula mutui   30
    nec certare iuvat mero
nec vincire novis tempora floribus.

4.1

Venus, are we at war again,
truce-breaker? Spare me, I implore you, spare,
    I'm not the man I used to be
in Cinara's benign regime. Forbear,

    o cruel mother of desires,
to tease a heart hardened by fifty years
    of tender tyranny; attend
instead to young men and their coaxing prayers.

    Seek, if you must, a worthier
victim for roasting in your oven; swoop
    on Paulus Maximus' roof-tree
to revel with your shimmering swan-troop.

    High-born and handsome, in the courts
his eloquence has often tipped the balance,
    he'll bear your conquering standard far
afield, a paladin of all the talents,

    and when his lavish rival owns
defeat, and bows to his triumphant laughter,
    he'll set your marble image near
the Alban lakes beneath a citrus rafter.

    There shall you savour rich perfume
of incense, there the music of a choir
    shall charm you, harmonising with
the Berecynthian horn, the flute, the lyre.

    There boys and virgins twice a day
shall dance like Salii on snowy feet
    in honour of your godhead, while
the ground reverberates to triple beat.

    I find no joy in girl or boy,
no hope of love requited now,
    no fun in tipsy rivalries,
no thrill in fresh-cut flowers on my brow.

sed cur heu, Ligurine, cur
manat rara meas lacrima per genas?
    cur facunda parum decoro
inter verba cadit lingua silentio?

    nocturnis ego somniis
iam captum teneo, iam volucrem sequor
    te per gramina Martii
campi, te per aquas, dure, volubilis.   40

4.2

Pindarum quisquis studet aemulari,
Iulle, ceratis ope Daedalea
nititur pennis vitreo daturus
    nomina ponto.

monte decurrens velut amnis, imbres
quem super notas aluere ripas,
fervet immensusque ruit profundo
    Pindarus ore,

laurea donandus Apollinari,
seu per audaces nova dithyrambos   10
verba devolvit numerisque fertur
    lege solutis,

seu deos regesque canit, deorum
sanguinem, per quos cecidere iusta
morte Centauri, cecidit tremendae
    flamma Chimaerae,

sive quos Elea domum reducit
palma caelestis pugilemve equumve
dicit et centum potiore signis
    munere donat,   20

flebili sponsae iuvenemve raptum
plorat et viris animumque moresque
aureos educit in astra nigroque
    invidet Orco.

So why, my Ligurinus, does
the lonely teardrop trickle down my cheek?
    why does my fluent tongue ... stall,
ineptly silent even as I speak?

    You haunt my dreams, eluding me:
I hold you, then as you escape I seem
    to chase you, hard-heart, through the field
of Mars and then the Tiber's gushing stream.

4.2

Whoever seeks to soar like Pindar risks
the fate of Icarus; his only fame,
Iullus, will be to leave to some marine
    expanse his name.

For Pindar is Apollo's laureate,
and like a mountain stream that bursts its bounds
and seethes and swirls storm-swollen, he deep-throat-
    edly resounds

in mighty onrush irresistible:
sometimes new-minted words he will unfold,
in daring dithyrambs transported, by
    no law controlled;

sometimes he celebrates the gods or their
descendant kings, who justly put to death
the Centaurs or the dread Chimaera with
    its scorching breath;

sometimes a boxer or a charioteer,
already raised to heaven by first prize,
with praise a hundred times more durable
    he dignifies;

sometimes he mourns a young man taken from
his weeping bride, extols some golden deed
of shining virtue to the stars, grudging
    the grave its greed.

multa Dircaeum levat aura cycnum,
tendit, Antoni, quotiens in altos
nubium tractus: ego apis Matinae
    more modoque

grata carpentis thyma per laborem
plurimum circa nemus uvidique   30
Tiburis ripas operosa parvus
    carmina fingo.

concines maiore poeta plectro
Caesarem, quandoque trahet feroces
per sacrum clivum merita decorus
    fronde Sugambros,

quo nihil maius meliusve terris
fata donavere bonique divi
nec dabunt, quamvis redeant in aurum
    tempora priscum.   40

concines laetosque dies et Urbis
publicum ludum super impetrato
fortis Augusti reditu forumque
    litibus orbum.

tum meae, si quid loquar audiendum,
vocis accedet bona pars, et 'o sol
pulcher! o laudande!' canam, recepto
    Caesare felix.

tuque dum procedis, 'io triumphe'
non semel dicemus 'io triumphe'   50
civitas omnis, dabimusque divis
    tura benignis.

te decem tauri totidemque vaccae,
me tener solvet vitulus, relicta
matre qui largis iuvenescit herbis
    in mea vota,

Yes, many a current lifts the Theban swan,
Antonius, when he sets out to climb
into the empyrean, while in style
   and stature I'm

a Matine bumblebee, flitting in search
of nectar round the fragrant glades and streams
of Tibur, effortfully fashioning
   my humdrum themes.

But you, a poet of more lofty tone,
shall sing of Caesar on the sacred way
leading the fierce Sugambri, garlanded
   with hard-won bay –

Caesar, the best and finest gift that fate
and kindly gods have ever sent to men,
or could send, even should the golden age
   come round again.

You'll sing of holidays and public games,
of law courts closed and general joy in Rome
at prayers answered and relief to have
   Augustus home.

Then I, if any word of mine can take
a part, shall raise my voice among the rout.
'Hail glorious sun, all hail and praise!' I shall
   in welcome shout.

As you ride in the triumph train, 'Hurrah!'
we'll cheer, 'Hurrah!' the whole of Rome will cry
time and again, and burn incense to thank
   the gods on high.

Ten bulls, ten cows you'll offer; my release
will be a single calf, just weaned, and now
turned loose in generous pastures, fattening
   to pay my vow.

fronte curvatos imitatus ignis
tertium lunae referentis ortum,
    qua notam duxit, niveus videri,
      cetera fulvus.   60

4.3

    Quem tu, Melpomene, semel
nascentem placido lumine videris,
    illum non labor Isthmius
clarabit pugilem, non equus impiger

    curru ducet Achaico
victorem, neque res bellica Deliis
    ornatum foliis ducem,
quod regum tumidas contuderit minas,

    ostendet Capitolio:
sed quae Tibur aquae fertile praefluunt   10
    et spissae nemorum comae
fingent Aeolio carmine nobilem.

    Romae principis urbium
dignatur suboles inter amabilis
    vatum ponere me choros,
et iam dente minus mordeor invido.

    o, testudinis aureae
dulcem quae strepitum, Pieri, temperas,
    o mutis quoque piscibus
donatura cycni, si libeat, sonum,   20

    totum muneris hoc tui est,
quod monstror digito praetereuntium
    Romanae fidicen lyrae:
quod spiro et placeo, si placeo, tuum est.

Upon his brow he bears a mark shaped like
a crescent moon of three days, barely grown;
    this blaze is snowy-white, and all the rest
      is chestnut brown.

4.3

    He, on whose birth, Melpomene,
you've looked with kindly eye, will never wear
      the hard-won laurels of the boxing ring;
no Grecian chariot with its racing pair

    will hurtle him to victory;
no feat of arms will furnish him renown
      and carry him in triumph to
the Capitol's acclaim, for putting down

    the arrogance of petty kings;
but Tibur, where the waters laze along
      replenishing the leafy glades,
shall bring him honour for Aeolian song.

    In Rome, the queen of cities, I
am now accorded by the nation's youth
      the cherished rank of poet, so
I suffer less the stab of envy's tooth.

    O you who sweetly modulate
the golden tones of tortoiseshell, my Muse,
      who can the music of the swan
evoke from voiceless fishes if you choose,

    my fame as Rome's first lyricist,
stared at by passers-by, to you I owe;
      my inspiration and my power
to please, if any, you alone bestow.

4.4

Qualem ministrum fulminis alitem,
cui rex deorum regnum in avis vagas
   permisit expertus fidelem
     Iuppiter in Ganymede flavo,

olim iuventas et patrius vigor
nido laborum protulit inscium,
   vernique iam nimbis remotis
     insolitos docuere nisus

venti paventem, mox in ovilia
demisit hostem vividus impetus,   10
   nunc in reluctantis dracones
     egit amor dapis atque pugnae,

qualemve laetis caprea pascuis
intenta fulvae matris ab ubere
   iam lacte depulsum leonem
     dente novo peritura vidit,

videre Raetis bella sub Alpibus
Drusum gerentem Vindelici – quibus
   mos unde deductus per omne
     tempus Amazonia securi   20

dextras obarmet, quaerere distuli,
nec scire fas est omnia – sed diu
   lateque victrices catervae
     consiliis iuvenis revictae

sensere, quid mens rite, quid indoles
nutrita faustis sub penetralibus
   posset, quid Augusti paternus
     in pueros animus Nerones.

fortes creantur fortibus et bonis;
est in iuvencis, est in equis patrum   30
   virtus, neque imbellem feroces
     progenerant aquilae columbam;

4.4

Like the winged guardian of the thunderbolt,
on whom almighty Jupiter conferred,
    as fee for Ganymede's abduction,
      kingship over every other bird,

who first was launched untutored from the nest
by youthful dash and natural energies,
    and then the unfamiliar motions
      hesitantly practised in the breeze

of cloudless spring, but soon on tender lambs
swooped fiercely in exhilarating flight,
    and now attacks defiant snakes for
      joy of battle and for appetite;

or like a new-weaned lion cub that's left
its tawny mother, which a kid, intent
    on carefree grazing, spies too late when
      lacerating death is imminent;

so Drusus thrusting through the Raetian Alps
appeared to the Vindelici (whose taste
    for Amazonian axes to its
      ancient origin has not been traced –

research which I've deferred; no man can be
omniscient), and, though to victory
    accustomed far and wide, their troops were
      humbled by a young man's strategy,

and learned the power of sound environment
allied to virtue and innate good sense,
    and what the Neros could achieve when
      guided by Augustus' influence.

Brave men are fathered by the brave and good;
stallions and bulls inherit from the sire
    their courage; timid doves are never
      generated from the eagle's fire;

doctrina sed vim promovet insitam,
rectique cultus pectora roborant;
   utcumque defecere mores,
     indecorant bene nata culpae.

quid debeas, o Roma, Neronibus,
testis Metaurum flumen et Hasdrubal
   devictus et pulcher fugatis
     ille dies Latio tenebris,   40

qui primus alma risit adorea,
dirus per urbis Afer ut Italas
   ceu flamma per taedas vel Eurus
     per Siculas equitavit undas.

post hoc secundis usque laboribus
Romana pubes crevit, et impio
   vastata Poenorum tumultu
     fana deos habuere rectos,

dixitque tandem perfidus Hannibal
'cervi, luporum praeda rapacium,
   sectamur ultro, quos opimus
     fallere et effugere est triumphus.   50

gens, quae cremato fortis ab Ilio
iactata Tuscis aequoribus sacra
   natosque maturosque patres
     pertulit Ausonias ad urbis,

duris ut ilex tonsa bipennibus
nigrae feraci frondis in Algido,
   per damna, per caedis, ab ipso
     ducit opes animumque ferro.   60

non hydra secto corpore firmior
vinci dolentem crevit in Herculem,
   monstrumve submisere Colchi
     maius Echioniaeve Thebae.

but training supplements the native strength,
right standards fortify the character;
    when public morals falter, well-born
        families are tainted by the slur.

How great your debt, o Rome, to Nero's line
Metaurus' stream attests, that famous day
    of Hasdrubal's defeat, when all the
        clouds that menaced you were blown away,

that first refreshing smile of glory since
the African terror through Italy
    had galloped like a forest fire, or
        storm-wind spurring the Sicilian sea.

From then young Roman forces prospered and
increased, and statues which the Punic horde
    had sacrilegiously thrown down were
        in their temples righted and restored,

until at last false Hannibal complained:
'We are like deer pursuing wolves, the prey
    not predators; triumph for us would
        be some ruse to get us clean away.

The people who found strength in blazing Troy
to sail across the storm-tossed Tuscan sea
    and bring their gods, their children and their
        parents to these shores successfully

are like a holm-oak savaged by the axe
on Algidus, where dark-leaved trees abound;
    through loss and carnage they can summon
        heart and spirit from the very wound.

Against the never-yielding Hercules
no faster did the severed Hydra grow;
    no monster spawned in Colchis or in
        Thebes was so resilient a foe.

merses profundo: pulchrior evenit:
luctere: multa proruet integrum
    cum laude victorem geretque
        proelia coniugibus loquenda.

Carthagini iam non ego nuntios
mittam superbos: occidit, occidit   70
    spes omnis et fortuna nostri
        nominis Hasdrubale interempto.'

nil Claudiae non perficiunt manus,
quas et benigno numine Iuppiter
    defendit et curae sagaces
        expediunt per acuta belli.

4.5

Divis orte bonis, optime Romulae
custos gentis, abes iam nimium diu;
maturum reditum pollicitus patrum
    sancto concilio, redi.

lucem redde tuae, dux bone, patriae:
instar veris enim vultus ubi tuus
adfulsit populo, gratior it dies
    et soles melius nitent.

ut mater iuvenem, quem Notus invido
flatu Carpathii trans maris aequora   10
cunctantem spatio longius annuo
    dulci distinet a domo,

votis omnibusque et precibus vocat,
curvo nec faciem litore dimovet:
sic desideriis icta fidelibus
    quaerit patria Caesarem.

tutus bos etenim rura perambulat,
nutrit rura Ceres almaque Faustitas,
pacatum volitant per mare navitae,
    culpari metuit fides,   20

Submerge them deep, they come out fairer still;
grapple with them, and, to widespread acclaim,
    while you're unmarked and think you've won, they'll
        throw you and take home a tale of fame.

I cannot now send proud despatches home
to Carthage; lost, all lost, our hoped-for prize
    and all our noble reputation,
        lost with brother Hasdrubal's demise.'

Naught is beyond the reach of Claudians,
with Jove's transcendent favour for defence,
    and safely steered through reefs of war by
        hard work and astute intelligence.

4.5

Blessed by the gods at birth, you've been abroad
too long, best guardian of the folk of Rome;
    the Senate heard your promise of a swift
        return; come now, come home.

Restore your radiance to your countrymen,
for when they see your face it's like the spring,
    the sun shines brighter, with new grace
        suffusing everything.

As when a young man is by adverse gales
beyond the open sea's expanse restrained,
    for longer than the season's normal span
        from hearth and home detained,

his mother falls to omens, vows and prayers,
and ever seaward longing eyes she turns;
    so now with heartfelt loyalty the whole
        of Rome for Caesar yearns.

For safely oxen roam the fields, which are
enriched by Ceres and Prosperity;
    in peace the merchant skims the sea; deceit
        defers to probity;

nullis polluitur casta domus stupris,
mos et lex maculosum edomuit nefas,
laudantur simili prole puerperae,
    culpam poena premit comes.

quis Parthum paveat, quis gelidum Scythen,
quis Germania quos horrida parturit
fetus, incolumi Caesare? quis ferae
    bellum curet Hiberiae?

condit quisque diem collibus in suis,
et vitem viduas ducit ad arbores;   30
hinc ad vina redit laetus et alteris
    te mensis adhibet deum;

te multa prece, te prosequitur mero
defuso pateris et Laribus tuum
miscet numen, uti Graecia Castoris
    et magni memor Herculis.

'longas o utinam, dux bone, ferias
praestes Hesperiae!' dicimus integro
sicci mane die, dicimus uvidi,
    cum sol Oceano subest.   40

4.6

Dive, quem proles Niobea magnae
vindicem linguae Tityosque raptor
sensit et Troiae prope victor altae
    Phthius Achilles,

ceteris maior, tibi miles impar,
filius quamvis Thetidis marinae
Dardanas turris quateret tremenda
    cuspide pugnax.

ille, mordaci velut icta ferro
pinus aut impulsa cupressus Euro,   10
procidit late posuitque collum in
    pulvere Teucro.

no family by scandal is disgraced;
respected laws all vices override;
the baby smiles his father's smile; no crime
  from punishment can hide.

Who could feel menaced by the Parthian,
or ice-bound Scyth, the warriors of Spain,
or hordes begotten in the German woods,
  with Caesar safe again?

Each man is grafting vines to virgin trees
in his own vineyard through the working day,
then after eating, with his wine content,
  to your name he will pray;

he importunes you with libations from
his bowl; you with his household deities
are honoured, like Castor among the Greeks
  and mighty Hercules.

'Long be the carefree time that Caesar grants
to Italy.' This prayer is on our lips
(dry in the morning, moistened later, as
  the sun in Ocean dips).

4.6

Great god, whose power punished Tityos
the rapist, Niobe's vainglorious boast,
and, near to victory, Achilles, who
  excelled the host

of Troy, but could not equal you, for all
his goddess mother's influence, and though
the Teucrian towers quaked before his spear's
  ferocious blow;

he, like a pine beneath the axe's bite,
or like a cypress by the gale concussed,
fell sprawling and laid down his neck upon
  Dardanian dust.

ille non inclusus equo Minervae
sacra mentito male feriatos
Troas et laetam Priami choreis
    falleret aulam;

sed palam captis gravis, heu nefas! heu!
nescios fari pueros Achivis
ureret flammis, etiam latentem
    matris in alvo,   20

ni tuis victus Venerisque gratae
vocibus divum pater adnuisset
rebus Aeneae potiore ductos
    alite muros.

doctor argutae fidicen Thaliae,
Phoebe, qui Xantho lavis amne crines,
Dauniae defende decus Camenae,
    levis Agyieu.

spiritum Phoebus mihi, Phoebus artem
carminis nomenque dedit poetae.   30
virginum primae puerique claris
    patribus orti,

Deliae tutela deae fugaces
lyncas et cervos cohibentis arcu,
Lesbium servate pedem meique
    pollicis ictum,

rite Latonae puerum canentes,
rite crescentem face Noctilucam,
prosperam frugum celeremque pronos
    volvere mensis.   40

nupta iam dices 'ego dis amicum
saeculo festas referente luces,
reddidi carmen, docilis modorum
    vatis Horati.'

He was not one to skulk in ambush in
that falsely sacred horse, plotting the fall
of Trojan dupes too soon carousing in
   King Priam's hall;

his deeds were open, but – outrageously –
he would have visited barbaric doom
by fire on babes in arms, and even those
   still in the womb,

had not the father of the gods, induced
by you with gracious Venus' aid, conceded
the favour which for founding city walls
   Aeneas needed.

Lyric instructor of sweet-voiced Thalia,
Phoebus, whose hair is bathed in Xanthus' stream,
smooth-cheeked Agyieus, bless the Daunian Muse
   with high esteem.

Phoebus the breath of song, Phoebus the art,
bestowed on me, Phoebus the poet's fame.
Now, chorus, high-born virgins and young men
   of noble name,

wards of the Delian goddess, whose arrow
can check the lynx or stag in full retreat,
observe the Sapphic metre and my thumb's
   controlling beat;

in strict time sing of Leto's son, in time
of her whose crescent beacon shines at night,
who blesses crops and rolls the months along
   their onward flight.

One day you'll boast: 'A hymn was sung when first
the secular festivities returned;
the choir included me, and Horace wrote
   the words we learned.'

4.7

Diffugere nives, redeunt iam gramina campis
    arboribusque comae;
mutat terra vices, et decrescentia ripas
    flumina praetereunt;

Gratia cum Nymphis geminisque sororibus audet
    ducere nuda choros.
immortalia ne speres, monet annus et almum
    quae rapit hora diem:

frigora mitescunt Zephyris, ver proterit aestas
    interitura simul   10
pomifer autumnus fruges effuderit, et mox
    bruma recurrit iners.

damna tamen celeres reparant caelestia lunae:
    nos ubi decidimus
quo pater Aeneas, quo Tullus dives et Ancus,
    pulvis et umbra sumus.

quis scit an adiciant hodiernae crastina summae
    tempora di superi?
cuncta manus avidas fugient heredis, amico
    quae dederis animo.   20

cum semel occideris et de te splendida Minos
    fecerit arbitria,
non, Torquate, genus, non te facundia, non te
    restituet pietas;

infernis neque enim tenebris Diana pudicum
    liberat Hippolytum,
nec Lethaea valet Theseus abrumpere caro
    vincula Pirithoo.

4.7

The snow has run off, grass-shoots reappear in the fields
  and the woodlands their leaves have regained;
all nature is changing, the streams are subsiding and now
  once again by their banks are contained.

The Graces have ventured to cast off their clothes and to dance
  with the Nymphs in a mingled display.
'Forget immortality' whisper the year and the hours,
  which pillage the life-giving day.

Chill winds become zephyrs, hotfoot on the traces of spring
  presses summer, soon vanishing, then,
once autumn has offered its harvest of apples, it's back
  to the numbness of winter again.

Swift moons, when in heaven they dwindle, recover, but we,
  when we to the region descend
whither father Aeneas and Tullus and Ancus have gone,
  are shadow and dust to the end.

Who knows if the sky-dwelling gods to the tale of your days
  will a single tomorrow concede?
But what you devote to the personal joy of your heart
  you deny to your heir and his greed.

When you die and illustrious Minos pronounces on you
  the result of the just inquisition,
neither rank, my Torquatus, nor virtue, nor eloquent plea
  can secure for you any remission.

Diana cannot set the stainless Hippolytus free,
  from the darkness he cannot abscond;
nor can Theseus deliver Pirithous, dear as he is,
  from the grip of oblivion's bond.

4.8

Donarem pateras grataque commodus,
Censorine, meis aera sodalibus,
donarem tripodas, praemia fortium
Graiorum, neque tu pessima munerum

ferres, divite me scilicet artium
quas aut Parrhasius protulit aut Scopas,
hic saxo, liquidis ille coloribus
sollers nunc hominem ponere, nunc deum.

sed non haec mihi vis, non tibi talium
res est aut animus deliciarum egens.   10
gaudes carminibus; carmina possumus
donare et pretium dicere muneri.

non incisa notis marmora publicis,
per quae spiritus et vita redit bonis
post mortem ducibus, non celeres fugae
reiectaeque retrorsum Hannibalis minae,

non incendia Carthaginis impiae
eius, qui domita nomen ab Africa
lucratus rediit, clarius indicant
laudes quam Calabrae Pierides: neque,   20

si chartae sileant quod bene feceris,
mercedem tuleris. quid foret Iliae
Mavortisque puer, si taciturnitas
obstaret meritis invida Romuli?

ereptum Stygiis fluctibus Aeacum
virtus et favor et lingua potentium
vatum divitibus consecrat insulis.
dignum laude virum Musa vetat mori:

caelo Musa beat. sic Iovis interest
optatis epulis impiger Hercules,   30
clarum Tyndaridae sidus ab infimis
quassas eripiunt aequoribus ratis,
ornatus viridi tempora pampino
Liber vota bonos ducit ad exitus.

4.8

Rich gifts I'd gladly give to all my friends,
libation bowls and bronzes, Censorinus,
I'd give tripods, those prizes dear to Greek
heroes, and no one's gift should be as fine as

your own – that is, if I was rich in works
of art such as exalted Scopas' name
in sculpture, or in paint Parrhasius,
each highly skilled both men and gods to frame.

But I have no such store, nor you such need,
nor would such luxuries your taste entice;
your joy is in poems, and poems I
can give, and to the gift assign its price.

No works in marble publicly inscribed,
which after deaths of worthy men recall
their breathing presence, nor the driving back
and hurried getaway of Hannibal,

nor wicked Carthage burning – none of these
can promulgate the praises of the man
who bought his name by African conquest
as clearly as Calabrian Muses can.

Without a written record you may lose
deserved rewards. Of Romulus what fame
would live, though born to Mars and Ilia,
if lack of mention had suppressed his name?

The power, goodwill and eloquence of poets
extracted Aeacus from Styx's waves
and sanctified him in the happy isles.
Praiseworthy men the Muse from Lethe saves,

and blesses in the sky. Thus at Jove's feast,
his cherished goal, sits tireless Hercules,
and thus the constellation of the Twins
can rescue battered ships from drowning seas,
and Bacchus, wreathing vine-leaves on his brow,
to glad fulfilment guides his votaries.

4.9

Ne forte credas interitura, quae
longe sonantem natus ad Aufidum
　　non ante vulgatas per artis
　　　　verba loquor socianda chordis:

non, si priores Maeonius tenet
sedes Homerus, Pindaricae latent
　　Ceaeque et Alcaei minaces
　　　　Stesichorive graves Camenae;

nec, si quid olim lusit Anacreon,
delevit aetas; spirat adhuc amor　　　　　　　　　　10
　　vivuntque commissi calores
　　　　Aeoliae fidibus puellae.

non sola comptos arsit adulteri
crinis et aurum vestibus illitum
　　mirata regalisque cultus
　　　　et comites Helene Lacaena,

primusve Teucer tela Cydonio
direxit arcu; non semel Ilios
　　vexata; non pugnavit ingens
　　　　Idomeneus Sthenelusve solus　　　　　　　　　20

dicenda Musis proelia; non ferox
Hector vel acer Deiphobus gravis
　　excepit ictus pro pudicis
　　　　coniugibus puerisque primus.

vixere fortes ante Agamemnona
multi; sed omnes illacrimabiles
　　urgentur ignotique longa
　　　　nocte, carent quia vate sacro.

paulum sepultae distat inertiae
celata virtus, non ego te meis　　　　　　　　　　30
　　chartis inornatum silebo,
　　　　totve tuos patiar labores

4.9

Born on the banks of sounding Aufidus,
by arts not earlier paraded I
   speak out in words well suited to
     the lyre; do not imagine they will die.

While Homer's name pre-eminently holds
the honoured place, the works of dignified
   Stesichorus, Simonides and
     Pindar and Alcaeus have not died.

The humour of Anacreon has not
succumbed to time; whatever Sappho yearned
   still lives and breathes forever, into
     passionate Aeolian verses burned.

Helen was not the only gaping girl
to be seduced by well-combed curls, by sheen
   of gold-embroidered robes, by fawning
     royal retinue and princely mien.

Teucer was not the first in Crete to aim
a deadly arrow; there was not just one
   assault on Troy; Idomeneus and
     brawny Sthenelus were not alone

in fighting epic battles; not the first
were Hector and Deïphobus to bear
   the weight of grievous blows, defending
     blameless wives and children in their care.

Before the dawn of Agamemnon's day
a host of brave men lived, but who can show it?
   Unmourned, unnamed, engulfed in endless
     night they rot, because they lack a poet.

The unsung hero and the coward are
alike, once dead; but my pen shall ensure
   that your name, Lollius, is known and
     honoured, that your labours shan't endure

impune, Lolli, carpere lividas
obliviones. est animus tibi
   rerumque prudens et secundis
     temporibus dubiisque rectus,

vindex avarae fraudis et abstinens
ducentis ad se cuncta pecuniae,
   consulque non unius anni,
     sed quotiens bonus atque fidus   40

iudex honestum praetulit utili,
reiecit alto dona nocentium
   vultu, per obstantis catervas
     explicuit sua victor arma.

non possidentem multa vocaveris
recte beatum: rectius occupat
   nomen beati, qui deorum
     muneribus sapienter uti

duramque callet pauperiem pati
peiusque leto flagitium timet,   50
   non ille pro caris amicis
     aut patria timidus perire.

4.10

O crudelis adhuc et Veneris muneribus potens,
insperata tuae cum veniet pluma superbiae,
et, quae nunc umeris involitant, deciderint comae,
nunc et qui color est puniceae flore prior rosae,

mutatus, Ligurine, in faciem verterit hispidam,
dices 'heu' quotiens te speculo videris alterum,
'quae mens est hodie, cur eadem non puero fuit,
vel cur his animis incolumes non redeunt genae?'

unaided the oblivion meted out
by envy. Your judgment gives true insight,
   whether affairs are prosperous or
     perilous, unfailingly upright;

avenger of the crimes of greed, immune
to money's universal canker, ready
   to bear beyond its year a consul's
     burden, as a judge honest and steady,

prepared to sacrifice expedience
to principle, with scorn to turn aside
   the guilty gift, to vindicate the
     right, though by hostile cohorts defied.

We must not misdescribe as happy him
who merely has piled up great wealth, that name
   he only who can wisely use the
     gifts which fortune sends can justly claim,

who's hardened to the pains of poverty
who honour more than life itself will cherish;
   that man will stand by friends and country,
     not dismayed on their behalf to perish.

4.10

Warder of love's potent promise, stony-hearted hitherto,
when the uninvited badge of man's estate surprises you,
when the airy curls are shorn which round your shoulders now cascade,
when your colour, which surpasses now the rose's crimson shade,

loses lustre, Ligurinus, darkened by invading hair,
you will ask, as in the mirror at your future self you stare:
'Why did boyhood's temper never match how I in manhood burn?
Why to manhood's mood can boyhood's unmarred features not return?'

4.11

Est mihi nonum superantis annum
plenus Albani cadus; est in horto,
Phylli, nectendis apium coronis;
　　est hederae vis

multa, qua crinis religata fulges;
ridet argento domus; ara castis
vincta verbenis avet immolato
　　spargier agno;

cuncta festinat manus, huc et illuc
cursitant mixtae pueris puellae;　　　　　　　　　　10
sordidum flammae trepidant rotantes
　　vertice fumum.

ut tamen noris quibus advoceris
gaudiis, Idus tibi sunt agendae
qui dies mensem Veneris marinae
　　findit Aprilem,

iure sollemnis mihi sanctiorque
paene natali proprio, quod ex hac
luce Maecenas meus adfluentis
　　ordinat annos.　　　　　　　　　　　　　　　　20

Telephum, quem tu petis, occupavit
non tuae sortis iuvenem puella
dives et lasciva tenetque grata
　　compede vinctum.

terret ambustus Phaethon avaras
spes, et exemplum grave praebet ales
Pegasus terrenum equitem gravatus
　　Bellerophontem,

semper ut te digna sequare et ultra
quam licet sperare nefas putando　　　　　　　　30
disparem vites. age iam, meorum
　　finis amorum –

216

4.11

Dear Phyllis, I've a cask of Alban here,
a vintage nine years old, awaiting you;
a garden full of parsley for our wreaths;
   a mountain too

of ivy to set off your glossy curls;
a green-decked altar standing by to bear
an offered lamb; the house is smiling with
   my silverware;

a swarm of maids and boys are scurrying
about; this flap among my household folk
infects the fire, which whirls aloft a plume
   of sooty smoke.

Let me explain the special treat to which
you are invited: we shall celebrate
the Ides of April (Venus' sacred month),
   a solemn date

to me, and almost more to be revered
than my own birthday, since it is the day
from which my own Maecenas counts the years
   which come his way.

Your eye's on Telephus, but that young man's
beyond your reach, and he's been snapped up by
a glamorous heiress, and rejoices in
   her tyranny.

Ambition should recoil from Phaëthon's
charred cinders; sky-borne Pegasus, by scorning
the burden of his earthbound rider, gives
   a weighty warning

to stick to your own level, think it wrong
to aim too high, and so avoid the blame
of an unequal match. But come, my dear,
   my final flame

non enim posthac alia calebo
femina – condisce modos, amanda
voce quos reddas: minuentur atrae
    carmine curae.

4.12

Iam veris comites, quae mare temperant,
impellunt animae lintea Thraciae;
iam nec prata rigent nec fluvii strepunt
    hiberna nive turgidi.

nidum ponit Ityn flebiliter gemens
infelix avis et Cecropiae domus
aeternum opprobrium, quod male barbaras
    regum est ulta libidines.

dicunt in tenero gramine pinguium
custodes ovium carmina fistula   10
delectantque deum cui pecus et nigri
    colles Arcadiae placent.

adduxere sitim tempora, Vergili:
sed pressum Calibus ducere Liberum
si gestis, iuvenum nobilium cliens,
    nardo vina merebere.

nardi parvus onyx eliciet cadum,
qui nunc Sulpiciis accubat horreis,
spes donare novas largus amaraque
    curarum eluere efficax.   20

ad quae si properas gaudia, cum tua
velox merce veni: non ego te meis
immunem meditor tingere poculis,
    plena dives ut in domo.

verum pone moras et studium lucri,
nigrorumque memor, dum licet, ignium
misce stultitiam consiliis brevem:
    dulce est desipere in loco.

(for henceforth I shall never kindle to
another woman), learn a new refrain
to render in your lovely voice; a song
    shall banish pain.

4.12

The streams no longer roar with melted snow,
the fields have thawed, the gentle Thracian breeze,
spring's ally, wafts the early sails across
    serenely tempered seas.

The swallow builds her nest, lamenting for
her son – as well she may, who so disgraced
the house of Cecrops by grotesque revenge
    upon a deed unchaste.

The shepherds, Virgil, pipe their country tunes
to flocks that fatten on the tender grasses,
charming the god who loves the beasts, and haunts
    the dark Arcadian passes.

This weather brings a thirst; I plan to drink
some good Calenian, but if you intend
to join me, you must barter, even you,
    whom noble youths befriend.

A modest jar of spikenard will fetch
a generous cask from my supplier's hoard,
and see your bitter tensions soothed away,
    your cheerful hopes restored.

If these enticements tempt you, leave at once –
but bring the merchandise to pay your share;
from me you can't expect such lavishness
    as from a millionaire.

Don't stop to make more money, bear in mind
your pyre awaits you. Now's the time to season
prudence with folly; it's a joy to take
    a holiday from reason.

4.13

Audivere, Lyce, di mea vota, di
audivere, Lyce: fis anus, et tamen
    vis formosa videri
        ludisque et bibis impudens

et cantu tremulo pota Cupidinem
lentum sollicitas. ille virentis et
    doctae psallere Chiae
        pulchris excubat in genis.

importunus enim transvolat aridas
quercus et refugit te, quia luridi   10
    dentes te, quia rugae
        turpant et capitis nives.

nec Coae referunt iam tibi purpurae
nec cari lapides tempora quae semel
    notis condita fastis
        inclusit volucris dies.

quo fugit Venus, heu, quove color? decens
quo motus? quid habes illius, illius,
    quae spirabat amores,
        quae me surpuerat mihi,   20

felix post Cinaram notaque et artium
gratarum facies? sed Cinarae brevis
    annos fata dederunt,
        servatura diu parem

cornicis vetulae temporibus Lycen,
possent ut iuvenes visere fervidi
    multo non sine risu
        dilapsam in cineres facem.

4.13

The gods have heard my prayers, Lyce, the gods
my prayers have heard. You're growing old, but still
    you yearn for beauty, shameless
      you play around, you swill,

with tremulous tunes you tipsily besiege
reluctant Cupid. He has spied meanwhile
    Chia the young musician,
      and lurks within her smile.

Unheeding he flits past the withered trunks,
from signs of ageing he recoils in fright,
    your yellow teeth, your wrinkles,
      your hair of slushy white.

Your days are in the archives now, locked up
in history, those halcyon days of yore,
    which now no precious jewels,
      no see-through silks restore.

But oh, where is the lure, the life, the lithe
mobility? What now is left to see
    of her whose breath was love, who
      infatuated me? –

that artful charmer favoured beyond all
save Cinara, for whom the fates contrived
    a dignified release, while
      Lyce too long survived,

a rival for the ancient crow, the butt
of cruel mocking from the young and brash,
    who watch her flame die down to
      incinerated ash.

4.14

Quae cura patrum quaeve Quiritium
plenis honorum muneribus tuas,
    Auguste, virtutes in aevum
        per titulos memoresque fastus

aeternet, o, qua sol habitabilis
illustrat oras, maxime principum?
    quem legis expertes Latinae
        Vindelici didicere nuper,

quid Marte posses, milite nam tuo
Drusus Genaunos, implacidum genus,   10
    Breunosque veloces et arces
        Alpibus impositas tremendis

deiecit acer plus vice simplici;
maior Neronum mox grave proelium
    commisit immanisque Raetos
        auspiciis pepulit secundis,

spectandus in certamine Martio,
devota morti pectora liberae
    quantis fatigaret ruinis,
        indomitas prope qualis undas   20

exercet Auster, Pleiadum choro
scindente nubes, impiger hostium
    vexare turmas et frementem
        mittere equum medios per ignis.

sic tauriformis volvitur Aufidus,
qui regna Dauni praefluit Apuli,
    cum saevit horrendamque cultis
        diluviem meditatur agris,

ut barbarorum Claudius agmina
ferrata vasto diruit impetu   30
    primosque et extremos metendo
        stravit humum sine clade victor,

4.14

Augustus, greatest prince in all the sun's
domain, what blaze of honours by the state
   of Rome conferred, however lavish,
      adequately could commemorate

your virtues for all future ages? What
inscriptions, what official eulogies?
   Vindelici, unused to Latin
      laws, have just been taught your expertise

in war, for Drusus with your soldiery
restless Genauni and Breuni suppressed,
   and, keen to pay in double measure,
      toppled all their formidable nest

of strongholds down the Alpine mountainside.
The elder Nero then, with heaven's aid,
   the fearsome Raeti, by a heavy
      stroke of arms, in headlong rout dismayed;

conspicuous on the field of battle were
his shattering assaults upon the flanks
   of forces sworn to die for freedom,
      like a hurricane tormenting banks

of breakers under cloud-wrack fretted by
the wheeling Pleiades, he did not tire
   of harrying their lines, with snorting
      charger spurred across their ring of fire.

Like bull-formed Aufidus, who irrigates
the realms of Daunus, when in angry mood
   his torrent rages, threatening for
      cultivated fields disastrous flood,

with such an irresistible onset
steel-clad formations Claudius overturned,
   and, scything from the first rank to the
      last, for Rome a bloodless triumph earned,

te copias, te consilium et tuos
praebente divos. nam tibi, quo die
    portus Alexandrea supplex
        et vacuam patefecit aulam,

fortuna lustro prospera tertio
belli secundos reddidit exitus,
    laudemque et optatum peractis
        imperiis decus arrogavit.   40

te Cantaber non ante domabilis
Medusque et Indus, te profugus Scythes
    miratur, o tutela praesens
        Italiae dominaeque Romae.

te, fontium qui celat origines,
Nilusque et Hister, te rapidus Tigris,
    te beluosus qui remotis
        obstrepit Oceanus Britannis,

te non paventis funera Galliae
duraeque tellus audit Hiberiae,   50
    te caede gaudentes Sugambri
        compositis venerantur armis.

4.15

Phoebus volentem proelia me loqui
victas et urbis increpuit lyra,
    ne parva Tyrrhenum per aequor
        vela darem. tua, Caesar, aetas

fruges et agris rettulit uberes,
et signa nostro restituit Iovi
    derepta Parthorum superbis
        postibus et vacuum duellis

Ianum Quirini clausit et ordinem
rectum evaganti frena licentiae   10
    iniecit emovitque culpas
        et veteres revocavit artis,

relying on your troops, your strategy,
your auspices; for on the very date
   when Alexandria's port and palace
     meekly opened up to you their gate,

fifteen years later prosperous fortune
again the war with happy outcome crowned,
   and added to the glorious list of
     victories for which you are renowned.

O mighty bulwark of all Italy
and Rome her queen, the world holds you in awe,
   the Scythian, the Indian, the
     Mede, and Cantabri untamed before.

Worldwide all rivers, Nile with hidden source,
Danube and Tigris of resistless motion,
   and that which washes distant Britain's
     shores, with many monsters teeming, Ocean,

worldwide all countries, death-defying Gaul
and hardy Spain – all hear you and obey,
   and murderous Sugambri, laying
     down their arms, to you their homage pay.

4.15

I meant to write of conquests and campaigns,
but Phoebus twanged a discord to restrain
   the launch of my frail craft upon so
     daunting an expanse. Caesar, your reign

has brought abundance to our fields once more,
has called our standards back from gloating doors
   in Parthia to Jupiter in
     Rome, has swept the whole world clean of wars

and closed the shrine of Janus, has the curse
of flagrant immorality outlawed,
   has banished vice, and has the worthy
     virtues of our ancestors restored,

per quas Latinum nomen et Italae
crevere vires, famaque et imperi
   porrecta maiestas ad ortus
      solis ab Hesperio cubili.

custode rerum Caesare non furor
civilis aut vis exiget otium,
   non ira, quae procudit ensis
      et miseras inimicat urbis.   20

non qui profundum Danuvium bibunt
edicta rumpent Iulia, non Getae,
   non Seres infidive Persae,
      non Tanain prope flumen orti.

nosque et profestis lucibus et sacris
inter iocosi munera Liberi,
   cum prole matronisque nostris,
      rite deos prius apprecati,

virtute functos more patrum duces
Lydis remixto carmine tibiis   30
   Troiamque et Anchisen et almae
      progeniem Veneris canemus.

by which the fame of Latium and the power
of Italy developed and expressed
   the majesty of empire, spread to
      sunrise from its setting in the west.

While Caesar rules no civil recklessness
or strife can mar the state's tranquillity,
   nor anger which makes cities arm and
      feud in ruinous hostility.

No distant tribes, not Getae, nor Chinese,
nor scheming Babylonians, nor they
   who drink from Don or Danube – none will
      Caesar's ordinances disobey.

And we on work-days and on holidays
by Bacchus's good humour elevated,
   among our womenfolk and children,
      once the gods have duly been placated,

shall sing to music of the Lydian flute
of old-style leaders and their chivalry,
   of Troy and of Anchises, and of
      gracious Venus's posterity.

Notes

Throughout these notes:

Horace is referred to simply as 'H'.

A bracketed number after a name indicates the number of syllables the name carries in the English version.

Bold numbers in brackets (mostly in Book 3) refer to the Augustan policies (numbered in Appendix 3) which are relevant.

The technical names of the Latin metres (see Appendix 2) are given only where each metre first occurs (see on 1.11).

The acknowledged Greek lyric poets (see on 1.1.35) are referred to as 'the Greek Nine'.

BOOK 1

1.1

H starts with a catalogue of pursuits, but takes care to frame it at each end with two lines addressed to **Maecenas**, thus paying his benefactor the compliment of opening his great work with his name. The catalogue lists a series of consuming ambitions and obsessions attractive to others, except at the end, where H's own position is described, and in the middle (often the key part of an ode), which sketches the leisure pursuits so frequently featured in the Odes.

Metre. 1st Asclepiad (there are five varieties with this name), occurring only at the very beginning and the very end of this collection, and once in Book 4.

13 whatever your munificence: H refers to the munificence of Attalus, king of Pergamum, who in 133 BC had bequeathed his kingdom to the Roman people.

32 my Muses: H names Euterpe and Polyhymnia, but at the time he wrote the Muses had not been allotted the individual spheres of influence which they later acquired. In 3.4 H makes a solemn address to Calliope, and he also mentions Clio (1.12) and Thalia (4.6), but it is for Melpomene that he reserves his most personal thanks (3.30, 4.3). Part of his poetic strategy is to introduce the Latin Muse(s), *Camena(e)*.

34 Lesbos: H's principal models, Alcaeus and Sappho, both came from Lesbos.

35 the lyricists of Greece: The Alexandrian scholars had named a canon of nine Greek lyric poets (the Greek Nine), including Alcaeus, Sappho and Pindar (others mentioned in the Odes are Stesichorus, Anacreon and Simonides). H is declaring his ambition to be considered their equal.

1.2

This ode is full of difficult contemporary references and should not be tackled until the reader has enjoyed others which are more accessible.

Next after his patron H addresses **Caesar** (Augustus). Alarm has been caused by portents, including a flood of the Tiber; the recent history is of Civil War: what god will save Rome? Apollo? Venus? Mars? Surely Mercury in the shape of the youthful Augustus, fresh from avenging the murder of Julius Caesar.

Metre. This is the Sapphic metre, the second commonest (twenty-five odes plus the Secular Hymn).

5   **Pyrrha's age**: a time of flood, when all mankind was destroyed except Pyrrha and her husband, Deucalion.

7   **Proteus**: a sea god who tended marine animals.

13   **We've seen … Tiber's waves thrown back**: a flood of the Tiber is recorded in January 27 BC, just after Augustus had caused consternation by proposing to retire into private life; a suitable date for the dramatic setting.

13–20   **the flood**: the allusions here are dense and complex. Ilia was the priestess of **Vesta**, and therefore sworn to chastity. But through rape by Mars she became the mother of Romulus and Remus (and hence ancestress of the Julian line and the murdered Julius Caesar). For this she was thrown into the Tiber, whose river-god, however, rescued and married her. All this explains Ilia's **indignation** and her **river-mate's** vengeance, which was excessive because what Jupiter had in mind for Rome was not destruction but revival under Augustus. **Numa's monuments** included the Temple of Vesta and the house of the Pontifex Maximus (*regia*), an office held by Julius Caesar. The passage is thus packed with references to the assassination of Julius Caesar, which started the Civil War, and to which H returns in line 43.

15   **king-ly**: The division of a word between two lines is a licence very rarely indulged in by H. Here it has been encouraged by the splitting of *u-xorius* at lines 19–20; in both cases the justification is the overflow being described.

21   **civil war**: the first mention of a recurrent theme, the waste, wickedness and guilt of Romans fighting Romans, and thereby **reducing** their own numbers.

37   **sport prolonged**: Mars is represented as enjoying the bloodshed.

44   **the regicides**: punishment of his adoptive father's murderers was a central policy of Octavian, but the term is not exact since Caesar was never king, a title he refused, only perpetual dictator and god.

48   **the robber breeze**: H is referring to the departure of Romulus, who was reputed to have been snatched up by the wind, and never seen again.

49   **mighty triumphs**: these must be the victories of Octavian (Augustus) at Philippi (42 BC) and Actium (31 BC); it is clear from line 43 that they are in the past.

1.3

H turns to his great friend, the poet **Virgil**, who is on the point of departing for Greece by sea. H moves on to deplore the practice of sea travel, something of a hobbyhorse of his, and from there to condemn ambition.

Metre. 4th Asclepiad, the commonest metre (twelve odes) after Alcaics and Sapphics.

1   **Goddess of Cyprus**: Venus, who is often known as Cypris.

2   **Helen's brothers**: Castor and Pollux, the heavenly twins, sons of Jupiter and Leda; a constellation of good omen because of its association with the phenomenon of St Elmo's fire, which was then, as now, believed by sailors to herald the end of a storm.

14   **Hyades** (3): a constellation believed to bring rain at its rising and setting.

19   **Acroceraunian headland**: a notorious promontory on the north-west coast of Greece, where Octavian was nearly wrecked after Actium.

27   **Prometheus** (3): a son of Iapetus who mocked the gods and smuggled fire from heaven to earth in a fennel stalk. He was punished by being chained to a rock with a vulture devouring his liver.

33   **Daedalus**: built the Labyrinth for King Minos of Crete, who then imprisoned him in it. He escaped with his son, Icarus, by flying with home-made wings. Icarus flew too near the sun and melted the wax by which his wings were attached, giving his name to the sea into which he fell.

36   **Hercules**: the last of Hercules' labours was the abduction of Cerberus from the underworld.

40   **wrathful thunderbolt**: ostensibly H is condemning what we would see as enterprise and progress. But perhaps it is partly the Civil War, again, which is the crime he is denouncing. In

230

3.4 it is Jupiter's thunderbolt which puts paid to the Giants in a metaphor for Octavian's victory in the Civil War.

1.4

H now addresses Lucius **Sestius**, consul in the year that Books 1-3 were published (23 BC). Sestius, like H, had fought with Brutus at Philippi and was a conspicuous beneficiary of Augustus' policy of clemency (see Appendix 3 (**2**)). He came from a wealthy family which owned potteries on the coast north of Rome. The hauling of ships down the beach in readiness for the sailing season would be a familiar sight there.

Metre. 3rd Archilochian, an unusual rhythm which never recurs. The end of the long lines carries a heavy (limping) beat, which the translation attempts to imitate.
5 **Dancing returns**: spring brings dancing, as in 4.7; these two odes make an interesting comparison.
8 **workshops of Etna**: H refers explicitly to the Cyclopes, Sicilian giants who were employed in forging thunderbolts for Jupiter in foundries beneath Etna, under the supervision of **Vulcan** (the god of fire and husband of Venus). The word used for **workshops** would be appropriate to the Sestius potteries.
14 **death**: the transition from thoughts of spring to thoughts of death is implied by the succession of the seasons (compare again 4.7, where the connection of thought is explicit). Here the moral drawn in the last stanza is that pleasures should be enjoyed before they are lost.

1.5

H interpolates a lighthearted love poem into the parade of grandees. Assuming from the start what turns out to be his habitual role in matters of the heart, that of an amused and ironic middle-aged observer who has seen it all and is now above the fray (like, say, Don Alfonso in *Così fan tutte*), he addresses **Pyrrha**, a serial charmer. This is perhaps the most translated poem in history; in *Ad Pyrrham* (1959) Sir Ronald Storrs published 144 versions, about one third of his collection, and the tide has not ceased to flow since. It was chosen by Milton for his experiment in literal translation (mentioned in the Introduction), which is set out at the end of this note.

Metre. 3rd Asclepiad, occurring in seven odes. On the page it is not readily distinguishable from the Alcaic, but the last two lines of the stanza are shorter and lighter.
6 **your sea**: Pyrrha is likened to the sea, and her moods to the weather. The metaphor is sustained to the end.
13 **as for me**: In a typical twist we learn that H too has been shipwrecked in this sea. He has hung up (**offered**) his dripping garments as a gesture of retirement and in gratitude to **Neptune** (see also 3.28) for his deliverance. His first love poem is also his first (but not his last) farewell to love.

Milton's version:

> What slender youth bedew'd with liquid odours
> Courts thee on Roses in some pleasant Cave,
> > Pyrrha for whom bind'st thou
> > In wreaths thy golden hair
>
> Plain in thy neatness; O how oft shall he
> On Faith and changed Gods complain: and Seas
> > Rough with black winds and storms
> > Unwonted shall admire:

Who now enjoys thee credulous, all Gold,
Who alwayes vacant, alwayes amiable
    Hopes thee; of flattering gales
    Unmindfull. Hapless they

To whom thou untry'd seem'st fair. Me in my vow'd
Picture the sacred wall declares t' have hung
    My dank and dropping weeds
    To the stern God of Sea.

It will be noticed that unattributed descriptions (unwonted, credulous, all gold) tend to ambiguity; and the word order, strained as it is, fails to capture some of the subtleties of the inflected Latin (e.g. in the first line *te* is embraced both by the slender youth and the many roses; in the second stanza the sense is deliberately held back by deferring the last two nouns).

1.6

H turns to **Agrippa**, the general and admiral whose victories paved the way for the triumph of Octavian in the Civil War. Not for the last time H declines the honour of celebrating warfare in epic verse, suggesting that Varius is more worthy. By this means he succeeds in complimenting Agrippa, Varius and, in passing, Augustus too, besides escaping the unwelcome task.

Metre. 2nd Asclepiad, occurring nine times; in these translations the only difference from the Sapphic is an extra foot in the last line of the stanza.

1 **Varius**: a friend of Virgil and of H, who wrote epics on Julius Caesar and Augustus, and also a tragedy about Thyestes, none of which has survived. At this time (before the publication of the *Aeneid*) he was regarded as Rome's leading epic poet.

6-8 **Achilles' tantrums ... two-faced Ulysses**: the somewhat unelevated terms in which H refers to the two Homeric epics ('wrath' and 'resourceful' would be the more conventional language) are designed to underline his unfitness for the epic role. **Pelops' descendants** included Thyestes, Atreus, Aegisthus, Agamemnon and Orestes.

14-15 **Meriones ... Diomedes**: Diomedes (4) was the chivalrous hero who in the *Iliad* succeeded in wounding Mars himself, with the help of Athene (Pallas). Meriones figures in the *Iliad* as the charioteer of Idomeneus, but elsewhere he is found associated with Diomedes. This relatively obscure character is probably there to complete an analogy, Diomedes and Meriones standing for Augustus and Agrippa.

17 **My war-songs**: needless to say there are no such songs to be found in the Odes, but the last two lines are a fair prospectus for the nature of H's personal poetry.

1.7

A poem of deeply perplexing transitions in Pindaric style. What follows draws heavily on the exposition of West 1995. H addresses **Plancus**, who was consul in 42 BC, the fateful year of Philippi (see also 3.14). For the next decade he had served under Antony (the arch-demon of the Civil War, whom H never names) in the east, but in 32 BC, before Actium (where Antony was defeated), he deserted Antony and returned to Rome. Like Sestius (see 1.4) he was a beneficiary of the policy of clemency, and it was he who in 27 BC proposed the name of Augustus for Octavian. The eve of his departure for Rome provides the most convincing moment for the parallel with Teucer developed below.

Metre. 1st Archilochian, which recurs only once (1.28).

1-11: a list of Greek cities, familiar no doubt to Plancus from his Asian service, somewhat tendentiously described (the praise of Athens is **unending**, and the olive, sacred to Pallas, is plucked anywhere). **Mytilene** (4). **Tempe** (2).

12–14: H prefers (genuinely, see 2.6) **Tibur** (the modern Tivoli), situated on the River **Anio,** founded by **Tiburnus,** home of the Sibyl **Albunea,** and evidently Plancus' place of retirement (line 21).

15–21: a transition from the waters of Tibur through the **rain**, which (unlike the praise of Athens) is not incessant, to Plancus and his troubles, which a third liquid will alleviate.

21–32: the parallel. **Teucer** was the son of Telamon, king of **Salamis**. He distinguished himself at the siege of Troy, but he returned home without his brother Ajax, who had come to an ignominious end. His father blamed him for this, and exiled him. He sailed to Cyprus where he founded a new Salamis. There are two points of contact with Plancus: first Plancus, when in a position of influence, did nothing to prevent the proscription of his brother (or cousin): secondly he set off for an unpredictable reception from a theatre where he could have expected to remain with honour.

1.8

The parade of grandees is over, though not yet the parade of metres. H slips into his avuncular role as amused observer of young lovers. An unbroken series of bantering questions directed at the more experienced **Lydia**, and all suggesting the same answer, exposes the failings of young **Sybaris** (the name suggests none too subtly his idle and luxurious disposition), who is neglecting his military training (required by Augustan policy, on the advice of Maecenas).

Metre. Greater Sapphic (the long lines being the Sapphic rhythm with an additional four syllables). This is the only example.

3   training ground: the Campus Martius, an open space in north-west Rome beside the Tiber, sacred to Mars, and used for military training.

13–16   malingering like the son of Thetis: Thetis was a sea nymph, and her son was Achilles, the greatest of the Greek warriors at Troy. To keep him away from the impending Trojan war, where he was doomed to die, she sent him to the island of Scyros disguised as a girl, where, however, he was detected by Ulysses. The implications of draft-dodging and effeminacy lend bite to the banter. But it was Thetis who hid Achilles, and it is Lydia who is getting the blame here.

1.9

This is a dramatic monologue, one of H's favourite forms, consisting of one side of a dialogue. The reader is left to deduce the unstated details of the dramatic context. The ode starts and finishes with two unforgettable images. But how does it move from the stillness of frozen winter via a violent storm to a warm summer evening? This question has puzzled readers down the centuries. The answer lies in the relationship depicted between the speaker and the addressee, and the exchange between them which can be inferred.

Metre. At last we have come to H's commonest metre, the Alcaic (thirty-seven odes), demanding in its discipline but flexible in its range.

1   Soracte (3): a mountain north of Rome. The vision is of cold and calm.

5   Thaliarchus: the name means 'Ruler of the Feast', he must be understood as a slave, and a boy lover, who, we learn, is outgrowing the role. H's first priority is for warmth.

9–12: the storm is not a description of the actual weather outside. The speaker (H) remarks that the gods can calm storms. The sequence of these three stanzas – from cold to the need for warmth, and then to reassurance that storms pass – suggests that the initial cold was emotional as well as physical. There was a quarrel before the start, and what follows suggests that it was sexual in nature: a proposition has been made and rejected. The older man looks out of the window, collects himself, and proceeds to offer generous advice: 'It's time for you to turn your attention to girls' (like Lycidas at the end of 1.4, and others later).

18 Now: the milder weather is not a contradiction of the first stanza; the scene is what is suitable to the young man's time of life (**your time**).

21–4: the last stanza is often quoted as the prime example of the artistry of word order, which Latin permits, which H exploits, and which English cannot hope to imitate.

1.10

The first ode to address a god. We might have expected Bacchus, but **Mercury** turns out to be H's favourite. Reasons appear from what he says here, and later we shall find H explicitly calling himself a follower of Mercury (2.17).

Metre. Sapphic, the first metre to be repeated, although the parade is not quite finished.

3   wrestling: the practice of wrestling in a public gymnasium was inherited from Greece, and was regarded as a civilising component of physical education.

6   first to tune the … **lyre**: the first act of Mercury (Hermes) was to kill a tortoise, and string its shell with sheep-gut, thus inventing the lyre; a prime reason for H's allegiance.

7   playful: it is not the thieving but the playfulness which appeals to H, who so often is poking quiet fun at his friends.

9–12: Still on the day of his birth, Mercury stole **Apollo**'s cattle, and while he was looking for them stole his **quiver** as well.

13–16: This incident is from the *Iliad*: Mercury convoyed king **Priam** through the Greek camp to Achilles' tent, to ransom the body of his son, Hector. Similarly H attributes his escape from Philippi to Mercury's protection (2.7).

19   respected equally: another attribute dear to H, who prided himself on rising from humble origins to a position of influence (3.30). As a boy he was taunted with being the son of a freedman; yet he was offered the post of secretary to Augustus.

1.11

A dramatic monologue, taking the form of a gentle admonition to a young girl who has evidently been consulting horoscopes.

Metre. 5th, or Greater, Asclepiad, and the end of the parade. No further routine references to metre will be made, except to draw attention to the three additional metres which occur later (each once only). The translation is the only consciously borrowed metre: readers of Tennyson may recognise the couplets of *Locksley Hall*, which are one syllable shorter than the Latin.

1   Leuconoe (4): the name suggests naivety, and the instructions about the wine suggest a slave girl.

5   wearing out the Tuscan sea: the Tyrrhenian sea, on the west of Italy. Usually the sea is seen as wearing down the shore; here the image is reversed.

7–8   gather in: the metaphor behind H's best known aphorism, starting with the pruning, is from viticulture. Despite the reticence it is clear that this is a love poem, culminating in the age-old persuasion of the man to the woman. Later the same metre is used for the same purpose, but addressed to a boy, and in a very different tone (4.10).

1.12

An ambitious ode modelled on Pindar (one of the Greek Nine, who figures most prominently in Book 4), who also began and ended with Jupiter. Enlisting the aid of the Muse, **Clio**, H asks whose praise he should sing. He proceeds to praise first gods, then demi-gods, then, with a transition to the Roman Muse, men distinguished in the history of Rome, leading up to Augustus, who rules under Jupiter.

5-6 Helicon … Pindus … Haemus: Greek mountains connected either to the Muses or Orpheus.

7 Orpheus (2): the legendary musician who charmed animals and trees with the lyre. One authority names Clio as his mother, though another Muse, Calliope, is the usual candidate.

25 Hercules and Leda's twins: H turns to the demi-gods (mortals who became gods). Leda's twins were Castor and Pollux, whose influence through St Elmo's fire was met in 1.3.2.

33-6: here H moves to Rome. **Camena** is the Roman Muse, and **Romulus** (another demi-god) was the founder and first king of Rome. These names delimit the span of Roman history inhabited by the names in the next two stanzas: the monarchy from Romulus and **Numa** Pompilius, his successor, to **Tarquinius** Superbus, and then the Republic, ending with the death of the younger **Cato** by suicide after Julius Caesar's victory at Thapsus in 46 BC.

37-44: a list of hardy Roman warriors, not all successful, but exemplars of the old Republican virtues. **Cannae** was the scene of a crushing victory of Hannibal in 216 BC.

45 Marcellan fame: a cunning transition; C. Claudius Marcellus was the captor of Syracuse in 212 BC. His descendant of the same name was the nephew and intended heir of Augustus (he died, however, in the autumn of 23 BC, presumably after the publication of this ode).

48 the Julian star: a reference to the well attested comet which appeared after the death of Julius Caesar, and was believed to control the fortunes of his house. Without naming Augustus H has reached his destination, for Augustus was the adoptive son of Julius Caesar.

58-60: Augustus' earthly dominion will not usurp Jupiter's control of Olympus, nor interfere with his power to punish pollution with the thunderbolt.

1.13

An unusually vehement love poem, which moves from an angry culinary metaphor to a touching description of an ideal partnership.

1-12: the avuncular mask slips, as H affects the pose of a furiously jealous lover. But the metaphor from cooking suggests a parodic element. We are reminded of Sappho's minute description of her feelings, imitated by Catullus 51. The liver was regarded as the seat of sexual emotion.

16 ambrosia: the food of the gods; H actually mentions nectar, which is what they drank.

17-20: H moves to a serious Augustan conclusion, with a warning about fidelity leading to a sensitive picture of the ideal of harmonious, lifelong marriage.

1.14

H addresses a **ship** which is struggling to make port during a storm. It was recognised in antiquity that the ship is an allegory for the ship of state, a theme of Alcaeus. The dramatic date appears to be some time during the Civil War when there was fear of a new outbreak (line 1), but attempts to be more specific are perilous.

6 unfrapped: frapping ('undergirding' in the language of Acts 27.17) is the practice of passing ropes under a damaged hull in order to bind it together.

9 your gods: ships were protected by statues of gods placed in niches at the stern.

18 desperate yearning: this very strong word is used of longing for Augustus in 4.5; this is perhaps a clue that the time is one of fear for Augustus' safety.

20 the Cyclades (3): the channels between the Cyclades were notoriously treacherous, but the specific reference may be another clue: Augustus may be making for Rome from somewhere beyond the Cyclades (for pursuit of this clue see West 1995).

1.15

This ode addresses no one, and is not a dramatic monologue; it falls into none of H's normal patterns. It consists almost entirely of a prophecy about the Trojan war, in direct speech, targeted scornfully at Paris, who caused the war by abducting Helen. It is said to be a shot at transposing epic into lyric in the manner of Bacchylides (one of the Greek Nine). It is Augustan in its condemnation of adultery (**5**).

1-4 false shepherd ... host ... Nereus: Paris was a son of Priam, king of Troy; called a shepherd because he was exposed at birth (by reason of prophecies about his future), but saved and brought up among shepherds. Later he was recognised and acknowledged; he was received at Sparta by its king, Menelaus, and proceeded to seduce his wife, Helen, who eloped with him to Troy. **Nereus** (2) was a sea god with the gift of prophecy, the father of the fifty Nereids.
12 aegis: a piece of body armour belonging to Pallas, usually represented as embossed with a gorgon's head on the midriff.
17-27: the names in these lines are all of Greek heroes who fought at Troy: **Ajax** is here the lesser Ajax (son of Oileus); **Laertes'** (3) **son** was Ulysses (Odysseus); **Tydeus'** (2) **son** was Diomedes, whom we met (in company with **Meriones**) in 1.6.
28 superior to his sire: H contradicts a taunt of Agamemnon in the *Iliad*, who calls Diomedes inferior to his father in battle (4.399).
33 furious detachment: an attempt to copy an oracular ambiguity in the Latin: the noun appears to refer to Achilles' troops, but with hindsight will be understood to mean his angry withdrawal from the fray.

Did H have any contemporary relevance in mind in choosing this episode for his epic exercise? The obvious analogue for the adulterous shepherd, whom he does not name here, is the adulterous general whom he refuses ever to name, Mark Antony. This idea is not at all new, but it suffered from the magisterial criticism of Fraenkel (188ff.). But when we find Paris threatened with heroes whom we have already identified with Augustus and his cause, Teucer (1.7), Meriones and Diomedes (1.6), and when the standing of the last is enhanced by a pointed contradiction of Homer, it is impossible to think that there was no contemporary component to H's intention.

1.16

This poem raises an immediate question by failing to name the addressee. An ancient speculation, which has attractions, is that she is to be identified with the Tyndaris of the next ode. Another question is who wrote the offending verses about the other: the natural answer would be that H wrote them about the addressee, but the Latin admits the opposite construction (and the translation preserves the ambiguity). The tone of the homily against anger is deliberately hyperbolical and mock serious, but there is no reason to doubt the final desire for a reconciliation.

1 daughter lovelier: Helen was the fairest, but her mother, Leda, was also noted for her beauty. Helen's (mortal) father was Tyndarus, and she is also known by her patronym, Tyndaris. Except for the purpose of giving this hint, there is no apparent reason for mentioning the mother.
5-8: this stanza instances ecstatic religious cults. The **Pythian** is Apollo, whose famous oracle was at his shrine in Delphi; the **Corybantes** (4) were priests of **Cybele** (3), a fertility goddess.
9-16: the catalogue even takes in Jupiter and the creation.
17 Thyestes (3): this reference is puzzling if H is pleading for the woman to give up her anger at his verses, for the obvious trend of the myth is that Thyestes was harmed not by his own anger, but by that of his brother Atreus (who served him his own children as a meal). It might help if we had the play on the subject by Varius, which would have been topical.

20 walls ploughed under: the classic instance of this was the ploughing of salt into the site of Carthage in 146 BC; another portentous reference.

22 I too: This sentence is difficult to accommodate to the picture of H apologising for his verses: on that view these lampoons must be the same as those of line 2, yet they appear to be a long time in the past.

28 recanted: the Latin word here was coined by H. Recantation is the other link with Tyndaris, for the celebrated case of recantation was by Stesichorus (one of the Greek Nine), who recanted an account of Helen being at Troy, substituting an alternative version, that it was only her phantom.

1.17

For the first time H speaks of his Sabine retreat. The tone is affectionate and contented. His flocks are protected by **Faunus**, the gods are smiling, the food is good. He offers **Tyndaris** sanctuary from the rough and tumble of the metropolitan social scene. The structure, as so often, hinges round the middle stanza, and the privileges of the goats in the first half have careful counterparts in the advantages offered to Tyndaris in the second.

1-2 Arcady … Lucretilis … Faunus: H identifies Faunus with Pan, who makes the journey from his seat in Arcadia to Lucretilis, the local Sabine mountain (illustrated on the cover of this book).

6 evil-smelling: H has an unsentimental attitude to animals, as is to be expected of one to whom animal sacrifice was a matter of everyday ritual.

10 Tyndaris: the sandwiching of the name hints at musical skill, which is common among the mature women in the Odes.

11 Ustica: a place near H's villa which cannot now be identified.

13-16: the contentment is also an expression of gratitude to his benefactor. For once H is not concerned to emphasise the frugality of his country diet.

18 Teian (2): the reference is to Anacreon (one of the Greek Nine), who came from Teos; the language is consistent with writing as well as performing.

19-20 Penelope … Circe (2): female characters from the *Odyssey*: Penelope was the faithful wife of Ulysses, and Circe the island enchantress who turned his companions into pigs.

22 wine of Lesbos: wine from the birthplace of Alcaeus and Sappho; it will be a very literary party.

1.18

H advises **Varus**, who is planting an estate at **Tibur**, to start with the **vine**. He praises wine, but warns of the violence and vices which result from over-indulgence. No less than four names for the god of wine are used, two Roman (**Bacchus** and **Liber**), and two Greek (**Euhius** (3) and **Bassareus** (3)), from the orgiastic cults of Dionysus.

1 Varus: this may be the Quintilius Varus whose death is mourned in 1.24. The line is imitated from Alcaeus.

3 always dry: this line is a parody of Hesiod, who speaks of the path of virtue being full of hardships.

8 Centaurs … Lapiths: the Lapiths were a tribe of Thessaly; the Centaurs were invited to the wedding of their king, Pirithous, where a drunken incident led to the battle commemorated in a frieze on the Parthenon.

9 Sithonians: a Thracian tribe; Sithon, from whom their name is taken, ravished his own daughter and was killed by Dionysus.

12 hidden emblems: H will not reveal the god's secrets (the language is intentionally obscure); he is anxious to maintain a reputation for discreet reticence.

13-16: the picture is of a wild Dionysiac procession. The participants are perversions of good qualities, produced by excessive drinking: love becomes blind self-love, glory becomes feather-headed vainglory, discretion becomes babbling indiscretion.

1.19

Though no more than an amused observer of the amorous scene, H finds himself driven to write of passion, but then comes the last stanza.

1 **cruel mother of desires**: i.e. Venus, mother of Cupid. H picks up this line at the very beginning of the second collection (4.1.5).
2 **Bacchus, son of ... Semele**: Semele (3) was loved by Jupiter, and was tricked by Juno into asking to see him. She was destroyed by his undisguised presence, but Jupiter saved their unborn child (Bacchus), and sewed him into his thigh, whence he was in due course born.
3 **Licence**: sexual freedom, here treated as a deity.
9 **Total onslaught**: there is no denying that this is passion.
11-12: political affairs have ceased to be important. The oxymoron of **aggressive** flight derives from the Parthian shot, delivered in retreat, notorious in Rome since the defeat of Carrhae (53 BC).
15-16 **she'll come**: the temperature has to be moderated. H is referring to Venus, not Glycera.

1.20

The second half of the book starts with another address to **Maecenas**, this time an invitation, adopting a complimentary but confidently familiar tone.

1 **quaff**: it is the material of the cups which will be modest, not the size (they are two-handled); there will be plenty to drink.
3 **that very day**: the allusion is to a known occasion when Maecenas, who had been ill, was spontaneously applauded on entering the theatre (mentioned again in 2.17).
5 **ancestral Tiber**: ancestral because Tiber was known as the Etruscan river, and Maecenas claimed descent from Etruscan royalty (see 3.29.1).
6 **noble knight**: another pointed reference, for Maecenas, despite his distinction and wealth, chose never to ascend above equestrian rank.
8 **Vatican**: one of the seven hills of Rome.
9-12: the wines mentioned are of higher quality, and come from further afield, than H's local Sabine. H's insistence on the point shows a measure of independence. An invitation in these terms reflects credit on both parties, and speaks of a friendship transcending the usual relationship between patron and client.

1.21

A hymn to Diana and her brother, Apollo, reminiscent of Catullus 34. Later H addressed the Secular Hymn to the same pair of deities.

3-4 **Latona ... Jove**: the parents of Apollo and Diana; their birth took place on the island of **Delos,** the only site where Latona (Greek: Leto) found sanctuary from the persecution of Juno.
6-8: these gods have a particular interest in the countryside, including mountains. Three mountains are mentioned here, establishing their connections with diverse areas, starting with Italy: **Algidus,** near Augustus' birthplace, Velitrae; **Erymanthus** (famous principally for the boar slain by Hercules) in Arcadia; **Gragus** in Lycia (Asia Minor).
9 **Tempe** (2).

15 Persia … Britain: opposite distant ends of the Roman world, not yet fully pacified; fit victims for any disasters that might be impending.

1.22

One of the best known and loved of the Odes, and deservedly so. It is even quoted by Shakespeare (*Tit. Andr.* 4.2.20). Yet the wicked reversal in the last stanza has been missed by many admirers of the first.

1-4: the portentous first stanza, which in reality is poking gentle fun at the Stoic concept of the virtuous man, lends itself to being taken too seriously. Fraenkel (p. 184) tells how it used to be sung at funerals in German schools as if it was a hymn (as a small boy, he confesses, he was 'very much puzzled' by the intrusion of Fuscus). Aristius **Fuscus** had already appeared in the Satires as a close friend of H, with a similar sense of humour.

5-8 Hydaspes (3): a river in the Punjab, famous for Alexander's defeat of Porus in 326 BC. **Syrtes** (2) confirms the Stoic connection, for in 47 BC it had been the scene of an epic march by the younger Cato, renowned for his Stoic virtues.

9 For: H uses the incident of the **wolf** to demonstrate the invulnerability of the virtuous man, thus claiming that status for himself.

10 Lalage: the name suggests a chatterbox.

13 Daunia: part of Apulia which included H's birthplace, Venusia.

17-22: H prepares to explain why extremes of climate can hold no terrors for him. Consistently with the opening we expect him to claim that virtue will be his protection.

22-4: but no, H stands his solemn opening on its head by attributing his safety to Lalage. (The sweet laughter is taken from Catullus 51, which is a direct translation of one of the few surviving poems of Sappho.)

1.23

A little gem. The difficulties here are textual; the text used has the approbation of Bentley and Housman, both of whom wrote about it in their most lively vein. The theme is from Anacreon, one of the Greek Nine.

1 Chloe: like Lycidas at the end of 1.4, she is at the threshold of sexual maturity.

9 wolf: in deference to English usage the size of the predator has been moderated.

1.24

A heartfelt lament for the death of a dear friend of both H and Virgil, which moves from epitaph to a reflection on the finality of death, tailored to Virgil.

3 Melpomene (4): see on 1.1.32.

5 Quintilius: consistently with the virtues singled out here, Quintilius is later praised by H in *Ars Poetica* as a penetrating and candid critic. Not to be confused with Quintilian, a writer of the next century whose *Institutio* contains comments on ancient authors, including H.

11 rectify life's terms: the legal flavour here reflects the Latin.

9-18: for the benefit of Virgil there are reminiscences of the *Aeneid* and the *Georgics* in these lines. Virgil's mourning recalls his famous line about 'tears of things'; **piety** is the repeatedly emphasised virtue of Aeneas; **Orpheus'** (2) failure to rescue his wife, Eurydice, from the underworld is an episode in *Georgics* 4, where the hostile reception of Orpheus by the nether gods is closer to the sinister picture of Mercury here than the more upbeat portrayal of the same role at the end of 1.10.

1.25

We glimpsed a fierce tone at the beginning of 1.13, but it had given way to mature reflection by the end. Here the attack mounts from unkind to vicious, to such an extent that Victorian translators (e.g. Conington, Wickham) disdained to notice the ode at all. Abuse of this kind was an established literary genre before H, and it is more consistent with his mood in the Epodes, but we shall meet it again.

12   moonless: the period between the waning of the old moon and the rising of the new was thought to be particularly stormy.
14   mares on heat: mares were considered exceptionally lustful. Virgil tells how they could be impregnated by the winds.
17: **ivy** is the emblem of Bacchus, and **myrtle** of Venus.

1.26

A short ode, but programmatic. H confidently addresses his Muse, reaffirming his intention to write lyrics in the Lesbian style. Rare rhythms suggest it may be of early date, before H had decided how the Alcaic metre worked best.

2   rebellions in the ... north: possibly a reference to Dacian Cotiso (see 3.8.18).
4   Tiridates (4): twice rebelled and took the throne of Parthia, and was eventually expelled.
7   Lamia: the Lamiae were a large and distinguished family. Since the crown probably denotes a military victory, this may be Lucius Lamia, who was legate in Spain in 24 BC. He was evidently a close friend. The same name recurs in 1.36 and 3.17.
9   Piplean: a rare label for a Muse; Piplea was a place in Pieria (the reputed home of the Muses from very early times), and said to be the site of the **Pierian** (4) spring.
10   the restrung lyre: H is claiming originality for his revival of the Lesbian lyric.

1.27

A dramatic monologue which explains itself without ambiguity. A drinking party (symposium) is in full swing, but a cup is thrown, and matters threaten to get out of hand. The elder statesman present intervenes, and to calm things down creates a deft diversion. This is the most conversational of the odes, and H at his most wickedly humorous.

3   good-tempered Bacchus: a stern opening to bring the young to heel. So far the wine's influence has been benevolent; in a moment there could be mayhem. In four lines the whole scene is illuminated.
8   reclining: the diners are, as normal, on couches, supporting themselves on one elbow.
9   sterner wine: the arbiter of drinking has prescribed Falernian, but the speaker has not yet taken it.
16-17   a decent class of mistress: a gently inserted needle. The sex of the partner is not specified, but the coming descriptions belong to a courtesan.
19   Charybdis: famous whirlpool, regarded as a female monster.
21-2   witch ... wizard ... god: a Pindaric climax. Thessaly was notorious for witches.
22-4: the **three-faced monstrosity** is the legendary Chimaera, part lion, part goat and part serpent (sometimes represented with three heads), which was killed by the hero Bellerophon riding the winged horse **Pegasus**.

1.28

Another dramatic monologue which, in contrast to the last ode, is notably opaque in character and purpose. An address to a dead mathematician leads to a list of mortals who died despite connections with the gods, with a special look at Pythagoras. Then at line 21 we learn that the speaker is himself a drowned sailor, who has never been buried. He cajoles and threatens a passing sailor to free his spirit with a ritual sprinkling of dust.

Metre. See 1.7: the second and last in this metre.

2 **Archytas**: a Pythagorean philosopher and mathematician from Tarentum (in Apulia) of the fourth century BC. The offered dust shows he has been duly buried.

7-9: **Tantalus** stole the food of the gods, and suffered eternal punishment for it. **Tithonus** (the 2nd syllable is stressed) was loved by Aurora, goddess of the dawn, who granted him immortality but not eternal youth; he withered away, and was changed into a grasshopper. **Minos,** king of Crete, was a lawgiver and confidante of Jupiter; he became the just judge of the underworld.

9-15: Pythagoras believed in the transmigration of souls. One day in the temple of Argos he recognised a shield hanging on the wall as one he had carried at the siege of Troy when he had been **Euphorbus,** a Trojan killed by Menelaus. When the shield was taken down and examined the name of Euphorbus was indeed found; ostensibly this is taken to prove that his spirit had lived on in Pythagoras, on whose death (*c*. 497 BC) it was removed to **Acheron** (a river in the underworld) for the second time.

16 **only once**: the speaker rejects the Pythagorean doctrine.

25 **squalls from the east**: it seems that the speaker and the passing sailor are, like Archytas, natives of **Tarentum**; a journey through the **Illyrian sea** would take them to Greece, and the east wind would be contrary, and would pass on to **Venusia** (H's birthplace in Apulia).

36 **three handfuls**: a minimal quantity of dust sufficed to release the spirit.

1.29

A bantering ode addressed to a young friend, **Iccius**, who has decided to go to war. By inference we learn a good deal about him. He likes to shoot a line and cut a dash; he has a taste for both sexes; he has money, a fine library and a passing fancy for Stoic philosophy, which, however, is not entirely consistent with his disposition or his latest resolve.

4 **Sheban princelings**: in 26-5 BC an expedition was sent to Arabia to gain a hold on the spice trade. It was unsuccessful, and if Iccius had joined it, he would probably not have returned. Sheba approximates to modern Yemen; mention of the Medes is an exaggeration, and the Chinese are fanciful embroidery.

16 leather: breastplates might be of leather, but the reference to Spain, which was famous for metals, makes metal at least equally plausible here.

1.30

H calls on **Venus** to come with her retinue from her eastern domain to **Glycera**'s house in **Rome**. In 1.19 he was on fire for Glycera, but shied away from passion, no doubt feeling his age. Here he is careful to include **Youth** among his helpers at the assignation. Implied also is the transfer from Greece to Rome of the inspiration for love poetry.

8 **Mercury**: in 1.10 we noted how congenial H finds Mercury. Naturally he wants his aid.

1.31

On 9 October 28 BC Augustus dedicated a new temple to **Apollo** in fulfilment of a vow made before Actium. In writing for this occasion H sidesteps the imperial theme, and frames a personal prayer addressed more to the god's healing aspect.

1   **the poet**: here the public poet, the bard.
3   **new liquor**: this language recalls a prayer for health in the coming year, traditionally offered at the *Meditrinalia* two days later.
8   **Liris**: the best wine came from the area in southern Latium watered by the river Liris.
13-16: the authenticity of this stanza has sometimes been called in question, but its sentiments are impeccably Horatian. (How far the last two lines are *true* is another matter.)
17-20: the bardic element has evaporated; the petition is personal and heartfelt.

1.32

Addressed to H's **lyre**, this is in form a hymn, but its tone is relaxed, familiar, a little less than solemn.

4   **a Latin chord**: H again emphasises his project of importing the Lesbian lyric to the Latin language.
5   **the citizen of Lesbos**: from the subject matter instanced it is quite clear that Alcaeus is meant, rather than Sappho. All the themes mentioned – war, shipwreck, wine, poetry and love (including homosexual love) – have already been encountered.
14   **tortoiseshell**: see on 1.10.6.

1.33

The lovesick **Albius** is thought to be none other than the elegist Tibullus, who was writing at the same time as H. A teasing homily on the tragi-comedy of love masks a criticism of Albius' literary style.

1   **Enough of moping**: too much unrelieved gloom is the implication.
6   **Pholoe** (3).
12   **the cruel joke**: don't take yourself so seriously.
13   **better love**: **Myrtale** (3) is a freedwoman, and no doubt a courtesan; the hint is that the better love was freeborn. Tactfully H softens the message by confessing to having shared the tribulations of love.

1.34

A short, partly ironic, reflection on religion, which leaves us sceptical of H's professed conversion and uncertain of his ultimate position.

1-5: a self-deprecating introduction. The **insane philosophy** is Epicureanism; the language contains reminiscences of its chief Roman apostle, Lucretius.
5-12: the Epicureans held (in common with modern science) that lightning is produced by clouds, and therefore could not occur without them. Thus lightning from a clear sky refuted the theory. It was, however, a literary commonplace, and we do not have to believe that H experienced it, or even seriously thought he did. **Diespiter** (4) is an archaic name for Jupiter. **Styx** is the river in the underworld over which all dead souls had to be ferried. **Taenarus** is one of the many names of the underworld.
12-16: H moves on simply to 'god', apparently equated with capricious Fortune, the subject of

242

the next ode. The image appears to be of a swooping bird, but such a range of sound is covered by the Latin that it is imprecise. The ambiguities serve H's purpose. He was an eclectic, making no pretence of any consistent philosophy

1.35

A hymn to the goddess, Fortune. It is a grim picture, unrelieved by H's lightness of touch, leading to an eloquent denunciation of the godlessness of the Civil War. This tone suggests a public pretext, perhaps the celebration of refurbishment of the temple at Antium under Augustan policy (**9**).

9-10: the whole world, Roman and barbarian, dreads the disfavour of Fortune. **Latium** (2 in English) is included as her home.

17-20: this vivid scene may describe a painted representation in the temple. The attributes appear to be instruments of torture, though some take them as tools of the building trade. Either way the anvil (line 38) will be on hand.

21 white-gloved: the priests of *Fides* (Loyalty) had their hands wrapped in white cloth.

22-4: a very obscure passage. When Fortune deserts a house, her attendants, **Hope** and **Loyalty**, go with her.

25-8: it is no surprise that the mortal hangers-on also desert; here there is a measure of characteristically acute observation.

29-32: in 27-6 BC Augustus planned expeditions to Britain, and the Arabian expedition also took place. Iccius (1.19) may have been one of the **young swarm**.

38-40: the prayer is to turn aggression outwards instead of inwards.

1.36

A celebration to mark the safe return of **Numida**, which seems, from the flattering prominence given to **Lamia** (H's friend of 1.26), to have been written at his suggestion. This could explain a certain want of conviction.

4 Spain: Numida has evidently been on military service.

9 manhood's robe: at about the age of fifteen a Roman boy was initiated into manhood, and assumed adult dress (the *toga virilis*).

10 chalk… in white: days of good omen were marked in white on the Roman calendar.

12 acrobatic dancing: the reference is to the *Salii* (see on 1.37.4).

13 thirsty Damalis: a drinking contest is on foot; Damalis is clearly a professional, and the implication seems to be that she must keep herself reasonably sober for the pleasure of Numida.

15-16: there is a language of flowers here: roses for death, lilies for transient youth, celery (longer lasting in a wreath) for the contrast.

1.37

The naval battle of Actium (31 BC) removed the last obstacle to the personal ascendancy of Octavian. He defeated the combined fleets of Antony and Cleopatra, who fled to Egypt, where they both in due course committed suicide. This famous ode celebrates the victory in terms which attest the joy and relief with which it was greeted in Rome. The first five stanzas paint a vindictive picture of Cleopatra, in the manner presented by Octavian's propaganda, but the last three transform the tone to one of admiration for the nobility of her end. Magnanimity to a fallen foe was a traditional Roman virtue, and it was part of the Augustan policy of clemency which followed (**2**), but it was not what Cleopatra could have expected if she had lived to figure in a Roman triumph.

1: the famous first line is imitated from a fragment of Alcaeus, celebrating the death of a tyrant.

2 **deck with feasts**: as part of victory celebrations meals would be set for the gods outside their temples.

4 **Salian priests**: priests of Mars noted for their abandoned dancing and lavish feasts.

7 **that demented queen**: H refuses to name the hated Cleopatra, who was reputed to have boasted of her intention to sit in judgment on the Capitol. He does not deign even to mention Antony, who had purported to present to her and her children (one by Julius Caesar and three by Antony himself) all the Roman territories in Asia (the Donations of Alexandria, 34 BC).

10 **semi-men**: a gibe at the eunuchs of the Egyptian court.

13 **scarce one ship**: a gross exaggeration. The rout was started by the desertion of Cleopatra with her sixty ships; Antony followed, and most of his fleet capitulated intact.

17-20: the speed implied by the similes is misleading. There was almost a year between the battle and the suicides.

21-4: Cleopatra was said to have attempted suicide with a dagger; she also failed in an attempt to drag ships overland to the Red Sea, and escape south. H is here presenting her in a generous light.

30 **Liburnians**: fast lightweight galleys, originally favoured by Liburnian pirates, which discomforted Antony's armoured dreadnoughts.

Text: the received punctuation places a comma at he end of line 29. This creates a difficulty over the case of *saevis Liburnis*, which has divided commentators. Some treat it as ablative of place (i.e. being transported in the galleys), others as dative after *invidens* (i.e. begrudging the Liburnians that …). The postponement of the comma for two words eliminates this ambiguity and proposes an ablative of comparison.

1.38

A charming miniature to mitigate the heavy political aftertaste of Cleopatra, and close the first Book on a lighter note. Because of the importance of its position, commentators are inclined to treat this ode as a declaration of H's literary intentions. Perhaps. But what is explicit is the unostentatious enjoyment of wine and, yes, love (for **myrtle** belongs to Venus, and the young Ganymede is garlanded too). This seems to be enough for eight lines.

BOOK 2

2.1

A powerful ode addressed to Pollio, the widely respected soldier, statesman, writer and public benefactor, who, having been a lieutenant of Julius Caesar and later an adherent of Antony, refused the overtures of Octavian, and raised himself above the power struggle between him and Antony, declaring that he would the prize of the victor. He then lived a life of letters, and founded the first national library in Rome. He outlived H, dying in AD 4. The ode is packed with allusions to his personal history.

1 **Metellus' year**: Metellus was consul in 60 BC, the year when Julius Caesar and Pompey formed an alliance. Pollio was writing a history of the Civil Wars, which unhappily has not survived, and took that year as his starting point.

6 **a dangerous throw**: a reminiscence of Caesar's remark as he crossed the Rubicon: 'The die is cast.' Pollio was on his staff at the time (49 BC).

8 **live embers**: raking up recent quarrels was bound to be contentious. For all Augustus' clemency, he would be sure to scan the history. Putting a foot wrong could be fatal.

9 **your tragedies**: Pollio was also writing tragic drama, also lost.

15 **Dalmatian triumph**: after Caesar's assassination (44 BC) Pollio served under Antony. He was consul in 40 BC, and he won a triumph over the Parthini (39/8 BC), who were in Antony's sphere of influence; H quietly moves it to the neighbouring territory, which was in Octavian's sphere.

17   Now, now: the accent of immediacy may hint at public recitation, a practice initiated by Pollio; this would explain how H can describe the contents of a work as yet unpublished.

17-24: the descriptions fit the battle of Pharsalus (48 BC), where Caesar, aided by Pollio, defeated Pompey. The rump of the Pompeians, inspired by **Cato** (the Younger), carried on the struggle in Africa until their defeat at Thapsus (46 BC). Cato then committed suicide rather than live under a dictator.

25-8: a complex historical conceit. A Scipio (Africanus Minor) had destroyed Carthage in 146 BC, after which, according to a later story, the city's gods had been ritually summoned away to Rome (**forced to leave**). Jugurtha, king of neighbouring Numidia, was a thorn in Rome's side who was executed in 104 BC; a prominent opponent of his was Q. Metellus. The Pompeian commander at Thapsus (100 years after the destruction of Carthage) was Q. Metellus Pius Scipio, an adopted grandson of Q. Metellus and a member of the Scipio family. He, like Cato, committed suicide after his defeat. H represents him in particular, but also all the Roman dead on both sides, as a blood sacrifice to **Jugurtha's shade**.

29-36: another moving reflection on the Civil War (cf. 1.35.33-40), which could have been in Rupert Brooke's mind when he wrote 'If I should die …'. **Daunian** emphasises the effect on H's native region.

37-40: like Pollio withdrawing from politics, H pulls himself up and turns to lighter themes. Heavy politics do not reappear until the beginning of Book 3.

2.2

Sallustius Crispus was the great nephew of the historian Sallust, from whom he inherited great wealth, but like Maecenas he remained in equestrian rank. Later he succeeded Maecenas as the chief adviser of Augustus. He had a reputation for liberality. It is conjectured that he had Stoic leanings, because this ode, with its opaque thought connections, is heavily weighted with Stoic preoccupations.

1   buried: Sallust is known to have owned a copper mine.

5-8   Proculeius (4): a brother-in-law of Maecenas, who shared his fortune with his brothers.

9   taming greed: H is not implying greed on Sallust's part, rather he is assuming, and complimenting his known generosity.

10-12: the second **Punic land** was southern Spain where there were Carthaginian settlements. The concept of a single vast estate is a comment on the expansionist habits of the great landlords.

13   dropsy: the disease is compared to greed: indulgence aggravates both.

17   Phraates (3): king of Parthia, who was twice deposed by the Roman puppet, Tiridates (1.26), and twice recovered his throne.

18   misuse of words: the word for blessed (*beatus*) means both wealthy and happy; popular belief equates wealth with happiness, but to the Stoics the wise man was indifferent to wealth, and just as only the wise man could be truly virtuous and happy, only the wise man could be a true king.

2.3

After the Stoic homily an Epicurean monologue, enjoining moderation but also enjoyment of what life has to offer. Dellius was a notorious turncoat of the Civil Wars (*desultor* was the insult he earned – horse-leaper), who, like Plancus (1.4), defected from Antony to Octavian shortly before Actium, and was treated with clemency. This ode shows that he had retained his wealth, and was on friendly terms with H.

1-5: we do not know in what way **times** might have been **hard** for Dellius, why he needed reminding of his mortality, or why he might have been a **prey to gloom**. West conjectures that he may have been mourning a bereavement. This makes sense of the odd transition after stanza 5, since the inevitability of death assumes the character of a consolation.

9-12: the allurements of nature are there to tempt us to pleasure.

13 Call forth, then: it is evident that the setting is on Dellius' property, and he is being invited to order the entertainment. A natural distraction from grief.

16 the Sisters Three: the Fates (*Parcae*), who spin, and ultimately cut, the thread of a man's life.

24 Orcus: strictly another name for Pluto, god of the underworld, but habitually used for the underworld itself.

28 the ferry: Charon's ferry across the Styx.

2.4

In 1.27 we found H making fun of a young man's love affair. Here the whole ode is devoted to teasing his young friend Xanthias, who is half ashamed of having fallen for a slave girl.

1-12: these stanzas in mock-epic tone offer examples from mythology. The least tactless is **Tecmessa**, who was a support to Ajax in his madness. The other two brought nothing but trouble. **Briseis** (3) was the bone of contention whose confiscation caused the wrath of Achilles. The **ravished girl** was the prophetess Cassandra, who at the sack of Troy was raped by (the other) Ajax; **Atrides** (Agamemnon) took her home to Mycenae, where he was murdered by his wife, Clytemnestra. **The Thessalian** is Achilles, who laid waste the Trojan army and slaughtered **Hector**, the Trojan prince and champion, but did not live to see Troy fall.

14 son-in-law: a tease; Xanthias will not be thinking of marriage. If he is a Roman citizen he cannot marry a slave.

15 her gloom: it is hinted that Phyllis has a sulky expression.

17-18: it is also hinted that Xanthias is a snob, and that she is mercenary and unfaithful.

22 impartially: it is not to be supposed that this is the same Phyllis who is addressed in 4.11 (or is it?).

2.5

We have already seen H gently cajoling a young girl on the point of sexual maturity (1.23). This is a sensitive examination of a different case, a young girl whom H judges to be unready. It should be remembered that girls were considered old enough to marry at twelve. Quinn takes the ode to be addressed to a husband with a young wife. The Victorian translators censored the whole ode.

1-9: here we are shown the girl's standpoint; **sexual aggression**: the language is uncharacteristically coarse: H is making a serious point, and wishes to seize the attention.

9-20: we switch to the advantages to the man of restraint; **the bovine wooer**: H lightens the tone as he leaves the heifer metaphor. **Pholoe** (3).

20-4: by way of distraction we glide into the parallel case of the opposite sex; **Gyges** is another Lycidas (1.4.19).

The ode is addressed to someone, but unusually no one is named. Some commentators have taken H to be reproving himself. But in view of the nature of the language and the delicacy of the subject, tact is a sufficient explanation for the discreet silence.

2.6

H addresses his friend, **Septimius**, specifying his first and second choices for his retirement home.

1–4: this opening is a reminiscence of Catullus 11 (also in Sapphic metre), where a much longer list of destinations introduces a vicious message. The **Cantabri** were a warlike tribe in northern Spain. **Syrtes** (2).

6: we have already met H's love of **Tibur** (1.7). H acquired at least one property in or near Tibur, but probably not until after the publication of Odes 1–3.

7–8: H proceeds to undercut all the journeys imagined in the first stanza.

9–16 Tarentum: the founder may be Spartan, but the pleasures are indigenous and indulgent. The sheep were indeed **leather-coated,** to protect their valuable wool. **Hymettus** is a mountain close to Athens, famous for its honey. **Venafrum** is in central Italy.

22–4: This desired event did not take place. H, having died within two months of Maecenas (in 8 BC), was buried near to him on his estate on the Esquiline in Rome. Whether Septimius was among the mourners history does not relate.

2.7

One of the most politically sensitive of the Odes. H welcomes back to Roman citizenship Pompeius, an army friend who had fought with him on the losing side at Philippi (42 BC).

1 Brutus: the principled republican who was one of the assassins of Julius Caesar in 44 BC. He withdrew to the East and joined forces with Cassius, another leading conspirator. At Philippi in eastern Macedonia they were defeated by the forces of Octavian and Antony.

3 who ... has brought you back?: the answer is Augustus, under whose policy Pompeius' citizenship has been restored, as was H's.

10 mislaid my pretty shield: H is here following a long-standing tradition among the Greek lyric poets, who also made light of this military disgrace (e.g. Alcaeus, Anacreon).

11–12: Brutus and Cassius both committed suicide; the language is figurative rather than literal, and it expresses, twenty years later, the viewpoint of the victor.

14 concealed with mist: this form of divine rescue was a Homeric tradition, but the rescuer is H's own favourite (see on 1.10).

15–16: the marine metaphor, and Pompeius' name, suggest that he may have joined the fleet of Sextus Pompeius, Antony's admiral, who was not disposed of until after the sea battles of Mylae and Naulochus (36 BC).

20 the feast you owe to Jove: H lays on an entertainment to match that of the second stanza, but with good class Italian wine. If **owed**, the feast would be in fulfilment of a vow offered for safe return. Some have seen the mention of **Jove** as a veiled reference to Augustus.

22: H turns to the slaves with his orders. **Forgetfulness** is appropriate in view of their shared past; again the theme of clemency is underlined.

25 myrtle ... Venus' choice: we have already seen that myrtle denotes Venus (1.38), but she is named here for a special reason: the arbiter of drinking was chosen by dice, and the highest throw was called Venus.

2.8

Hyperbolic, and not wholly serious, condemnation of a too-successful courtesan. The last stanza was too indelicate for the Victorians.

1 Barine (3): the Greek name probably denotes a freedwoman; a high-class professional.

3 discolouration: a discoloured tooth would be black, but on the fingernail a white fleck was thought to expose a liar.

5 I might believe you: her lies are so notorious that she appears to be immune to divine wrath; any sign of punishment might suggest she had reformed. **You dazzle**: despite himself H betrays admiration; this is not a pitiless diatribe in the vein of 1.25.

9–12: these are the perjured oaths she swears.

14: as he hones … Cupid is having to work overtime to handle her lovers.

21-4 bull-calves: 2.5 has prepared us for this metaphor, which in turn prepares us for the last line. Stingy old men were a stock butt of comedy. The unfortunate brides are still virgins.

2.9

H's friend **Valgius**, whom he names elsewhere as one of the people whom he would particularly like his work to please, was himself a poet. H takes him to task for overdoing his laments for **Mystes** to the point of tedium and self-indulgence.

1-8: four examples of adverse natural conditions which do not last for ever.

9-12: but Valgius' grieving does last for ever. H imitates Virgil's description of Orpheus mourning Eurydice. **Mystes** (2) a slave-boy.

13-16: two more examples to the same effect as the first four, though closer to the point (excessive grief). This is unlike H; he is parodying what he complains of. **Nestor**, king of Pylos, survived the siege of Troy, where his son **Antilochus** was killed, and lived on for three lives of men. **Troilus** (3), Priam's youngest son, was killed by Achilles.

17-24: the unsympathetic nature of H's prescription for distracting Valgius (a good dose of imperial triumphalism to clear the poetic sinuses) suggests that his real criticism is literary.

2.10

The addressee of this ode is usually identified with **Licinius Murena** (see also 3.19), who was a brother of Maecenas' wife, Terentia. In 22 BC (within a year of the publication of Odes 1-3) he was put to death for complicity in a conspiracy against Augustus. The moralising of the ode, therefore, is not an empty academic exercise, but a delicate journey on tiptoe through a political minefield. H proceeds by an unbroken series of unexceptionable precepts, which nevertheless carry clear advice to Licinius.

1-4: although no friend of sea travel, H codes his messages in nautical metaphor.

5 the golden mean: this expression, first articulated here, is so familiar that we do not notice the paradox in the juxtaposition of moderation with gold, the symbol of wealth; the concept goes back at least to Aristotle. Syme (p. 504) remarked that if Murena had been content with it, he 'would have escaped his doom'.

15-16: the references to **Jove** perhaps serve to placate Augustus as well as console Licinius.

19 arrows: Apollo's arrows were deadly: at the beginning of the *Iliad* they inflict plague on the besieging Greeks.

21-4: a return to the nautical metaphor. In both stanzas avoidance of excess is counselled (**too close/ too-full**). The advice remains sound even in days of fore-and-aft sails.

2.11

The setting here is similar to 2.3, with H conversing in his friend's garden. Quinctius is of an age with H, but a worrier; he needs to be teased and diverted. The pleasant surroundings suggest an impromptu picnic, and this time feminine company is called for.

10 stormy moon: a ruddy moon was thought to portend stormy weather.

18-24: H suggests orders for the servants.

21 call-girl: Lyde (2) is clearly on call, and the Latin leaves no doubt about her profession, but she is a musician and has her own secluded house; a high-class courtesan.

2.12

In 1.6 H deflected the idea of writing about Agrippa's military exploits. Here, in response to prompting from **Maecenas**, he does the same with Augustus's (despite his own suggestion to Valgius in 2.9). The strategy, however, is different. In stanzas 1-3, instead of demonstrating ineptitude, he plays on epic memories, relating them to recent history.

1-4: the references evoke new as well as old. The **Numantians** of central Spain had ferociously resisted Rome between 195 and 133 BC, but in 26-5 BC Augustus fought their neighbours, the Cantabri; **Mylae** in northern Sicily was the scene of naval defeats of the Carthaginians (260 BC), and more recently of Sextus Pompeius (36 BC).

5 **drunken brawls**: perhaps a reference to the notorious drunkenness of Mark Antony.

7 **the earthborn Giants**: we have already met the overthrow of the Giants as a metaphor for victory in the Civil War (1.3.40); Augustus becomes **Hercules**.

11 **princelings in chains**: Augustus celebrated a triple triumph in 29 BC.

12 **your prose**: Maecenas is known to have written some florid verse, but not prose; the suggestion is not wholly serious.

13 **your Licymnia**: H turns to Licymnia, whose identity is disputed. There are commentators who believe he is writing of his own mistress, and the Latin is compatible with this view (although stanza 6 is undoubtedly addressed to Maecenas). The translation sides with those who identify her with Maecenas' wife Terentia (the name scans the same way – a code used by other Latin poets). It would require unusual freedom for a poet to speak of his patron's wife in these terms, but unusual freedom, friendship and intimacy do indeed characterise the relationship of H and Maecenas.

17-20: the details are not precise here, but some consider the conduct unbecoming for a respectable Roman matron. Even if it is, H may be describing events before she was married.

25-8: an unforgettable picture of a beautiful but indiscreet woman, who, if Suetonius is to be trusted, later betrayed to her brother, Licinius Murena, the danger he was in (see on 2.10), and thereby caused Maecenas' fall from grace.

2.13

This ode is prompted by a narrow escape from a falling branch. It is impossible to doubt that some such event occurred, since H mentions it in no less than three other places in the Odes (2.17.27, 3.4.27, 3.8.6). The movement is from burlesque to a serious reflection on the dangers of life, and ends with an enigmatic vision of the underworld which leaves the commentators still arguing over H's purpose.

1-12: The attack not only on the **tree**, but on the man who planted it, is overdone to the point of absurdity. H is amusing himself and us.

15 **Bosphorus**: it was believed that the current in the Bosphorus was always adverse to the southern approach.

18 **backward arrow**: the Parthian shot again (see on 1.19.11-12).

21-8: here the underworld vision is conventional enough. **Proserpine** was Pluto's queen; **Aeacus** (3) was one of the judges of the underworld. H's two principal models, **Sappho** and **Alcaeus** (3) are briefly compared, to the advantage of Alcaeus. The comparison continues in the next stanza, but the vision is about to turn surreal.

29-32: here, perhaps, is the key. The **triumph song** about expelling tyranny (which can be related to the fragment of Alcaeus which lay behind 1.37) is another reference to the ending of the Civil War and the relief this has brought.

33-40 **the hundred-headed hound**: this is Cerberus, but normally he has only three heads; here he is drooping 200 ears. Then a quiet close in respite from pain. After the compliment to

Augustus H seems to be implying an ambition on his part to emulate the magical powers of Alcaeus.

2.14

This ode is so well known and loved, so universal, that little need be said. Nothing is known of **Postumus**, but we may guess some of his foibles from what H chooses to say.

5 **hecatomb**: a sacrifice of a hundred animals; exaggeration of a similar order is found in the last stanza.

8: two Giants are named; **Tityos** (3) was a monster with three heads and bodies; **Geryon** (3) was so huge that his body covered nine acres.

9 **that stream**: the Styx.

18-19 **Cocytus,** another river of the Underworld. There follow two of the usual cast of notorious sinners: the **wicked brides** were the forty-nine daughters of Danaus who killed their bridegrooms (see further 3.11); **Sisyphus** was condemned to roll a stone to the top of a hill, but it always escaped him.

24 **hated cypress**: boughs of cypress were placed over the door of a house which held a dead body, and around funeral pyres.

25 **worthier**: presumably because he drinks the wine, instead of hoarding it; the only overt hint at a moral.

2.15

A purely political ode, addressed to no one. Thoroughly Augustan in sentiment, it reads like an extract from one of the Roman Odes (say 3.6, whose theme it partly shares). It first looks forward, deploring the trend of current extravagance, then harks back to a golden age of traditional Roman austerity and dignity.

3 **the Lucrine lake**: during the campaign against Sextus Pompeius (37-6 BC) Agrippa, by a feat of engineering, had converted this inland lagoon into a harbour; the thought of it being rivalled by a fishpond would not be welcome to Augustus.

4 **plane-trees**: give good shade, but, unlike the worthy **elm**, are useless for supporting vines.

10 **sunburn**: intolerance of the sun is treated as a mark of degeneracy.

10-12 **Romulus**: the first king of Rome. The elder **Cato** (the Censor: 234-149 BC) was a paragon of the ancient virtues (of which his **beard** was a minor example).

13: reminiscent of Macaulay (*Horatius* st. xxxii):

> Then lands were fairly portioned;
> Then spoils were fairly sold:
> The Romans were like brothers
> In the brave days of old.

17-20: **turf** was a primitive building material, **stone** being reserved for public buildings.

2.16

An ode full of Epicurean propositions dear to H's heart. **Peace** of mind is what is important, but it does not come from power or wealth; the simple life is best; ambition and restless change do not cheat cares; perfect happiness is unattainable; fortune favours people in different ways. And there is a closing comparison between the circumstances of **Grosphus**, a wealthy Sicilian landowner, and H himself.

10   lictors: official bodyguards for Roman magistrates, who cleared the way for them with their rods.

12   coffered vault: a symbol of wealth.

21-4 bronze-clad yacht: another symbol of wealth. **Knights parading**: a reference to the annual horseback parade of the equestrian order. Both allusions recur in 3.1.37-40.

29-32: **Achilles** and **Tithonus** (2nd syllable stressed) are opposite cases: the first meeting premature death, the second unable to die.

37   twice-dipped purple: serious wealth, with a reference back to the second stanza. **little lot**: this wordplay is an attempt to parallel a pun by H on the word for Fate (*Parca*), which also means 'frugal'.

2.17

Maecenas appears to have been ill and moaning about his prospects of recovery. In addition it seems that, like Leuconoe in 1.11, he has been consulting his horoscope. H reassures him. The ode is striking testimony to his affection for his patron.

5   half my soul: H used a similar expression in speaking of his friend Virgil in 1.3.

9-12: it is possible that such a vow was sworn when they shared the perils of the Actium campaign. In the event they both died in 8 BC; H was the survivor by less than two months.

13-16: H lightens the tone, as often, by use of unserious exaggeration.

17-22: H patronised Leuconoe over her astrology, but he meets Maecenas on his own ground, likening their horoscopes and pointing out their separate brushes with death.

26   glad applause: this was for his recovery from illness (see 1.20).

27-30: see 2.13; H attributes Maecenas' escape to Jupiter, but his own only to **Faunus** (Pan), the son of his favourite, Mercury (see 1.10).

2.18

This unusual ode starts on a personal note, but turns into a diatribe against a land-grabbing developer, who is addressed but not named.

Metre. Hipponactean (unique): distichs consisting of an alternation of shorts and longs unbroken except for the limping end of the long line. The effect is uncharacteristically monotonous. Also untypical is the rhythm, which does not fall into the usual pattern of quatrains (and is so printed only for uniformity), but has clear breaks dividing the whole into units of 14, 14 and 12 lines.

1-14: H expresses satisfaction with his unaffluent lot, contrasting it with luxuries which imply time-consuming organisation in assembling imported goods. **distinguished women**: the picture is of wives of clients attending on a wealthy patron. **Sabine country**: a reference to Maecenas' generosity to H.

15-16   Day aside by day ...: this apparently violent transition has a logic to it. The speed of the moon's progress from birth to death links the implied labour and bustle of the first part to the explicit themes of frantic, greedy activity in the next part, and death in the last.

17-28: the unattributed 'you' cannot be understood as Maecenas, despite the Sabine reference, in view of the indignation inherent in the description of evicted clients. It is best taken as an address to the generalised money-grubbing type that H is attacking.

29-40: wealth is no protection against death. **the escort of the dead** is Mercury (as described at the ends of 1.10 and 24): in this role he is unwelcome to the rich, but a relief to the poor. There is no known account of **Prometheus** (3) seeking to bribe him. The **Tantalids** included Pelops, Atreus, Thyestes, Agamemnon and Aegisthus, all of whom came to famously bad ends.

2.19

A hymn to Bacchus had to come, yet its form is totally unexpected, with barely a mention of wine. The shifts of tone are extreme, oscillating between burlesque and high seriousness.

1-4: the personal vision of a god was a respectable literary pose, but the parenthesis gives away the tongue in the cheek here.

5-8: teasing gives way to possession by the god. This is dangerous, it can bring poetical inspiration, but the loss of control can also bring destruction, so the god must be placated. The **thyrsus** is the ivy-tipped wand which induces Bacchic frenzy.

9-12 So may I: H is anxious not to reveal forbidden mysteries, but possession by the god licenses him. All the phenomena in this stanza were well known Bacchic effects (described, for example, by Euripides in the *Bacchae*).

13 Ariadne: after she had been deserted on Naxos by Theseus, the Cretan princess was befriended by Bacchus, who gave her a crown of seven stars, which later became a constellation (Titian's famous painting places them proleptically over her head in a sunlit sky).

15 Pentheus (2): king of Thebes, who prohibited the worship of Bacchus, and was torn to pieces by the maenads (the subject of the *Bacchae*).

16 Lycurgus: king of Thrace, outlawed wine and in a fury put his own son to death, and cut off his own legs, taking them for vine branches.

22 your father: Jupiter (see on 1.19.2). In H's version of the war with the Giants Bacchus evidently participates in the form of a lion. **Rhoetus** (2).

29-32: Bacchus made a journey to the underworld to rescue his mother Semele. Cerberus fawns on him both coming and going; it is unclear how many heads there are with a triple tongue – presumably not the hundred of 2.13.

2.20

To end this book H makes an audacious claim, but then undercuts it with an outrageous fantasy – all in the finest literary tradition.

6-7 poor and humble ... your creature: H uses the words of the backbiters, softening any reflection on Maecenas by the exceptional 'dear'. For H's origins see the Brief Life in the Introduction.

9-12: H is changing into a swan, the bird of Apollo, god of poetry, and also of Pindar. Swans were believed to be mute (as one variety is) except on the point of death, when they could produce the piercing beauty of the swansong (which is elusive).

13 Icarus: it is typical of H that he compares himself to Icarus, whose flight from the Labyrinth ended in disaster, rather than to his father, Daedalus, who was successful. The comparison is picked up at the beginning of 4.2.

16 Hyperborean: the home of the north wind; H is travelling to the limits of the world. The next stanza ranges the known Roman world.

21-4: a swan, like a great hero, has no need of a **tomb**.

BOOK 3

Note: Bold figures in brackets refer to the Augustan policies (numbered in Appendix 3) which are relevant.

3.1

After the solemn, programmatic opening stanza the reader is eased into the Roman sequence by an ode which ends on a familiar personal note. The political elements have almost all been touched on in the first two books. Abrupt transitions suit the oracular mode.

1-4: assuming a **priestly** role H banishes profane bystanders and addresses his novel themes to the **young** people of Rome (whose ranks have been thinned by the Civil Wars: 1.2.23-4) (**8**).

6 Jupiter: the overthrow of the **Giants** (with its unspoken analogy of Augustus and his opponents) will be more fully developed later (**3**). In Homer it is usually Zeus' nod which governs; in H a single **eyebrow** is enough.

9-16: career politicians were introduced in 1.1.7-8, and the fateful **urn** in 2.3.26, but here they are brought together to deflate ambition.

17-18   the guilty man: the allusion is to the lesson taught to Damocles by Dionysius of Syracuse, who seated him under **a naked sword** suspended by a single hair. But Damocles was merely naive in his envy of a tyrant's lot; relating the lesson to **guilt** is part of the political message.

25-32: see 2.16.13-16 (**7**). **Arcturus ... Kid**: constellations whose respective setting and rising bring storms.

33-7: see 2.18.20-2.

37-40: see 2.16.21-2.

45-8: a repetition of H's gratitude to Maecenas for his generosity.

3.2

A difficult ode aimed at young men of military age. They must be **tough** and skilled with weapons; they must inspire terror in the enemy; they must not shrink from **death** for their country (**1, 8**). From courage the focus shifts to **virtue**, which does not depend on popular opinion, and can even provide a route to Olympus. Finally there is a leap to the value of **discretion**, and the danger of associating with those who lack it (**9**). Some themes are outlined which are treated more fully later.

1-5: the **Parthian** menace figures again in 3.5 and 3.6 (**1**).

6-12: a scene borrowed from Homer, where heroes are pointed out from the walls of Troy. The **furious lion** is the young Roman.

13   a patriotic death: since the time of Wilfred Owen this is the most reviled line in the Odes, notwithstanding the comfort it must have brought to generations. It should be remembered that to H there was a fundamental distinction between a patriotic death, i.e. suffered while fighting Rome's enemies, and the useless, impious deaths inflicted by Roman on Roman in the Civil War he had experienced.

17-20: the glide from courage to **virtue** is seamless in Latin, since *virtus* includes courage. True virtue does not depend on public approval; H seems to refer to some specific event, now irretrievable.

21-4: the highest virtue can make a man into a demi-god; this anticipates the elevation of Augustus in the next ode.

25-9: **discretion** is a political virtue, as well as a religious one (see 1.18.11), and H had enough to be invited to become Augustus' secretary.

29-32: if a sinner is punished by a falling roof or a capsizing dinghy, it's best to be elsewhere.

3.3

The first of the full-scale Roman Odes. Its opening theme is the elevation of **Augustus** to the rank of an immortal demi-god (**9**), and much of it consists of a speech by **Juno** to the other Olympian gods, reluctantly consenting to the earlier elevation of **Quirinus** (Romulus), and developing into a prophecy of Rome's imperial destiny. As in Virgil's *Aeneid* (which attributes the colonisation of Latium to Aeneas, a Trojan and a refugee from the sack of Troy), Juno is hostile to **Troy**, for reasons which appear, but relents in favour of **Rome**. But she imposes the condition that Troy shall never be rebuilt (**10**). Ostensibly the context is mythological, but inevitably there are implied references to contemporary affairs.

1-8: a noble vision of the Stoic hero, unmoved by any disaster.

9-16: **Augustus** is placed in the middle of four others who became immortal by their outstanding services to mankind. Mention of the last, Romulus (**Quirinus**), introduces Juno's speech, who proceeds to enlarge on Rome's future. (When Octavian accepted the name Augustus, another suggested name had been Romulus.)

18-24: Juno's hostility is traced to (i) the judgment of Paris (the **unchaste judge**), in which the losers were **Juno** herself and **Minerva,** and Paris' reward from Venus was Helen (the **foreign woman/ Spartan harlot**), (ii) the ancient swindle of **Laomedon** (Priam's father), who built Troy's walls with the help of Neptune and Apollo, and then refused them their reward.

25-36: more hard words for Paris and Helen (easily related to Antony and Cleopatra: see on 1.15), but **Troy** has fallen and **Hector** is dead. **our quarrelling**: ostensibly the feuding of the gods described by Homer and Virgil, but calculated to remind readers of the Civil War (**3**). **my grandson**: Romulus, the son of Mars (son of Juno) and Ilia.

37-48: as long as **Priam** and **Paris** (named at last) remain dishonoured (**10**), **Rome** may prosper, dealing with the Parthian threat (**the Medes**), and dominating the known world, with a pointed reference to the Nile (Cleopatra) (**1**).

49-56: Rome must also avoid the Trojan vice of luxury, conquering for altruistic ends.

57-68: a final emphatic prohibition against the rebuilding of **Troy**. There is no record that Augustus ever contemplated this, but the Donations of Alexandria and the propaganda they inspired would be enough to give this solemn warning against the oriental menace a topical undertone.

69-72: this disclaimer, habitual elsewhere, seems inappropriate in the context of the first stanza of 3.1, whose influence will not expire until the end of 3.6. Perhaps the point is that long speeches of gods are beyond even the priestly role.

3.4

In its opening, its imagery, its transitions, its tone and its style this ode is modelled on Pindar. After the invocation of a Greek Muse, H recounts a mock-heroic adventure of his infancy, and declares his adherence to the Latin Muses (**Camenae**) (**4**). He then comes to Augustus, and describes the triumph of **Jupiter** (Augustus) over the **Titans** (Antony), with the aid of the gods (**3**). Finally the wickedness of uncontrolled force is proved by the eternal punishment of the Giants and notorious sexual sinners (**5**).

1-4: a Greek opening, but already the **Latin lyre** is proffered. **Calliope** (4) is called by Hesiod the noblest of the Muses.

5-8   You hear her?: H turns to his hearers (the young people of 3.1.4).

9-20: such early marks of divine favour had a good literary pedigree. We are now firmly in Italy: **Vultur** is a mountain in **Apulia**, H's birthplace; the names in stanza 4 are of obscure places in the locality. The event is not to be taken seriously (what use are leaves against bears and vipers?), but the last two lines are: **laurel** and **myrtle** are sacred to Apollo and Venus respectively, and the **numinous afflatus** is a bold claim to divine inspiration.

21-36: the shift to the Latin Muses represents H's central poetical objective. In stanza 7 he attributes to them his escape at **Philippi** (in 2.7 it was Mercury who saved him) and from the falling **branch** (in 2.17 it was Faunus). The escape at Cape **Palinurus** (named after Aeneas' helmsman, who fell overboard at night and was drowned) is not mentioned elsewhere, perhaps because it was too traumatic for levity. It was no doubt a storm at sea, and it may explain H's antipathy to sea travel.

37-42: after defeating Antony Augustus had to reward and demobilise a huge number of his veterans (**4**). On his way back from Actium Suetonius tells how Virgil and Maecenas read the

Georgics to him while he convalesced from an illness. The gentle advice refers to the policy of clemency (**2**).

42-64: the victor over the **Titans** is not named at first: ostensibly the description is of Jupiter, but it fits Augustus too; the gods fight for him against his enemies (**3**). Among the named Titans is **Rhoetus**, who in 2.19 was said to have been dealt with by Bacchus, but Bacchus does not figure here. A **shouldered** bow is out of use; the **Castalian** spring, sacred to Apollo and the Muses, was on Parnassus; **Patara** and Delos held notable shrines of Apollo.

65-8: **judicious force** is that of Augustus; that of his enemies is **uncontrolled**.

69-80: a series of examples of the penalties of uncontrolled force. The list progresses from brute violence to sexual assault, and ends by emphasising the inexorable nature of the punishment. Eruptions of Etna do not diminish the weight crushing the Giants; the **vulture** eternally gnaws the liver of Tityos. Even **Pirithous** (4, stressed on the 2nd), not a Giant but a Lapith and the great friend of Theseus, is for ever in chains, for his (unsuccessful) attempt to abduct Proserpina. A striking warning of sexual reforms to come (**5**).

3.5

Ostensibly this is a contribution to a debate about the prisoners of Carrhae, delivered by means of a historical analogy harking back to the Punic Wars. In reality the object seems to be more general, namely a plea for a return to ancient patriotic and military standards of the most austere and uncompromising kind (**6**). The closing picture of the honourable **Regulus** calmly returning to a barbarous end is perhaps the most vivid and affecting the Odes have to offer (Kipling featured it in an extra-canonical Stalky episode called *Regulus*: see *A Diversity of Creatures*, Macmillan 1917).

1-4: Jupiter's triumph over the Giants is said to have been announced by a thunderclap. The ode concentrates on the **Parthians** (Augustus' plans to pacify **Britain** never came to fruition) (**1**). H does not say **Augustus** will be a god, but that upon completing his conquests he will be treated as the equivalent.

5-12: 20,000 Romans surrendered at Carrhae (53 BC, thirty years ago). There is no record of any current debate about recovering them. **Marsians** and **Apulians**: sturdy countrymen from H's region (**4**). **Vesta's flame, the sacred shields**: traditional symbols of the perpetuity of Rome. **their dress**: the toga, another symbol of Rome.

13-18: the historical analogy. **Regulus** was the consul who in 256 BC (First Punic War), after initial successes, was defeated and captured by the Carthaginians. He was sent to Rome, under oath to return, to arrange an exchange of prisoners. Instead he argued in the Senate against the exchange, and duly returned to cruel torture and death. **unpitiable**: the Latin word is found only here.

18-40: powerful as it is, this speech probably bears little relation either to what Regulus said or to any current debate. **our standards**: did have a symbolic importance; they were recovered later by diplomacy. **wasteful cost**: earlier sources make no mention of ransom in Regulus' time; his argument was that the Carthaginian prisoners were more valuable than the Romans. **native courage … does not rekindle**: this argument could hardly apply to the Carrhae prisoners, who had by this time **grown old** (line 7).

41   **stripped of civil rights**: technically Regulus, as a prisoner of war, had forfeited his rights as a Roman citizen.

54   **judgment handed down**: Regulus is pictured as an advocate who has been arguing a case in court, or possibly as a patron who has been adjudicating among his dependent *clientes*.

55-6: for the pleasures of **Venafrum** and **Laconian** (Spartan) **Tarentum** see 2.6. The impact of this quiet close owes much to the word *Lacedaemonium*, not only for its inimitable rhythm but also for its connotations. Regulus' heroic submission to fate is not only deeply Roman, it is also Spartan. For another closing evocation of the same chord compare Housman (*Last Poems* xxv):

The King with half the East at heel is marched from lands of morning;
Their fighters drink the rivers up, their shafts benight the air.
And he that stands must die for naught, and home there's no returning.
The Spartans on the sea-wet rock sat down and combed their hair.

3.6

The last Roman Ode starts with the need to repair temples and honour the gods, attributing recent disasters to their neglect (**9**). H then switches to the corruption of family values and launches into a shocking depiction of a young wife prostituting herself with the connivance of her husband (**5, 8**), a scene which he contrasts with the sturdy virtues of the yeoman soldiers who laid the foundation of Rome's greatness (**4, 6**). It is a plea for sexual reform, which H must have known was in the air, and which followed in 18 BC. The final note is of ringing pessimism.

1-4: H is taking the safe course of advocating a policy which Augustus had inaugurated in 28 BC.
5-8: the Romans considered that their superior piety was their secret weapon. The troubles of the next two stanzas are attributed to neglect of the gods.
9-12 Monaeses was the Parthian general, **Pacorus** the son of their king, Orodus; in 40 and 36 BC they defeated, or at least discomforted, armies for which Antony was responsible. **unsacramented** refers to the need for auspices to be taken before battle by a properly appointed magistrate; it appears to be implied that Antony failed in this pious duty.
13-16: the impiety here is **insurrection**, i.e. the Civil War. There is a degree of exaggeration: unrest among the Dacians was not a serious threat to Rome. **Egyptians**: a reference to Actium, treating Antony as an Egyptian, and the Civil War as a mere distraction at the time (**3**).
17-20: it is a small step from Antony to H's central theme, the pollution of family life.
21-32: the Victorian censors red-pencilled this striking passage, thereby destroying the logical and artistic heart of the ode. Under the later *Lex Julia* the wife would have been liable to exile, and the conniving husband would have been an accessory to her crime (**5**).
33-44: H's best depiction of the brave days of old (**4, 6**). The names are from the great period of Roman conquests: **Pyrrhus,** king of Epirus, was defeated in 275 BC, the decisive naval victories of the first Punic War were Mylae (260 BC) and the Aegates Islands (241 BC), **Hannibal** was defeated in 202 BC and **Antiochus the Great,** king of Syria, in 190 BC (**1**).
45-8: no quiet close here. Summarising his analysis of the moral descent, H covers four generations in three lines. It is implicit, perhaps, that stern reforms could halt the downward trend.

3.7

After the thunder against sexual licence, a light-hearted tale (in a lighter metre) of young lovers wintering apart, and suffering temptations of the heart. H is incorrigible.

1-8: a reminder of how winter could interrupt sea travel in the days of sail; **Gyges** (the name hints at wealth), on his way back from the east was driven north and is having to wait for the spring sailing season at **Oricum** on the Adriatic coast of Greece. **Asterie** (**4**) means 'starry'.
10 he beguiles: i.e. the **go-between** beguiles Gyges.
13-16 Proetus (**2**): king of Argos, whose wife made advances to **Bellerophon,** and when they were rejected, accused him of trying to seduce her. **puritan** is the go-between's gloss for honourable; he will not have mentioned that Proetus' attempt failed.
17-20 Hippolyte (**4**): the wife of Acastus, who treated **Peleus** (**2**) in a similar fashion. The go-between is an expert in Greek mythology: his point is that it is dangerous to scorn such women.
21-4 as yet: a sly hint of what could happen reinforces the coming warning about **Enipeus** (**3**, stressed on the 2nd), who is doing his military training, like Sybaris in 1.8.

29-32: in the end the advice is impeccably Augustan.

3.8

A dramatic monologue. It is 1 March (the festival of the Matronalia). H is preparing a celebration at his Sabine villa. A cultivated guest arrives (not named until line 13) and raises an eyebrow: why is a **bachelor** observing a festival for married women?

6-8: that falling branch again. In 2.17 it was Faunus who saved H, and in 3.4 the Camenae, now **Bacchus**. **homicidal**: the Latin word is rare and deliberately over the top. **goat**: an eater of vines and therefore an appropriate victim for Bacchus.
11 Tullus: there are two candidates, father and son, consuls in 66 BC (the year *before* H's birth) and 33 BC respectively. The later date may be when H received his Sabine estate, which would make it appropriate.
12 in smoke matured: smoke was thought to improve wine, and the practice was to store it in some upper compartment through which the flues passed.
17-24: a favourite date to fit these topical allusions is 28 BC, which would pinpoint the dramatic date precisely.
25 Once more a private citizen: in 29 BC Octavian had returned from the campaigns of Actium and Egypt, and relieved Maecenas of his heavy, but temporary, public responsibilities as *Curator Urbis*.

3.9

The form of this ode is unique, a dialogue between two former lovers. The odd stanzas are spoken by the boy (unnamed, so ostensibly H) and the even stanzas by the girl (**Lydia**). The whole romance is gradually laid bare.

1-4: he implies that she was unfaithful; his comparison is oriental.
5-8: she returns the imputation; her comparison is Roman: **Ilia** was the mother of Romulus.
9-12: he admits his love for **Chloe**; he will **not shrink from** death for her.
13-16: her love is twice as strong, and it is returned; she will **embrace** death for him. **Calais** (3). **Thurii** (3), near the site of Sybaris, implies wealth.
17-20: he asks his question obliquely. **jilted**: the truth is out: he was the one who behaved badly.
21-4: she has trumped him at every turn; he is less attractive too. Yet in the last line she capitulates – but not completely: she says what she would like to do, not that she will.

By standing in the shoes of the boy H positions himself to hand the victory to the girl. But at the same time he has avoided his usual first-person pose, thereby ensuring that his role of middle-aged observer is not compromised.

3.10

The serenade of the lover shut out in the cold before the beloved's door is a time-honoured genre. This is H's idiosyncratic version, with several changes of mood.

1-4 Lyce (2): if she were Scythian (which she is not) her husband would be a jealous and cruel brute; even so she could not fail to pity poor H. **local**: in Scythia the north wind would be her neighbour.
6 the trees: a wealthy Roman townhouse, with colonnaded buildings surrounding a substantial garden (peristyle).
10 the bucket: the precise details of this proverb are obscure; it seems to approximate to the baby and the bathwater.

11-12   **Tuscan**: (Etruscan) a byword for luxurious living. **Penelope**: the wife of Ulysses, who fended off suitors for twenty years before he returned from the Trojan War.

15   **panting for his paramour**: an opportunistic argument for infidelity in the injured wife.

3.11

Lyde is ripe for marriage, but she is at a difficult age, flighty and out of hand. H takes seriously the task of writing something to induce a maturer attitude to marriage. After a lengthy invocation of both **Mercury** and the lyre, he hits on the myth of the wicked daughters of Danaus, forty-nine of whom killed their bridegrooms, and tells it through the mouth of the fiftieth, the heroic Hypermestra, who dared to disobey her treacherous father.

1-12: in 1.10 we learnt that **Mercury** invented the lyre; here he is invoked jointly with his invention. The minstrel **Amphion** was taught by Mercury, and when the walls of Thebes were being built his playing caused the stones to move into place on their own. **Lyde** (2) is behaving like the Lalage of 2.5.

13-20: these are exploits of the lyre in the hands of Orpheus, when he descended to the underworld in quest of Eurydice. The authenticity of the fifth stanza has been doubted.

21-9: three of the usual cast of sinners enduring perpetual punishment. The **Danaids** (3) were encountered in 2.14; their punishment was to fill a leaking vessel with water carried in sieves. H decides that their story will provide a suitably solemn warning for Lyde.

30-6: Danaus betrothed his daughters to the fifty sons of his hated brother, Aegyptus, but ordered them to kill their bridegrooms on their wedding night.

47   **exile**: the punishment of *relegatio* to a specified distance from Rome, without loss of civil rights, was attached to many matrimonial offences by the coming family legislation.

52   **my sorry tale**: though she does not yet know it, her tale was to end (possibly by divine intervention) in her happy union with Lynceus, whom she had saved. This would presumably be known to Lyde, or the message would be very two-edged, sanctifying her recalcitrance without dignifying marriage.

3.12

A study of a young girl distracted from her proper Roman pursuits by dreams of romance. Her name, **Neobule** (4), means 'new counsel', and hints that she is modern in her outlook; perhaps she is not unlike the Lyde of 3.11, seen from another angle.

Metre. Ionic (*a minore*) unique in Latin poetry; rapid but unvarying. The division into lines is arbitrary: here Quinn's layout is followed, in the interests of presenting four-line stanzas (see Appendix 2, Meineke's Law).

1-4: **daydreaming of love** or indulging in wine are liable to bring down stern rebuke upon the closely supervised girl. The breathless language reflects her imaginings.

5-8: But Neobule is luckier. She has the opportunity to admire the young men at military training on the Campus Martius. Her spinning and **weaving**, the traditional pursuits of the virtuous Roman matron, are being neglected as well as **Minerva's activities** – her books.

9-16: **Hebrus** (unlike Sybaris in 1.8) is to the fore in all the manly activities approved of by Augustus, swimming, riding, boxing, running and hunting both deer and boar. With a fair wind they will make a fine Augustan couple.

3.13

A hymn to the local **spring** which watered H's Sabine villa (whose site has long been identified, with some degree of plausibility, near the village of Licenza). Springs were not only valued sources of water (and minor deities), but were traditionally associated with the Muses and inspiration. H not only celebrates the qualities of the spring, but in pursuit of his object of Romanising Greek models he enrols it among the famous springs of Greek literature (Castalia, Hippocrene, Aganippe, Arethusa etc.). A memorably vivid and justly famous ode.

1-4   tomorrow's festival: annually on 13 October the festival of *Fontinalia* was celebrated by offering flowers and wine to springs: honour in return for water. H, however, is promising more, and presumably expecting more in return. He does not say what.

5-8: this uncompromising picture has provoked some, who deplore its heartlessness, while others commend its sensitivity. But to H animal sacrifice was a matter of routine. He describes the **kid** in order to guarantee its vigour and worth as a sacrifice.

13-16: it is a self-confident boast to claim that this ode will elevate the spring to the level of the famous Greek predecessors. Yet so it has proved: the modern site includes a landscaped and publicised Bandusian spring, and even forty years ago, before the modern development, the custodian would recite this ode on request. But the fame cuts both ways. The spring is **chattering,** it has a voice of its own, and its voice is bound to speak of H, as in effect it has. The **renown** is mutually conferred. Here, perhaps, is the extra benefit which prompts H's exceptional offering.

3.14

An ode to welcome Augustus back from campaigning in Spain (**1**). The first half is public, addressed to the populace assembled to witness the ceremonial; the second half turns to the preparations for H's private party. While it is much easier to relate to the second half, the first, with its focus on the Julian family, is an equally important component of this eulogy of the Augustan achievement.

1-4: the campaign was against the Cantabri in 26-5 BC; the army returned in 25 BC, but Augustus was too ill to make the journey until 24 BC. **Hercules** was also active in Spain, dealing with the monster Geryon, and he returned via the site of Rome; he is relevant also because his labours raised him to the status of demigod (see 3.4.9-16).

5-8   his wife: Livia, his second wife, who had divorced to marry Octavian. **his … sister**: Octavia, expediently married to, but slighted and divorced by, Antony. The family of a general returning in triumph would formally **process** to meet him.

9-10   sons … restored to safety: these included Marcellus, son of Octavia's first marriage, whose first campaign it had been. Great hopes were invested in him as Augustus' nephew and intended successor, but he died in 23 BC, just after the publication of these Odes.

17-29: H's wine will recall earlier civil disturbances, the Social (**Marsian**) War of 91-89 BC, and the Servile War of 73-1 BC, when the slaves revolted under **Spartacus**. **Neaera** (**3**).

27-8   Plancus' day: Plancus was consul in 42 BC, the year of Philippi (see 1.7), when H, in his **headstrong youth** fought on the wrong side (see 2.7). This final reference brings together the Augustan achievement of quieting civil unrest (**3**), the subsequent policy of reconciliation (**2**), and H's personal history. The coded allusions unify the ode.

3.15

H condemns Chloris, an aging mother who cannot resist aping the youthful indiscretions of her daughter, **Pholoe** (**3**).

10   Bassarid: a crazed devotee of Bacchus (Bassareus). H feels free to blame in a woman (who, since she has a teenage daughter, must be of an age with him) excess of the kind that he is happy to depict in himself (see 2.7.27-8, 3.19.17-20): a neat illustration of the double standards of the day.

11   Nothus: Greek for a bastard.

13-14   the local wool: wool-making was the proper pursuit for the Roman matron (compare Neobule in 3.12).

3.16

As in Book 1, the ode which starts the second half of the Book is addressed to **Maecenas**. This, however, is more complex than the spontaneity of 1.20. Ostensibly it is a homily on wealth and the evils of greed (**7**), not the most anodyne subject on which to admonish the prodigiously rich Maecenas. There is praise once more for the Sabine endowment, but with stress on its limited character; there is pointed rejection of opulence. But there is also sufficient tact not to alienate his benefactor. It is a calculated assertion of independence, which paves the way for 3.29.

1-8: **Acrisius**, king of Argos, warned by a prophecy that her son would kill him, **immured** his daughter Danae (**3**) (not to be confused with the Danaids) in a brazen tower. In vain, for **Jupiter** visited her in a shower of gold, and their son Perseus did accidentally kill his grandfather. H rationalises the myth by having Jupiter change into **money**, which will easily find a way past any **sentinel**.

9-16: three more examples of the power of money. The Theban **soothsayer**, Amphiaraus, was betrayed by his wife who was bribed by a necklace, which later brought ruin to her and their son. **Philip II** of Macedon, father of Alexander the Great, notoriously used **bribery** as a weapon. **pirates** may refer to Menas, the venal supporter of Sextus Pompeius after Philippi.

17-24: H switches to the present and himself. **I was right**: he seems to refer to a specific occasion when he refused a conspicuous position: perhaps this was when Augustus invited him to help deal with his correspondence, which could have brought him **opulence**; H declined on health grounds. **noble knight**: this tactful reference softens the hard words about wealth: H is reminding Maecenas of his own decision to remain a knight, rather than accept Senatorial rank.

25-8   my humble farm: H is treading a delicate line between independence and an appearance of ingratitude. **needy**: never satisfied (like the monopolist in 1.1.9).

31   proconsul: an ex-consul could become the governor of a province, an opportunity for great wealth.

38: this line corrects any image of poverty which constant praise of the simple life may have suggested. What H condemns is not a comfortable life, but greed and ostentation. What he commends is being satisfied with what is **enough** (see e.g. 3.1.25), and that is precisely the line he is drawing here. He is grateful, but his own man; he expresses independence without ingratitude. Maecenas was intelligent enough, and their friendship was strong enough, for the patron to understand.

3.17

Addressed to (L) **Aelius Lamia** (probably the Lamia of 1.26), a member of the distinguished Aelii family, and clearly a close friend of H. Half the ode consists of a parenthesis which is a preposterous parody of a fad for genealogies. **Lamus** was the founder of **Formiae** (**3**), which was reputed to be the home of the giant Laestrygonians, who devoured the companions of Ulysses (*Odyssey* 10); the derivation is doubly absurd since it is based not on the family name, but the later *cognomen*.

8   Liris: it appears that Lamia had a villa, known to H, at the wine-rich mouth of the Liris (see on 1.31.8).

15   your Genius: Lamia's personal attendant spirit, presumably to be feasted on his birthday. The coming storm offers the occasion for a general day off.

3.18

H has already told us that **Faunus** (Pan) often visits his farm (1.17); here he addresses a prayer to him for continued favour. Simple in language and versification, it sensitively evokes a rustic festival. Those who consider H's attitude to the gods as empty lip-service must wonder why an ode like this was written.

1 fleeing nymphs: amorousness is an attribute inherited from Pan; it explains the reference to love in the next stanza.
5 while: as always there is a bargain: the observances are the price of the favours.
9 December: the exact date is specified, the 5th (Nones).
13: the presence of the god protects lambs against wolves.
15-16: the countryman, dancing in triple time, appears to take revenge on the earth which costs him so much labour. A detail worthy of Bruegel, as Williams remarks.

3.19

A dramatic monologue whose implied setting defies precise analysis. For the first eight lines H complains to a boring companion that he does not understand what is going to happen. Then at line 9 a party is in full swing, and H is calling for toasts; it is midnight, and **Murena** (see 2.10) has just become an augur. As a way of uniting the two parts (there have been many suggestions) imagine that the bore has called on H, and invited him out to a party. As they make their way, instead of explaining what sort of party and where, he holds forth interminably on his genealogical and antiquarian interests. H explodes with lines 1-8. They then arrive at Murena's where his celebration is in progress, and H is put in charge of the drinking.

1-4: **Inachus**: the first king of Argos. **Codrus**: the last king of Athens, who gave his life for the city. **Aeacus' progeny**: included Peleus (father of Achilles) and Telamon (father of Teucer and Ajax), all of whom (except Peleus) fought at Ilium (Troy). There is a hint of the same fad as in 3.17.
10-17 the blend: a twelve-ladle measure is to contain three or nine ladles of wine (the balance being water): three for the Graces, nine for the Muses (naturally H's is the stronger).
18 welcome madness: the stronger mix has its effect on H.
22 roses: if it is winter (as suggested by the **frozen bones** of line 8), these must be a great extravagance, but Murena is paying.
23-8 Rhode (2, meaning rose): perhaps the partner of **Lycus** (meaning wolf); **Telephus** will be her age.

3.20

A mock-heroic opening turns into pantomime burlesque, but then into a glimpse of youthful beauty. A skilfully constructed cameo.

1-4: apparently a serious warning couched in a Homeric lion-simile. **Pyrrhus**: at best only a Pyrrhic victory can be expected. **Nearchus** (3) means 'the young ruler'.
5-10: but now we learn that the lioness is a formidable woman, intent on protecting her boy from Pyrrhus' clutches, a fearsome proposition of a different order. When she starts to sharpen her teeth (not her claws) the comedy breaks cover.
11-16: farce gives way to contemplation of the beautiful unshorn boy, stripped for the gymnasium. **Nireus** (2) is mentioned in Homer only for his beauty. **Ganymede**: another beautiful boy, who was carried off from Ida by an eagle (instructed by Jupiter: see 4.4.3-4), and became the cupbearer of the gods.

261

3.21

This is a good-humoured parody of the hymn form, addressed not to a god, but to a wine jar. H is entertaining and Messalla Corvinus, a distinguished man and patron of the poet Tibullus, is among the guests. The fiction of the jar's divinity is maintained throughout, the opening invocation developing into a recital of the god's benefits, and finally a celebratory concourse of deities.

1-6 **my birth-year**: 65 BC when Manlius Torquatus was consul. In place of the usual recital of the god's names, a list of wine's effects is given. Only at the end of the first stanza is it revealed that no god is being invoked.

7-8 **descend**: the same petition is addressed to Calliope at the start of 3.4 (for the lofty storage of wine see on 3.8.12). **Corvinus** seems to have been put in charge of the drinking.

11 **Elder Cato**: the devotion of Cato the Censor (d. 149 BC) to the stern ancient morality was legendary.

14-16: despite his disapproval of indiscretion (see e.g. 3.2) H appears to acknowledge therapeutic value in unburdening oneself under the influence of alcohol.

3.22

A dedicatory hymn to Diana, reminiscent of Catullus 34 and of similar Greek epigrams. H dedicates a tree near his villa and also promises the annual sacrifice of a young boar. No reason is given.

1-4: the **triple godhead** of Diana denotes her functions on earth and also above it (as Luna, the moon) and below it (as Hecate). Two of her functions are mentioned, both earthly: as custodian of the countryside and as saviour of women in childbirth: this last dominates the first stanza.

5-8: a double offering, dedication and annual sacrifice. As in 3.13 the vigour of the victim is observed and guaranteed.

Two questions arise. First, why the double offering? No bargain is mentioned, but it is not far to seek. The first stanza suggests that there has been a difficult birth to a woman on H's estate: that Diana was invoked (three times, perhaps), and that a vow was made. The offering could be the fulfilment of such a vow, in return for a successful delivery. So, secondly, what has the birth to do with H? Again the answer is not far to seek: Quinn notes (at p. 282) the possibility that H 'could claim more than token status as father'.

3.23

Overwhelmingly the human cast of the Odes is metropolitan in character: grandees, poets, friends, courtesans, girlfriends and a range of supporting Roman extras. **Phidyle** (3) is a unique exception. She is a responsible countrywoman, doing the woman's work on a farm. She is neither patronised nor wooed, but respected. This is H in his country hat. His Sabine 'farm' was in fact (as he discloses elsewhere) an estate comprising a home farm, which needed a bailiff and seven slaves to run it, plus five tenanted holdings. Phidyle could be the wife of the bailiff or a tenant farmer.

1-8: it is the woman's part to tend the **domestic deities**. H prescribes the ideal offerings: if every **new moon** is meant, the programme seems surprisingly extravagant, but perhaps it is a single annual occasion.

9-16: **Algidus**: a mountain in the **Alban** hills south of Rome, where the priests raised cattle for sacrifice on official occasions. H contrasts the requirements of Phidyle's household gods, which are **little** not only in scope, but in the physical size of their images.

17-20: this should not be seen as a pre-Christian shift of emphasis to the individual's state of mind. Roman ritual was understood as a form of bargain, but a sacrifice could be limited by what was available. The **pinch of salt and meal** was routinely scattered on sacrifices and offered to the household gods at mealtimes.

3.24

This is a diatribe combining a number of Augustan themes, but lacking the humanity (there is no addressee, nor is H personally present), inspiration and imaginative energy of the Roman Odes, employing a less flexible metre, and unrelieved by humour or even irony. It appears to be a partisan contribution to a debate over moral reform (**5**), but some of the arguments lack conviction.

1-8 **Your**: generalised (the reader). Riches won't save you from your fate. The **nails** are wielded by Necessity (as in 1.35.17).
9-16: the northern nomads have a better economic system (one wonders how many of H's readers found this argument convincing). The **share** is the share of work.
17-24: their wives are kinder and chaste, because they are not protected by a dowry.
25-32: the benevolent ruler (Augustus) must legislate against vice, but expect no thanks in this world.
33-44: but a change in behaviour is needed as well; sea trade (that hobbyhorse from 1.3) is driven by greed.
45-50: if we sincerely regret the past (i.e. the Civil Wars) we must despise wealth and get rid of it by public donation **on the Capitol** or by throwing it away (**7**).
51-64: we must also provide a sterner education for the younger generation, which is soft and vicious (**8**), and no wonder when their grasping fathers set such a bad example. Greed is never satisfied.

3.25

Like 2.19 this is a hymn to **Bacchus**, but there H was less than wholly serious. This is different: it is a dithyramb. From the first line H is possessed by the god, conscious of the privilege of inspiration but also of the attendant dangers. On a more mundane level he claims novelty for his themes, that is the treating of topical politics in lyric verse, and he is aware of the risk of putting a foot wrong.

4-6: just as Julius Caesar was deified after his death, and was believed to have been commemorated by a star (see on 1.12.48), H anticipates that Augustus will be deified and admitted to the stars after his death; a delicate topic, indirectly alluded to.
11 **Rhodope** (3): a mountain range in western Thrace: traditional scenery for Bacchic revels.

3.26

Back to H's lighter vein. The fifth ode from the beginning of this collection (1.5) was in the nature of a farewell to love, so (ostensibly) is this, the fifth from the end. The opening is apparently serious, but the solemnity goes off the rails, and it is not until the last word that the real point is revealed.

1-6: the military metaphor is a commonplace of ancient love poetry, as is the setting of the lover besieging the beloved's door (3.10 was a non-military example).
8 **bows**: torches fine, crowbars fine, but what use are bows and arrows against doors and doorkeepers? As in 3.20, H has deliberately gone over the top.
9-10: H appeals to Venus. **Cyprus** was her birthplace, and she had a shrine at **Memphis** in Egypt.

The absence of **Thracian** winter in Egypt hardly seems to deserve mention, but the point is that H is relying on Venus not to be cold in her response.

11-12   disdain: this gives the game away: **Chloe** has said no. If Venus flicks her she will presumably relent.

3.27

This extraordinary ode falls into two parts. The first 6 stanzas are a farewell to a girlfriend, **Galatea** (4), ending with forebodings about the sea journey she is to undertake. Then in 13 stanzas the story of **Europa**'s abduction by Jupiter is told, mostly through a breathless, almost hysterical, soliloquy by Europa herself. Finally she is curtly addressed by **Venus**. Apart from stanzas 4 to 6 and 19, the tone is high camp parody. The relevance of the second part to the first is problematic (see further below).

1-12: the number of adverse omens, and the promise to **rouse the raven** (i.e. cook the auspices) show that this episode of augury is not to be taken seriously. The reference to **dear friends** defines H's relationship to Galatea (4).

13-16: she is leaving by sea, and from what follows we may infer she is going with a man who has swept her off her feet, so it is for good. H wishes her well. His Europa narrative must carry a message for her. Its tone implies an easy intellectual intimacy between them.

17-25   Orion plunges: Orion sets in November, a bad time for storms. **well known to me**: H may be thinking of his experience off Cape Palinurus (see 3.4.28). **Thus**: i.e. in a storm like this. **Europa** was daughter of a king of Phoenicia: she was abducted to Crete by Jupiter in the form of a white **bull**.

37   Whence, whither: questions tumble out. The language and thought processes in this speech are too silly to be anything but parody.

42   the ivory gate: dreams (in Homer and Virgil) issue from two gates, one of horn, one of ivory: the former are true, the latter false.

46-8   break his … horns: this overheated hyperbole is in its turn meanly parodied by Venus in line 72.

67   with bow unstrung: Cuipid's bow is no longer needed; its work has been done by attracting Europa to the bull.

73-6: Europa became by Jupiter the mother of Minos and Rhadamanthus, both ultimately judges in the underworld, and Sarpedon; she married Asterius, the king of Crete, who accepted them as his. The **continent** to which Jupiter had carried her bears her name. H seems to be saying to Galatea, in a code which he expects her to understand, that there is every hope that her new departure will end well, and perhaps very well.

3.28

H's final, final farewell to love and love poetry (for this collection anyway). In his first (1.5) he ended with thanks to **Neptune**, and here he celebrates Neptune's festival (23 July). A dramatic monologue with a brisk opening, which glides into a mood of nostalgic melancholy.

1-2   How else: it seems that H intends to start drinking, but **Lyde** (2) has suggested it's a bit early. Her status is undefined: she can be ordered about, but there is a personal bond too.

2-8: H responds a little testily with a volley of military metaphors. Never mind wisdom, it's a day for the very best wine. **Bibulus** was consul in 59 BC, a procrastinating colleague of Julius Caesar; his name is equally appropriate in Latin and English.

9-10   we'll sing: H goes first with Neptune (obviously) and the Nereids (whose **green hair** is memorably portrayed by J.W.M. Turner in *Ulysses Deriding Polyphemus*: Tate Britain). Whether he would have sung, recited or read is a matter of ancient debate.

11-12: she will sing and accompany herself. **Leto** (Latona) was the mother of Diana/Cynthia (**goddess of the moon**) by Jupiter. While pregnant she was hounded by the jealous Juno, and the earth refused to harbour her; it was Neptune who took pity on her and provided the island of Delos for the birth.

13-16: we come to Venus, who was born from the foam of the sea. She does not need to be named: her temple at **Paphos** (Cyprus) and her chariot drawn by **swans** (see also 4.1.10) identify her. For all the reticence of the last line, the end of this day unquestionably belongs to her.

3.29

The last ode of the first collection, except for the epilogue. A monument to the friendship of H and **Maecenas**, it nevertheless ends with a sturdy declaration of independence. In the centre is the most developed statement of H's philosophy of living for the present moment.

1-16: H starts by exaggerating **Maecenas' Etruscan** pretensions, and tempting him with lavish hospitality. He pictures him in his **pile that reaches to the clouds** (i.e. his tower on the Esquiline, from which Nero later watched Rome burning), gazing at distant landmarks east of Rome, Tibur, Aefula near **Praeneste** (3), and Tusculum (founded by Telegonus, a son of Ulysses by **Circe** (2) who unwittingly killed his father), and urges him to take a break from **Rome**. The food, it seems, will be simple after all.

17-24: a scatter of astronomical learning describes the heat of Rome in the first half of July; the country is hot too, but there is shade to be found. **Cepheus** (2).

25-8 constitutional affairs: these imply the time immediately after Actium, when Maecenas was in charge of Rome as *Curator Urbis* during Augustus' absence (see 3.8); the areas mentioned as giving concern are hyperbolically distant.

29-48: it is no use trying to see into the future: the present is what matters. The rest goes by like the Tiber (the **Tuscan**, i.e. Etruscan, river, flowing into the Tyrrhenian sea), tranquil and turbulent by turns. Live each day for itself; what you experience or achieve cannot be undone.

49-56 Fortune: imagined as a bird (compare 1.34.14). **honest penury**: H declares himself ready, if need be, to lose his privileges and embrace poverty: she will be a bride with no dowry, like those of the Getae, praised in 3.24.

57-64: a storm at sea holds no material terrors for H, since he has no cargo to lose. He will paddle his own canoe to safety, guided by the heavenly Twins (see on 1.3.2).

3.30

Finally the epilogue, which has acquired iconic status as the best known of the Odes. It expresses H's confidence (well founded, as history has shown) that the Odes will live, his affection for his rural origin, his summary of his lyric achievement, and his obligation to his Muse. Augustan attitudes are inherent, but of Maecenas there is nothing. It is a proud self-assessment.

Metre. The last is the same as the first. As a unique exception rhyme is not used here, apart from the final couplet.

2 the Pyramids: the reference to the tombs of Egyptian royalty must hint at the overthrow of Cleopatra.

7 the undertaker: H mentions the homely goddess of funerals: the claim is ambitious, but the tone deflates it.

8-9: another ambitious claim, which, however, has proved to be a serious underestimate. The **Capitol** may veil another dig at Cleopatra and her egregious boast (see on 1.37.7).

10-12: instead of claiming far-flung readership (as in 2.20), H speaks of his Apulian roots. **Daunus** was the reputed founder, and **Aufidus** the local river (which will hardly believe what it hears).

13-16: H keeps his largest claim to last: it is that he has achieved the status which he coveted at the end of 1.1. The reference to **Italy** rather than Rome or the Latin language is significantly

Augustan (**4**). **measures** embrace themes and style as well as metres. For **Melpomene** (4) see note on 1.1.32. H leaves it ambiguous whether the **vindicated praise** is owed to him or the Muse. The **crown** is **of Delphic bays** because it comes from Apollo, the god of poetry (and champion of Augustus at Actium), whose most famous shrine was at Delphi.

It is worth quoting the laconic paraphrase which Kipling wrote in the margin of his Horace:

> What I have done I have done.
> It is first–class work and I know it.
> And nothing under the sun
> Shall 'minish or overthrow it.
> Certified. BC 21:
> Q.H. Flaccus.
> Poet.

SECULAR HYMN

The question whether the Odes were sung, read or recited has never been settled, but there is no doubt about this hymn. It was written for public oral (sung) performance, no doubt before large audiences, by two choirs of young people, twenty-seven boys and twenty-seven girls. The metre is familiar from the Odes (Sapphic, the second most frequent), but in such a context it is not surprising to find that the subtleties of tone and nuance typical of the Odes are lacking. Difficulties of audibility alone would be enough to explain this, but besides, the official, ritual nature of the occasion would dictate it.

1   **Diana … Phoebus**: these two deities, appropriate to the girls and boys respectively, dominate the beginning, middle and end of the hymn.
5   **Sibyl's verses**: the Sibylline books, which contained the original writings of the ancient prophetesses known as Sibyls, were destroyed when the Capitol was burnt in 82 BC, but other texts of theirs were then collected, and kept in the care of a college of fifteen men, who were given the responsibility of organising the Festival (see line 70).
9-12   **Sun**: another manifestation of Phoebus is separately invoked.
13-16   **Ilithyia** (4): a Greek goddess of childbirth, here apparently treated (like **Lucina**) as another manifestation of Diana, although she was individually honoured in the Festival.
18   **domestic legislation**: Augustus' reforms of the marriage laws, foreshadowed in the Roman Odes (**5**), had become law in 18 BC. The name **Childbearer** is otherwise unknown.
21-4: on the authority of the Sibylline verses the length of time between Festivals was determined at 110 years. There were separate sacrifices by day and by night on each of the three days.
25-32: other deities expressly honoured included the **Parcae**/Fates (text and meaning are uncertain here), **Earth/Ceres** (2), and Jupiter.
33-6: a return to Phoebus and Diana; possibly this stanza would have been split between the two choirs.
37-52: a tribute to the *Aeneid* of the recently deceased Virgil, which traces the pilgrimage **of Aeneas** (3, with stress on the 2nd), son of **Anchises** and Venus, from the fall of Troy to the origins of Rome. Augustus is the **heir** of line 50, since, as a member of the Julian family, he traced his ancestry to Aeneas' son, Iulus. Lines 51-2 are a paraphrase of a famous line of the *Aeneid*, *parcere subiectis et debellare superbos* (2), thereby casting Augustus, without the need to name him, as the epic exemplar of Roman authority.
53-60   **The Mede**: the Parthians had in 20 BC returned the standards lost at Carrhae (see 3.5). For **lictors** see on 2.16.10. **audience**: the Latin is appropriate to consulting an oracle. **well-stocked horn**: the cornucopia. The picture is of dominance abroad and prosperity at home.
61-72: back to Apollo, at whose Palatine temple the hymn was sung, and Diana.

73-6: to finish, a personal note for the young singers (compare the end of 4.6). **taught**: i.e. by H.

BOOK 4

4.1

H, now aged over fifty, returns to the role of world-weary poet of love. He gracefully sidesteps in favour of a young man who looks destined for stardom (he became consul two years later). But all is not quite what it was: the use of a Latin name (**Ligurinus**) is a departure, and the last three stanzas speak in a tone not heard before.

1-8   at war: resumes the military metaphor of 3.26. **Cinara** has no place in Books 1-3, but she recurs in 4.13, again affectionately drawn, **cruel mother of desires**: a deliberate self-quotation from 1.19, where H recoiled from too passionate an encounter.
9-28   Paulus (Fabius) Maximus: married Augustus' cousin, Marcia, but it is not known when. If the marriage was foreseen at the time of writing, it would explain his suitability for the attentions of Venus. **Berecynthian horn**: a Phrygian pipe used in orgiastic rites, and at wild parties. **Salii** (3): the Salian priests (see on 1.37.4).
29-40: there is nothing in Books 1-3 to compare with this. The mask of urbane detachment is put aside. H has found the self-assurance to speak from his heart. The object beyond his reach is a young boy, addressed again in 4.10. **stall**: the English metre misses a beat here in deference to the sense: curiously H does the opposite, with an extra syllable eliding hypermetrically. **the field of Mars**: the Campus Martius (see on 1.8.3). **gushing**: the Tiber has the fluency which has deserted H, and carries the boy away.

4.2

H addresses **Iullus Antonius**, a son of Mark Antony brought up by Augustus' sister, Octavia, married to her daughter, Marcella, praetor in 13 BC and consul in 10 BC. Despite his new prestige H, as in the past, declines the public role of composing a Pindaric ode to greet a triumph of Augustus, but takes the opportunity to praise **Pindar** (in Pindaric manner), Iullus and Augustus.

1-4   Icarus: the son of Daedalus, whose flight from the Labyrinth ended in his fatal plunge into the sea, which was named Icarian after him (see on 2.20.13). **Iullus** (2: the I is consonantal).
5-12   Pindar: the great Theban lyric poet (one of the Greek Nine): H produces a creditable pastiche of the style he describes. The Romans had not analysed the complex metres Pindar used, hence **by no law controlled**.
13-24: H lists the principal subjects of Pindar's verse: dithyrambs (hymns to Dionysus), paeans and hymns to other gods and heroes, odes in celebration of victories at public games, and funerary dirges and eulogies.
25-32: in comparison with Pindar, the soaring swan, H is no more than a hardworking bee (a simile taken from Pindar). **Matine** denotes an area in H's native Apulia.
33-6   you, a poet of more lofty tone: Iullus is known to have written an epic poem on Diomedes. **leading**: i.e. in triumph; the **Sugambri** were a German tribe who defeated M. Lollius in 16 BC. Augustus thereupon undertook an expedition against them and was away until 13 BC. The dramatic date of the ode is when his return is imminent.
37-52: H imagines the victory ode, and his part as a mere spectator of the triumphal procession. In fact it never took place: Augustus refused the triumph. The text of lines 49/50 is uncertain.
53-60: the ode dies away in a close description of H's intended sacrifice (compare 3.13). Caesar's safe return is important enough for him to have vowed a sacrifice, and to have singled out and fattened up a particular animal for the purpose.

4.3

In this ode, addressed to the same Muse as 3.30, H draws together the themes of the first and last odes of Books 1-3, but he does it from the maturer perspective of the public recognition accorded through the Secular Hymn. The bold ambition stated at the end of 1.1 has been achieved; the backbiters have been silenced, and he has become a celebrity, pointed out in the street as The Roman Lyric Poet. Gone are the equivocation and assertiveness of 3.30. He lays his success wholeheartedly at the feet of his Muse. It sets the seal on his proudest literary achievement.

1-9: a catalogue of distinctions which the Muse does not bestow, recalling the longer catalogue of pursuits in 1.1. **Melpomene** (4).
10-12   Tibur has provided the cool glade that figured in 1.1.31, and the fame that H craved at 1.1.35-6. It is perhaps no coincidence that flowing water, the traditional source of inspiration, is found in the middle of 1.1 as well as here. **Aeolian**: the Greek dialect of Alcaeus and Sappho.
13-16: it is Rome's **youth**, the young singers of the Secular Hymn, who have demonstrated H's distinction, and put an end to the carping which greeted Books 1-3.
17-24: finally a graceful hymn of gratitude to Melpomene, recalling 3.30. It is a swansong, with a touch of humour from the fishes and a candid confession of delight in star status (it was not, after all, an era of mass communication). Any grudging undertone in 3.30 is superseded and handsomely repaired.

4.4

Here H wears the mantle of poet laureate in celebrating the victory over the **Vindelici** and **Raeti** (situated roughly in the modem Tyrol) in 15 BC of **Nero Claudius Drusus**, son of Tiberius Claudius Nero and Livia (but born in 38 BC, just after she had divorced, and married Augustus), and now the stepson and chosen heir of Augustus. In fact Drusus shared command with his elder brother, another Tiberius Claudius Nero (later the emperor Tiberius), who has to wait until 4.14 for a share of the credit. In the event Augustus outlived Drusus, and was succeeded by the currently unfavoured Tiberius. Despite the warning in 4.2 this ode is consciously Pindaric in style, with its elaborate opening simile, containing an extraordinary parenthesis. It is also profoundly Augustan, not only in its express compliment to the emperor, but also in its revival of themes from the Roman Odes (**1**, **4**, **6**, **8**, **9**, **10**).

1-28: an heroic double simile, comparing **Drusus** first to an eagle, then to a lion cub, summarising the campaign, and ending in eulogy of the **Nero** family and **Augustus. guardian of the thunderbolt**: the eagle. **Ganymede's abduction**: see on 3.20.16. The young eagle's predatory development is described in stages which can be related to the spectacular military progress of the young Drusus. **Amazonian axes**: this inconsequential parenthesis is explicable as Pindaric pastiche, possibly parodic.
29-36: Pindar insisted on the value of good breeding, and H adds the Augustan requirement of proper education (compare the end of 3.24). **well-born families are tainted**: H could not foresee that in 2 BC (six years after his death) Augustus would exile his own daughter, Julia, for immorality, and execute among others the addressee of 4.2 for complicity.
37-72: H traces the distinction of the **Neros** back to C. Claudius Nero, one of the consuls who defeated **Hasdrubal** at the **River Metaurus** in 207 BC, thus preventing him from relieving his beleaguered brother, Hannibal. **the African terror**: the Carthaginian general, **Hannibal**, who had invaded Italy across the Alps in 218, but after early victories found himself cut off. **false Hannibal**: a stock Roman insult for Carthaginians: Livy speaks of Hannibal's 'more than Punic treachery'. **blazing Troy**: this stanza describes the theme of the *Aeneid*, in which Aeneas, after escaping from burning Troy, sails to Latium where Rome will be founded. The **holm-oak** is said to be invigorated by brutal pruning. **Hydra**: one of the labours of Hercules was to kill this many-headed monster, which immediately grew two new heads whenever one

was cut off. Jason at **Colchis** and Cadmus at **Thebes** (1) had to contend with dragons whose teeth, when sown, sprang up as armed warriors. **lost, all lost**: the failure of Hasdrubal to make the junction did indeed make Hannibal's position in Italy untenable; in 203 BC he was recalled, and the Second Punic War was determined in Africa.

73-6 Claudians: here a simile for the Neros. It is an irony of history that, despite this glowing prophecy (which some editors include in Hannibal's speech), the name of Nero is now exclusively linked to the infamous emperor (37-68 AD).

4.5

Like 3.14, this ode is concerned with the return of Augustus from abroad. But here the dramatic date is some ten years later (like 4.2). Here H does not address the people, but makes a direct personal appeal to Augustus. The result has warmth and a touch of humour at the end, but lacks the easy spontaneity, irony and affection of his approaches to Maecenas. The benefits of Augustus' rule are recited, and the close is a striking picture of the working farmer (**7**), perhaps one of Augustus' military veterans, contentedly pouring libations to him (**9**).

16 yearns: much more than mere hope (see on 1.14.18).

17-24: cattle are safe from lawlessness, agriculture is settled (**4**). **Ceres** (**2**). The sea has been cleared of pirates (**3**). **respected laws**: the moral legislation anticipated in Book 3 was passed in 18 BC (**5**). **his father's smile**: the baby's resemblance to his father proclaims the chastity of his mother.

25-8: the standards held by the **Parthians** were recovered in 20 BC. The other references are to Augustus' recent campaigns (**1**).

29-36 virgin trees: the vine was 'married' to a tree on which it was trained. Worship of Augustus was frowned upon, but in 24 BC the Senate had decreed that **libations** could be poured to him. H is careful to equate him only to the demigods **Castor** and **Hercules**, as in 3.3.9. The shy joke at the end has a charm of its own.

4.6

Here the first six stanzas are a hymn to **Phoebus** (Apollo), leading up to his part in assisting the founding of Rome by **Aeneas**. His role then changes to that of the god of lyric poetry, and finally H turns to address a chorus of young people, as if coaching them for a performance of the Secular Hymn. It is not possible to understand this as a single coherent scene, but it is the Secular Hymn which provides the thread. The opening hymn is a more complex treatment of Apollo's part in the *Aeneid* theme, touched on there; the transition enables H to re-emphasise his sense of fulfilment in being chosen for the task; the end is explicitly about the Secular Festival. Examples of similar transitions from hymn to addressing a chorus can be found in Pindar.

1-2 Great god: unnamed until line 26, but immediately identifiable from two examples of Apollo's vengeance, both for offences against his mother, Latona. **Tityos** (3), one of the traditional sinners, attempted to ravish her. **Niobe** (3, with stress on the 1st) insulted her because she had only two children (Apollo and Diana); Niobe's many children paid the price along with her: all were turned to stone, bequeathing a vocabulary of pathos to European sculpture.

3-20 Achilles: the third victim, who, before the fall of Troy, was shot in his vulnerable heel by Paris, with the aid of Apollo (the rest of him was invulnerable because his **goddess mother**, Thetis, dipped him in Styx as a baby, holding him by the foot). This hymn hinges on Achilles' **outrageous** brutality, contrasted with the stealthy **plotting** of Ulysses in the wooden **horse**. The Augustan attitude to **Trojan dupes** … **carousing** is not forgotten (**10**). **Teucrian** and **Dardanian** are variants of Trojan.

21-4: as in the Secular Hymn, H acknowledges the *Aeneid*, where Apollo and Venus assist **Aeneas**

(3, with stress on the 2nd) and his fugitive band of Trojans. H goes further and implies that without Apollo's intervention Achilles would have slaughtered them all.

25–30: the change of direction to H's personal concerns. **Thalia** (3, with stress on the 2nd): a Muse – Apollo has taught the lyre even to the Muses. **Agyieus** (3, with stress on the 2nd): another name for Apollo; the **smooth cheeks** lead into the final passage by emphasising his eternal youth. **Daunian Muse**: a bold expression: H is not merely assimilating the Muse to the Italian Camena, but he is appropriating her to his birthplace (compare 3.30).

31–44: finally the address to the chorus about to rehearse, or perform, the Secular Hymn. Diana, **Leto's** (Latona's) other child, huntress and moon-goddess, is brought into the picture. This ode, like the Secular Hymn, is in the **Sapphic** metre. The instructions to the chorus are much relied on by those who argue that the Odes were sung; but the argument is weak, since the Hymn, unlike the Odes, was indisputably designed for public performance. **Horace**: the only place where H utters his own name. The **boast,** unlike that of Niobe, will be venial and true: not an insult to Leto's children, but a tribute.

4.7

A.E. Housman considered this the most beautiful poem in Latin (see below), and translated it (*More Poems* v). Its theme, moving from the arrival of spring to the succession of the seasons and then to reflections on mortality, is obviously similar to that of 1.4. But the differences are significant: the addressee, who is a lawyer not a politician, is less to the fore; Venus is not dancing with the Graces and hints of happy love are supplanted by love's impotence; the transition to mortality is derived logically from the relentless speed of the seasons; the moral (enjoy what you have) is the same, but it is explicit, and is based on the solemn truths of the human condition: life is uncertain, and death is inescapable and irreversible.

Metre. 2nd Archilochian (unique): a shortened elegiac couplet, with only half of the second line.
15 Tullus and Ancus: early kings of Rome.
21–4 Minos: see note on 1.28.7-9. This stanza is tailored to **Torquatus'** profession.
25–8: in the end Venus, or rather the frustration of love, makes a powerful contribution to the impact of this ode. **Hippolytus** was the son of **Theseus** (2) by the Amazon queen, Hippolyte: he was devoted to the cult of **Diana**, and when his stepmother, Phaedra, made advances to him, he repulsed them: she then traduced him, and he was cursed by Theseus, whose father, Neptune, roused a bull from the sea, which killed him. Hippolytus is not a sinner, but he is dead (the present tense denotes the continuing fact), and for all the injustice of his fate, he is beyond the rescue even of Diana. For **Pirithous** (4, with stress on the 2nd) see on 3.4.69-80: Theseus cannot help him, and what is worse Pirithous has forgotten him. It is perhaps this reference to **oblivion** which most moved Housman, for he too had a Pirithous (Moses Jackson) from whom he was separated by life: he addressed a Latin elegy to him, which contains a reminiscence of this passage.

4.8

There are several strange things about this ode. Uniquely, the number of lines it contains is not a multiple of four. It commits a historical howler, and possibly a mythical solecism. And there are other oddities, mentioned below. Many attempts have been made at emending it, the most attractive being the removal of lines 17 (the howler) and 33 (almost a complete repetition of 3.25.20), but the translator has to take it as it stands. The corruption, if any, is old, and difficult to explain.

The addressee is probably the **Censorinus** who was consul in 39 BC, and who, like the addressee of the next ode, was one of the college of fifteen who superintended the Secular Festival. The theme, more elaborately and convincingly developed in the next ode, is the power of the poet to bestow immortality.

1-12: a lighthearted preamble, which implies some occasion for giving presents. A sustained metaphor of financial reward is introduced, which tends to emphasise the monetary value of poetry. **Scopas** and **Parrhasius** were famous Greek artists of the early fourth century BC, whose works would be very valuable.

13-20: the man who **bought his name** in Africa, by **driving back … Hannibal** to end the Second Punic War (202 BC), was Scipio Africanus *Major*, and this is confirmed by the reference to **Calabrian Muses**, denoting Ennius, whose patron he was, and whose *Annals* included an account of that war. But the **burning** of **Carthage** was not until the end of the Third Punic War (146 BC) at the hands of Scipio Africanus *Minor*.

21-4: H moves on to the demigods. It is unique to find **Romulus** identified by the names of both parents as well as his own.

25-8: we met **Aeacus** (3) in 2.13 as a judge of the underworld (far from the isles of the blessed), and he interrupts the list of demigods. It looks as if he has been confused with Rhadamanthus, another underworld judge, whom, however, Homer places in the isles of the blessed, and who was a son of Jupiter (and Europa). **Lethe** (2): the underworld river of oblivion.

29-34   the Twins: Castor and Pollux. In 3.3.9-15 the immortality of this same list of demigods was attributed to their heroic steadfastness, not to the power of poetry.

4.9

No man ever had such a resoundingly eloquent memorial as this eulogy of M. Lollius, consul in 21 BC and one of the fifteen controllers of the Secular Festival, yet the eloquence is all in the first half before Lollius is even named. Having dwelt on the finality of death in 4.7, H elaborates the theme of 4.8, the power of poetry to defeat death. He goes further in claiming that not only the epic Homer but also the lyric poets have immortality in their gift, and proceeds to lend his support to Lollius in terms which some have found half-hearted. How far Lollius deserved his support is controversial: he was an enemy of Tiberius, and was virulently attacked for corruption by later historians. The fact remains that Augustus, no friend of inefficiency or corruption, maintained his confidence in him, which is no doubt how this ode came to be written.

1-4: reminiscent of the first stanza and the last ode of Book 3: H openly resumes laureate mode. This is another text for the music theorists.

5-12: **Homer** apart, all the names are of Greek lyric poets. The claim that lyric poetry will confer immortality was not made in Books 1-3 (except in the case of the Bandusian spring: 3.13). **Stesichorus, Simonides, Anacreon** (all stressed on the 2nd) were all members of the Greek Nine. The prominence of **Sappho** corrects the grudging impression given in 2.13.

13-28: all the names are of Greek or Trojan heroes in the *Iliad*, the earliest source available for heroic exploits. H makes the same striking point six times over, leading up to the famous stanza about **Agamemnon**. **Idomeneus** and **Deiphobus** (both 4, with stress on the 2nd).

29-44: the reference to **envy** shows H is aware of the charges against Lollius. He meets the suspicion of corruption head-on. The military allusion to **cohorts** is more oblique. In 16 BC Lollius had suffered a defeat by the Sugambri, who had captured a standard: he was supplanted by Tiberius. This minor reverse was magnified into a disaster (see Syme p. 429).

45-52: H returns to one of his hobbyhorses, the Stoic distinction between wealth and happiness (see e.g. the end of 2.2): the implication is that Lollius passes the test, a high compliment, since he was immensely wealthy.

4.10

This short ode in its rare metre is the counterpart of 1.11. The obvious difference is that it is addressed not to a young girl, but to a boy on the edge of manhood (like the Lycidas of 1.4.19, Thaliarchus of 1.9, Gyges of 2.5.20 and Nearchus of 3.20). The persuasion to love is express instead of implied, though the argument is the same (naturally the ode is unnoticed by the Victorian translators). The striking difference is in the tone. H's approach to Leuconoe is light, detached, avuncular, patronising. Here, speaking in a persona at least ten years older, he is genuinely aware of time's winged chariot drawing near. As at the end of 4.1, his words come from the heart.

1   **hitherto**: this word demonstrates the persuasive nature of the poem: the speaker still entertains hopes.
3   **when the ... curls are shorn**: this would be on assuming the man's toga, at about the age of fifteen.

4.11

Positively H's last farewell to love, this and the next are the two odes nearest in tone to the relaxed, candid, ironical friendship of Books 1-3. H invites **Phyllis** to an intimate supper. He is taking a lot of trouble, and explains that it is **Maecenas'** birthday (this Book's sole reference to Maecenas). He advises her not to pursue **Telephus** (not the most tactful gambit) and invites her to sing (better).

1-12 **Dear Phyllis ... a mountain ... flap**: this is in the nature of a letter, and the tone here is conversational. **Alban**: H is more prosperous now: he is preparing a wine second only to Falernian and Caecuban, and superior to the Sabine he was offering to Maecenas in 1.20. With home-grown garlands, a lamb sacrifice and silverware he is pulling out all the stops.
13-20 **my own Maecenas**: a warm label, elsewhere applied only to Lamia (1.26). **the years which come his way**: an expression which seems to hint at the ill-health which Maecenas suffered at the end of his life.
21-31: The transition is abrupt and apparently insensitive, but H is affecting a new urgency in matters of the heart (see 4.10), and he is no longer in a mood to mince his words. Besides we may infer that Phyllis too is no longer young, and is close enough to him not to take offence. **Phaethon** (3) was a son of Apollo who insisted on driving the chariot of the sun; the horses bolted, and he was scorched to death. **Pegasus** was the winged horse with whose aid Bellerophon destroyed the Chimaera (see 1.27), but he then attempted to fly to the heavens and was thrown. H undercuts this ponderous moral by the wordplay of **burden** and **weighty**.
31-6: the warmth and affection of acknowledged desire: in this Book there is no self-irony in H's forays of the heart. **learn a new refrain to render**: H is giving her words to sing: here at last there is evidence that H sometimes expected his lyrics to be sung. **pain**: both have unwelcome prospects to face: she the loss of Telephus, he the onset of old age and the departure of love.

4.12

Another spring ode, this time addressed to **Virgil**, who also figures in 1.3 and 1.24. He had by this time been dead for some six years, and the sly reference to noble youths (see below) could only fit a much earlier stage in his career. As a result many commentators have concluded that this Virgil is not the poet. That involves supposing that H would have allowed his readers to confuse with his great friend another unknown, and unintroduced, Virgil. It is more probable that this ode was kept back from the first collection and then brought out, perhaps polished up, when H was preparing this second, unplanned, collection. H teases Virgil for money-grubbing in a manner which nostalgically recalls a long-standing friendship warm enough to permit it.

5-8: pleasant as the weather is, there are ominous undertones (see also lines 19, 26), which start with this myth of sex, cruelty and cannibalism. Procne, a descendant of **Cecrops** (king of Athens), was married to Tereus, who seduced her sister, Philomela, cut out her tongue and imprisoned her in a tower. In **revenge** Procne killed their infant **son**, Itys, and served him up to Tereus at a banquet. All the protagonists were changed into birds, Procne becoming a **swallow**.

9-12: this pastoral stanza, particularly the reference to **Arcadia**, points to the poet Virgil, whose pastoral *Eclogues* were published about the time that H was introduced to him (39/8 BC). The **god** is Pan (Faunus to H).

13-20 Calenian: good quality wine (attributed to Maecenas in 1.20), to be paid for at least in part by Virgil's contribution. The invitation is reminiscent of Catullus 13, where, however, the guest has to bring the wine. **noble youths**: both Maecenas and Octavian were some six years younger than Virgil, who joined Maecenas' circle after the publication of the *Eclogues*. Thus the dramatic date of the ode appears to be the mid-30s BC.

21-4 millionaire: used as a modern measure of affluence. In terms of sesterces H would almost certainly have been a millionaire at the date of publication, but probably not at the dramatic date (though the invitation does seem to be to his Sabine estate).

27-8: one of the remarks for which H is blessed by posterity.

4.13

This ode starts with the same cruel gloating over an older woman as 1.25, but the comparison is revealing. The earlier ode ends as it began, a barren literary exercise. But here there is a transition in the middle stanza, which acknowledges earlier, happier days, and the second half is transformed by the entry of H himself as a former lover, and his second reference to **Cinara** (see 4.1). Another passage of genuine personal warmth. Even the Victorians did not refuse to translate it.

1 Lyce (2, with stress on the 2nd): self-reference would take us back to the threat at the end of 3.10 of H the doorstep lover.

9 dried out trunks: The same heartless metaphor of desiccation occurs at the end of 1.25.

16 see-through: silk from Cos was famous for its transparency.

28 incinerated: the torch has consumed itself; there appears to be a deliberate play on the name Cinara (stressed on the 1st).

4.14

H reverts to the victory over the **Vindelici** and **Raeti** (15 BC), attributed largely to Drusus in 4.4. This time the spotlight is on the contribution of Tiberius, although the first mention goes to Drusus. But first and last the praise is for **Augustus**, whose worldwide achievements are catalogued in a closing crescendo.

10 Genauni and Breuni: like the Raeti, neighbours of the Vindelici.

14 The elder Nero: Tiberius, Drusus' elder brother.

22 Pleiades: a constellation associated with equinoctial storms.

25-6 Aufidus … Daunus: see on 3.30.10-12.

30 Claudius: here Tiberius again.

33-40: after the debacle of Actium, **Alexandria** surrendered in 30 BC. This transition paves the way for a recital of Augustus' victories similar to that which he himself claimed in his *Res Gestae* (**1**).

48 Ocean: traditionally a river encircling the world.

4.15

The finale of the first collection was devoted to H, his literary achievement and his Muse. In this collection that function has been performed by 4.3, and here we have instead a summary of the achievements of **Augustus** at home and abroad. It is an Augustan inventory which does not overlook the contributions of Virgil and (by implication and self-reference) H himself.

1-4: see 2.1, with its recoil at the end.

5: agricultural regeneration (see 4.5.17-18) (**4**).

6-8: the Parthian standards, when recovered in 20 BC, were first placed on the Capitol (**1**).

8-9: the closing of the **shrine of Janus** symbolised a time of complete peace; Augustus had by this time done it twice (in 29 and 25 BC) (**3**).

10-16: the moral legislation (**5**), and the return to ancient traditions (**6**).

17-20: the ending of Civil War, so frequently deplored by H (**2, 3**).

21-4: the worldwide empire (**1**).

25-32: back to the brave days of old, updated perhaps by the libations to Augustus of 4.5, and expressed primarily in the Augustan epic of Virgil, the *Aeneid,* but enriched also by the **Lydian** (Greek) influence imported by H. **Venus's posterity** includes not only Aeneas (son of **Anchises** and Venus), but also, through his son, Iulus, and the Julian line, Augustus himself. A suitably allusive note to close the Odes (**4, 7, 8, 9**).

Glossary of Names

Acheron   one of the rivers of the underworld, used for the underworld itself.

Achilles   the leading Greek hero at the siege of Troy, whose wrath is the theme of the *Iliad*.

Aeolia   part of Asia Minor including Lesbos, the homeland of Alcaeus and Sappho.

Agamemnon   king of Mycenae, son of Atreus and brother of Menelaus, leader of the Greek expedition to Troy.

Ajax   the name of two Greek heroes at Troy, one the son of Telamon, the other (lesser) of Oileus.

Alban   in the region of Alba Longa, in Latium; good quality wine.

Albunea   a grove in Tibur which took its name from the Sibyl who lived in it.

Alcaeus   lyric poet from Lesbos, H's chief model in the Odes, after whom his most frequent metre is named.

Algidus   mountain in Latium.

Amazons   tribe of warrior women from Cappadocia.

Amphion   a son of Jupiter who became a legendary musician.

Anacreon   Greek lyric poet famous for poems of love and wine.

Anchises   father of Aeneas by Venus.

Antium   town in Latium with a famous temple of Fortune.

Apulia   region in south Italy containing Venusia, H's birthplace.

Arcadia   region in the central Peloponnese, traditionally frequented by Pan.

Argive   alternative for Greek (from **Argos)**.

Ariadne   daughter of king Minos of Crete who rescued Theseus from the labyrinth.

Atreus   king of Mycenae, father of the **Atrides,** namely Agamemnon, leader of the Greeks at Troy, and Menelaus, husband of Helen.

Attica   region of Greece containing Athens.

Aufidus   river in H's native Apulia.

Aulon   a mountain in Calabria near Tarentum.

Bacchanal/Bacchant   a devotee of Bacchus.

Baiae   fashionable seaside resort on the bay of Naples.

Bassareus/id   alternative name for Bacchus and his devotee.

Bellerophon   hero renowned for chastity and for slaying the Chimaera with the aid of Pegasus, on whom he then flew too high and was thrown.

Cadiz   used to denote the distant west.

Caecuban   top class wine.

Calabria   region in south-eastern Italy, birthplace of the early Latin poet, Ennius.

Calenian   high class wine from Cales in Campania.

Camena(e)   the Latin Muse(s).

Cantabri   warlike tribe in north-west Spain finally subdued by Agrippa in 20 BC.

Capitol   one of the hills of Rome, site of temple to Jupiter, Juno and Minerva.

Carthage   Rome's great north African rival in three Punic Wars between 264 and 46 BC, during the second of which Hannibal invaded Italy.

Castor   see note on 1.3.2.

Cato the Elder   (234-149 BC) exemplar of the old Roman virtues.

Cato the Younger   (95-46 BC) supporter of Pompey who after the battle of Thapsus committed suicide rather than live under the dictatorship of Julius Caesar.

Centaurs   half-men, half-horses, notorious for their battle with the Lapiths at the wedding of Pirithous.

Cerberus   three-headed watchdog of the underworld.

Ceres   goddess of the harvest, Greek Demeter, worshipped in the Eleusinian mysteries.

Chimaera   see note on 1.27.22-4.

Circe   enchantress encountered by Ulysses on his journey home from Troy, recounted in the *Odyssey*.

Crassus   member of he 1st Triumvirate who was defeated and killed by the Parthians at Carrhae in 53 BC.

Croesus   king of Lydia of legendary wealth.

Cyclades   islands in the Aegean around Delos.

Cyprus   island associated with Venus.

Dacia   province north of the Danube.

Danaids   daughters of **Danaus**, king of Argos; see notes on 3.11.

Daunia   northern region of H's birthplace, Apulia, named after its legendary king, **Daunus**.

Delian   of Delos, the island where Latona gave birth to Apollo and Diana.

Falernian   top class wine.

Faunus   god of the countryside, equivalent of the Greek Pan.

Formian   high class wine.

Garganus   a mountainous promontory in Apulia.

Geloni   a Scythian tribe.

Getae   a Thracian tribe on the lower Danube.

Gyges   giant with fifty heads and a hundred hands.

Hannibal   Carthaginian general who invaded Italy across the Alps in the Second Punic War.

Hasdrubal   brother of Hannibal, who attempted to relieve him in southern Italy but was defeated at the River Metaurus in 207 BC.

Hector   son of Priam and the leading Trojan hero, who was killed by Achilles.

Helen   wife of Menelaus, king of Sparta, whose abduction by Paris to Troy was the cause of the Trojan war.

Hercules   son of Jupiter and Alcmena, whose heroic labours qualified him for immortality as a demigod.

Ilia   see note on 1.2.13-20.

Iulus   son of Aeneas, founder of the Julian line, to which Augustus was heir through his adoption by Julius Caesar.

Ixion   attempted to seduce Juno, and was condemned to eternal torment in the underworld.

Janus   god of gateways, who looks both ways, to the future and the past, for whom the first month is named.

Lacedaemonian, Laconian   Spartan.

Lapiths   see note on 1.18.8.

Latium   central Italy west of the Apennines, including Rome, giving its name to **Latin**.

Latona   mother of Apollo and Diana (Greek Leto): see further note on 3.28.11-12.

Liber   alternative name for Bacchus.

Maecenas   H's patron, benefactor and friend. Augustus' chief minister until soon after the publication of Books 1-3, when he fell from grace, possibly through the indiscretion of his wife (see note on 2.12.25-8). He is mentioned only once in Book 4 (4.11.19).

Maenad   frenzied female devotee of Bacchus.

Marsians   sturdy allies of Rome from central Italy.

Massic   high class wine.

Medes   properly Persians, but routinely used by H to mean Parthians.

Melpomene   a Muse (see note on 1.1.32).

Mercury   the messenger of the gods and H's personal favourite among the gods (see notes on 1.10).

Midas   king of Phrygia whose touch turned everything to gold.

Naiad   woodland nymph.

Niphates   a mountain range in Armenia.

Numa   philosopher who was persuaded to become the successor to Romulus as king of Rome.

Octavian Gaius Octavius, great-nephew of Julius Caesar, who adopted him as a son in the name of Gaius Julius Caesar Octavianus; he took the name of Augustus in 27 BC.

Orcus see note on 2.3.24.

Orion great huntsman who attempted the virtue of Diana, but became a constellation.

Orpheus see note on 1.12.7.

Pallas alternative name for the goddess known to the Greeks as Athene and to the Romans as Minerva.

Parcae the Fates.

Paris see note on 1.15.1-4.

Parthia country south-east of the Caspian Sea, whose territory in H's time included Persia. With their victory at Carrhae in 53 BC and more recent successes against Antony (see 3.6.9-12) the Parthians were considered a serious threat to Rome in the east. For the Parthian shot of their horsemen see note on 1.19.11 -12. H regularly refers to them as Medes or Persians, thus equating the Romans to the Greeks in their historic resistance to Persia.

Pelion mountain in Thessalia.

Persia see on **Parthia** and **Medes**.

Pindar the great Greek lyric poet from Thebes (see 4.2.5-24 and notes).

Pieria district on the slopes of Mt Olympus, traditional home of the Muses.

Pluto god of the underworld.

Praeneste ancient Etruscan city east of Rome.

Priam king of Troy.

Procyon a star in the constellation of Canis Minor.

Prometheus formed the first man and woman from clay, and stole fire from heaven and gave it to mortals, for which Jupiter had him chained to a rock in the Caucasus, and sent an eagle to devour his liver, which was perpetually renewed (only H puts his punishment in the underworld: 2.13).

Proserpine queen of the underworld.

Punic Carthaginian.

Quirinus another name for Romulus.

Raeti see notes on 4.4.

Regulus see note on 3.5.13-18.

Rhoetus a Giant.

Romulus son of Mars and Ilia and first king of Rome.

Salians see note on 1.37.4.

Sappho Lesbian poetess, one of H's chief models, after whom his second most frequent metre is named.

Saturn father of Jupiter, Neptune and Pluto.

Scythia land north of the Black Sea.

Styx best known river in the underworld, across which everyone had to be ferried by Charon.

Sugambri see note on 4.2.33-6.

Syrtes notoriously dangerous sands on the north African coast, the scene of an heroic march by Cato the Younger in 47 BC.

Taenarus the southernmost promontory of the Peloponnese (Matapan), where a cave was considered to be the entrance to the underworld; hence a synonym for the underworld.

Tantalus father of Pelops, whose ill-fated descendants included Atreus, Thyestes and Agamemnon; he stole the food of the gods and suffered eternal torment (being tantalised) in the underworld.

Tarentum town in Calabria (Taranto) originally colonised by the Spartans.

Teucer see note on 1.7.21-32.

Tempe valley in Thessaly renowned for its beauty.

Thebes chief city of Boeotia and home of Pindar.

Thrace vaguely defined country east of Macedon.

277

Thyestes   seduced the wife of his brother, Atreus, and suffered a horrible revenge; see note on 1.16.17.

Tibur   popular resort of the wealthy in the hills east of Rome.

Tityos   Giant who was subjected to eternal torment for attempting to rape Latona.

Tithonus   see note on 1.28.7–9.

Troy   legendary site of the Trojan war and setting of the *Iliad*. Refugees from its destruction become the ancestors of Rome in the *Aeneid*, but Augustan policy stigmatised it for luxury and decadence.

Tuscan /Tyrrhenian   Etruscan; the sea is on the western side of Italy.

Ulysses   Latin name of Odysseus.

Venusia   H's birthplace in northern Apulia.

Vesta   goddess of the hearth, served by the Vestal Virgins, who tended a perpetual flame in her temple.

Vindelici   tribe in the region of the Tyrol subdued by Drusus and Tiberius in 15 BC.

Virgil   author of the *Aeneid* who introduced H to Maecenas.

Vulcan   god of fire, husband of Venus.

Xanthus   river in Lycia sacred to Apollo.

Appendix 1

Chronology

BC

264-241	First Punic War
218	Hannibal invades across the Alps
218-201	Second Punic War
202	Scipio Africanus Major defeats Carthaginians at Zama.
149-146	Third Punic War
146	Scipio Africanus Minor destroys Carthage
88	Social War: Venusia captured and 3,000 prisoners taken (including Horace's father?)
70	Birth of Virgil
65	Manlius Consul: **Birth of Horace**
63	Birth of Octavian
59	First Triumvirate: Caesar, Crassus, Pompey
53	Crassus defeated by Parthians at Carrhae
49	Caesar crosses Rubicon: Civil War till 45
48	Caesar defeats Pompey at Pharsalus
46	Caesar defeats remaining Pompeians at Thapsus. Suicide of Cato
44	Caesar (dictator) assassinated
43	Second Triumvirate: Antony, Lepidus, Octavian
42	Plancus Consul: Antony and Octavian defeat Brutus and Cassius at **Philippi** (Horace runs away)
40	Antony marries Octavia: pact of Brundisium
38	Virgil introduces Horace to Maecenas
36-5	Campaigns against Sextus Pompeius
35	Horace *Satires* 1
34	Donations of Alexandria by Antony to Cleopatra and her children
33?	Horace receives Sabine estate
31	Octavian defeats Antony and Cleopatra at **Actium**
30	Suicides of Antony and Cleopatra in Alexandria: Horace *Epodes, Satires* 2 (?)
29	Triple triumph of Octavian
28	Temple of Palatine Apollo dedicated
27	Octavian takes name Augustus
26-5	Augustus campaigns in Spain
23	Sestius Consul: **Horace *Odes* 1-3**
20	Standards and prisoners taken at Carrhae recovered by diplomacy: Horace *Epistles* 1
19	Death of Virgil (*Aeneid* published posthumously)
18	Augustan marriage and social reforms (Julian Laws)
17	Secular Festival: **Horace *Secular Hymn***
16-13	Augustus in Gaul and Spain
15	Drusus and Tiberius defeat Raeti and Vindelici
13	**Horace *Odes* 4**
12-10	Horace *Epistles* 2 and *Ars Poetica* (?)
8	**Deaths of Maecenas and Horace**

AD

14	Death of Augustus

Appendix 2

Metres

There are one hundred and four odes (including the Secular Hymn), and they are written in thirteen different metres. The five most frequent metres account for ninety-one odes, and two more for another three each. That leaves only seven odes for the last six (rare) metres. The technical names refer to Greek origins, and their precise metrical structure can be found in works of greater learning. The following table lists them in descending order of frequency with the number of syllables in their lines and the number of syllables in the chosen equivalent.

Metre	Pattern ode	Syllables (Latin)	Syllables (English)	Number of odes
1. Alcaic	1.9	11,11,9,10	10,10+,9,9+	37
2. Sapphic	1.2	11,11,11,5	10,10+,10,4+	26
3. 4th Asclepiad	1.3	8,12	8,10+	12
4. 2nd Asclepiad	1.6	12,12,12,8	10,10+,10,6+	9
5. 3rd Asclepiad	1.5	12,12,7,8	10,10+,7,6	7
6. 1st Asclepiad	1.1	12	10(+)	3
7. 5th Asclepiad	1.11	16	15	3
8. 1st Archilochian	1.7	13-16,9-11	13-16,11-13	2
9. 2nd Archilochian	4.7	14-16,7	13-15,8-9+	1
10. 3rd Archilochian	1.4	16-18,11	15-18,10+	1
11. Greater Sapphic	1.8	7,15	7,15	1
12. Hipponactean	2.18	7,11	6,10	1
13. Ionic	3.12	8,8,16,8	10,10,16,10	1

The number of syllables in the Latin lines is unvarying, except in the Archilochians, where a long syllable can sometimes be resolved into two shorts: the figures indicate the range actually found. The same applies to the English, except that '+' indicates the possibility of an additional syllable at the end of the line (feminine ending), a licence which I have used only for the purpose of accommodating a rhyme (and therefore only in the even numbered lines: the bracketed + for the 1st Asclepiad denotes this restriction).

Part of the rationale behind my choice of metres was to make the English look the same on the page as the Latin. Thus the same indentation has been used for corresponding metres. But the object has been partially frustrated by a (to me) unexpected characteristic of English. In comparison with Latin it not only requires many more little words (articles, pronouns, auxiliaries etc), without which it ceases to be properly articulate, but it is also much richer in consonants (e.g. Latin has no monosyllable of comparable length to 'strengths'). The result is that, although almost all my lines have fewer syllables than H's, they invariably look longer on the page. I hope the reader will be able to distinguish by sight the common Alcaic metre from its lighter sister the 3rd Asclepiad, whose third and fourth lines are shorter and indented further.

The only English metre which I have consciously borrowed is that for the 5th Asclepiad, which comes from Tennyson's *Locksley Hall*. On the assumption (in itself a demanding one) that the Latin sense can fairly be represented in English by an equal number of syllables, it will be seen from the table that, apart from some of the rare metres, my practice has given me significantly restricted space in which to work. On the whole I have considered this a beneficial concession to discipline, on the ground that it is worse to add material than to eliminate what is inessential or peripheral.

Meineke's Law

In 1834 Meineke observed that all the Odes are written in quatrains, an observation which affects only the minority which are written in metres which repeat after only one or two lines. Statistically this is demonstrably correct, since all such odes have a number of lines which is a multiple of four, with the sole exception of 4.8 (which is suspected of corruption on other grounds). By comparison, the distich metres in the Epodes are equally divided between multiples of four and multiples of two, a chance distribution.

It is for this reason that the Latin is printed in four-line stanzas, even for the one- and two-line metres, and even though in a few cases H does not seem to have been thinking of four-line units. In 4.8 the temptation to excise two lines has been resisted, and it is given a six-line last stanza. 3.12 is a curious case: its unbroken succession of Ionic units makes it difficult to say where lines end. It is commonly printed with four stanzas of three lines. I have preferred Quinn's layout, which is the only way of defining a four-line stanza without a word running over the end of a line.

Appendix 3

Augustan Policies

The following summary leans heavily on the list in West (2002, pp. 3-11). One of its chief sources is the *Res Gestae*, Augustus' own account of his achievements.

1. Empire

Augustus claimed to have subjected the whole world to Roman rule. Many of the odes emphasise the distant reach of the empire (e.g. mentions of the Chinese). At the time of Books 1-3 Parthia was still seen as a serious threat, with its victories at Carrhae (53 BC) and more recently over Antony's forces (see on 3.6.9-12). By the time of Book 4 the standards lost at Carrhae had been recovered by peaceful diplomacy, but an expedition to Britain, which seems to have been expected (see 3.5.3), never materialised.

2. Clemency

As ultimate victor in the Civil War Augustus' policy towards the defeated was one of magnanimity and reconciliation (and H himself was a beneficiary), and nationally his approach was the same. It does not receive much explicit emphasis in the Roman Odes, but it is frequently implicit elsewhere (e.g. in choice of addressees, see 1.4, 1.7, 2.7).

These first two policies are embodied in Virgil's famous line (paraphrased in the Secular Hymn):

> *parcere subiectis et debellare superbos*
> [to spare the defeated and crush the defiant]

3. *Pax Augusta*

The restoration of peace, prosperity, order and security after years of intermittent Civil War was Augustus' greatest achievement. He claimed that the closing of the temple of Janus, a symbol of universal peace, occurred three times during his rule (see note on 4.15.8-9). H realised how fortunate he was to benefit from it.

4. Italy and rural life

Augustus drew his support more from the Italian provinces than from the traditional ruling classes in Rome, and his rule shifted the centre of gravity. He also claimed that the resettling of his veterans on the land revived agriculture and the sterling yeoman values of the past (see e.g. 3.6.33-44).

5. Moral legislation

Seeing civil strife as symptomatic of moral decline, Augustus embarked on a stringent programme of moral reform (which must have been projected before Books 1-3 were published, but was not enacted until 18 BC). Among other measures it made marriage compulsory between certain ages, and imposed severe penalties for adultery (see e.g. 3.6.17-32).

6. Past heroes

Augustus conspicuously honoured the early Republican heroes with their austere values (Regulus in 3.5 is an example, and see the list in 1.12.37-44).

7. Frugality

Augustus set a personal example in frugal living, and the moral legislation included measures to curb luxury and extravagance. The virtue of wanting no more than is enough and of indifference to wealth is a constant refrain throughout the Odes (see e.g. 2.16, 3.1.25-48).

8. Young people

Augustus recognised the importance of impressing the younger generation, and took a keen interest in the education and upbringing of children (see e.g. 3.2.1-16, 3.24.51-62).

9. Religion

Augustus was religious, and part of his programme was the restoration of damaged temples (see 3.6.1-8). As the adoptive son of Julius Caesar he could claim descent from Venus (see the final note on 4.15), and although H stops short of addressing him as a god, he was certain to be treated, like Caesar, as a god after his death.

10. Troy

The *Aeneid* tells the story of the arrival in Latium (a necessary prelude to the founding of Rome) of Aeneas, a refugee from the sack of Troy. But Troy stood also for luxury (Priam's court), immorality (Paris and Helen) and treachery (Laomedon's failure to pay his debts). This inheritance was held to account for the divine wrath which brought the Civil Wars; it also provided Augustus with ammunition in his propaganda war against Antony (see the speech of Juno in 3.3).

Appendix 4

Further Reading

SH = Secular Hymn.

Translations

Carne-Ross, D.S. and Haynes, K., *Horace in English* (Penguin, 1996). Anthology of translations of all dates, and all H's work; with introduction and other useful material.

Lee, G., *Horace Odes and Carmen Saeculare* (Francis Cairns, 1998). An ambitious approach to translation, attempting the full task of importing H's quantitative metres; with introduction, text and notes.

Leishman, J.B., *Translating Horace* (Bruno Cassirer. Oxford, 1956). The case for importing H's quantitative metres into English, with translations of thirty odes.

Lentin, A., *Horace The Odes* (Wordsworth, 1997). An anthology of translations, one for each ode in text order (no SH) by translators from the sixteenth century to date.

Marsh, E., *The Odes of Horace* (Macmillan, 1941). Verse translation by an old-style man of affairs and letters.

Michie, J., *The Odes of Horace* (Hart-Davis, 1964; Penguin, 1967). The best translation by a genuine poet.

West, D., *Horace: The Complete Odes and Epodes* (Oxford, 1997). English only, including SH, with short notes.

Wickham, E.C., *Horace for English Readers* (Oxford, 1903). Prose translation of all H's work by a Victorian scholar.

Commentaries

Fraenkel, E., *Horace* (Oxford, 1957). Comprehensive survey of all H's work: always magisterial in scholarship, at times suspect in literary judgment.

Gow, J., *Horace Odes and Epodes* (Cambridge, 1896). Valuable old-style school edition, including SH and useful introduction, notes and indexes.

Nisbet, R.G.M. and Hubbard, M., *A Commentary on Horace Odes Bk I* (Oxford, 1970) and *A Commentary on Horace Odes Bk II* (Oxford, 1978). Commentary only (no text); heavyweight modern scholarship, very strong on literary sources.

Nisbet, R.G.M. and Rudd, N., *A Commentary on Horace Odes Bk III* (Oxford, 2004). Sequel to the last two, which came too late to be of use in the preparation of this book.

Quinn, K., *Horace: The Odes* (Nelson, 1980). Similar scale to Gow, without SH, but more up to date.

West, D., *Horace Odes I: Carpe Diem* (Oxford, 1995), *Horace Odes II: Vatis Amici* (Oxford, 1998), *Horace Odes III: Dulce Periculum* (Oxford, 2002). All with text, translation and discursive commentary. Worth their weight in gold.

Williams, G., *The Third Book of Horace's Odes* (Oxford, 1969). Text, translation and smaller-scale modern commentary on Book 3 alone.

Historical background

Syme, R., *The Roman Revolution* (Oxford, 1939). For the contemporary history, including the parts played by many of the characters named in the Odes.

General survey

Hills, P., *Horace* (Duckworth, 2005). Good introduction to H's life and all his work, full of up to the minute insights.

Appendix 5

Index of Opening Words

Opening words are in bold and addressees in ordinary type, followed by other actors (if any) in parentheses, and the ode number.

Aeli vetusto Aelius Lamia 3.17
Aequam memento Dellius 2.3
Albi, ne doleas Albius (Glycera, Lycoris, Cyrus, Pholoe, Myrtale) 1.33
Angustam amice None 3.2
Audivere, Lyce Lyce (Chia, Cinara) 4.13
Bacchum in remotis Bacchus 2.19
Caelo supinas Phidyle 3.23
Caelo tonantem None 3.5
Cum tu, Lydia Lydia (Telephus) 1.13
Cur me querelis Maecenas 2.17
Delicta maiorum Roman 3.6
Descende caelo Calliope 3.4
Dianam tenerae Virgines, Pueri 1.21
Diffugere nives Torquatus 4.7
Dive, quem proles Apollo, Chorus 4.6
Divis orte bonis Augustus 4.5
Donarem pateras Censorinus 4.8
Donec gratus eram Lydia (Chloe, Calais) 3.9
Eheu fugaces Postumus 2.14
Est mihi nonum Phyllis (Telephus) 4.11
Et ture et fidibus None (Numida, Lamia, Damalis, Bassus) 1.36
Exegi monumentum Melpomene 3.30
Extremum Tanain Lyce 3.10
Faune, Nympharum Faunus 3.18
Festo quid potius Lyde 3.28
Herculis ritu Plebs (Neaera) 3.14
Iam pauca aratro None 2.15
Iam satis terris Mercury/Augustus 1.2
Iam veris comites Virgil 4.12
Icci, beatis Iccius 1.29
Ille et nefasto Arbos 2.13
Impios parrae Galatea (Europa, Venus) 3.27
Inclusam Danaen Maecenas 3.16
Intactis opulentior Unnamed 3.24
Integer vitae Fuscus (Lalage) 1.22
Intermissa, Venus, diu Venus (Cinara, Ligurinus) 4.1
Iustum et tenacem None (Juno) 3.3
Laudabunt alii Plancus (Teucer) 1.7
Lydia, dic, per omnis Lydia (Sybaris) 1.8
Maecenas atavis Maecenas 1.1
Martiis caelebs Maecenas 3.8
Mater saeva None (Glycera) 1.19